W9-DCE-613

MULTIPROTOCOL NETWORK MANAGEMENT
A practical guide to NetView for AIX

Larry Bennett

McGRAW-HILL BOOK COMPANY

London · New York · St Louis · San Francisco · Auckland · Bogotá · Caracas
Lisbon · Madrid · Mexico · Milan · Montreal · New Delhi · Panama · Paris
San Juan · São Paulo · Singapore · Sidney · Tokyo · Toronto

Published by
McGRAW-HILL Book Company Europe
Shoppenhangers Road, Maidenhead, Berkshire SL6 2QL, England
Telephone 01628 23432
Facsimile 01628 770224

British Library Cataloguing in Publications Data
Bennett, Larry
  Multiprotocol network management: a practical guide to NetView for AIX
  1. NetView for AIX (Computer program)   2. Computer network protocols
  I. Title
  004.6'2

  ISBN 0-07-709122-1

Library of Congress Cataloging-in-Publication Data
The CIP data of this title is available from the Library of Congress, Washington, DC, USA

McGraw-Hill

A Division of The **McGraw·Hill** *Companies*

1234 CUP 99876

Typeset by David Penfold, Edgerton Publishing Services, Huddersfield
Printed and bound in Great Britain at the University Press, Cambridge

Printed on permanent paper in compliance with ISO Standard 9706

To my family

CONTENTS

Advanced Peer-to-Peer Networking, AIX, AnyNet, APPN, DB2, DB2/6000, MVS/ESA, NetView, Nways, OS/2, RISC System/6000, RMONitor, S/390, SystemView, Trouble Ticket, VM/ESA, and VTAM are trademarks of IBM Corporation

AFS and Andrew File System are trademarks of Transarc Inc.

Apple and Macintosh are trademarks of Apple Computer Corporation

DECnet and Digital UNIX are trademarks of Digital Equipment Corporation

Ethernet is a trademark of Xerox Corporation

HP-UX and OpenView are trademarks of Hewlett-Packard Company

INGRES is a trademark of ASK Group Inc.

IPX and NetWare are trademarks of Novell Inc.

Motif is a trademark of the Open Software Foundation

NFS, Network File System, Solaris and SunOS are trademarks of Sun Microsystems

PostScript is a trademark of Adobe Systems Inc.

The X Window System and Kerberos are trademarks of the Massachusetts Institute of Technology

UNIX is a technology trademark of the X/Open Comapny Ltd

Windows and Windows NT are trademarks of Microsoft Corporation

ONE

INTRODUCTION

Many people's idea of network management is a room full of large consoles on which are drawn multicoloured lines and shapes, flashing here and there. The system presents a complete and easy-to-understand representation of the network and hides the ten million combinations of protocols, media and communications gear that lurk malevolently below. A team of cool, confident operators sits in the dimly lit room before this electronic marvel—in the style of Mission Control in Houston—as the system alerts them to difficulties in the network and guides them through the solutions. Windows pop up, zooming into the network and presenting the operators with any fact or figure they may require.

Others see the network management system in quite different terms, as a dark room in which computers coldly calculate away at the network performing, through sophisticated automation and artificial intelligence, all management the network requires.

Then there are those, having a taste for obscure terminology and travel to exotic locations, who believe that the standards documents to which a network management system adheres must, when placed end to end, span the longest terrestrial link the system is expected to manage. At last report, they were debating the number of sub-committees required to address the ecological issues of conformance testing.

And then there are the rest of us humble folk who are concerned with systems that can help manage real networks today, saving for future generations the network management nirvana that surely awaits them, and focusing instead on more pressing problems. In this book, we will look at how to build real network management solutions using IBM's NetView for AIX.

1.1 NETVIEW

In the mid-1980s at IBM's networking laboratory in Research Triangle Park, North Carolina, a clever developer with a secret ambition to work in the advertising trade coined the brand name 'NetView'. Since then NetView has been used to designate many IBM network management

1

systems, most notably the mainframe-based system first shipped in 1986 for management of IBM Systems Network Architecture (SNA) and other networks. In the last few years, the name has also been given to IBM's UNIX-based network management systems. As open systems have gained more attention, NetView for many people means these products more than the mainframe NetView. In this book, since we're interested in a particular UNIX-based system, NetView will mean IBM's NetView for AIX product.

The NetView we're concerned with first came into being in June 1991 when IBM shipped a product called AIX NetView/6000. This was based on a product from Hewlett-Packard called OpenView, which like NetView is a general-purpose management system based on the Simple Network Management Protocol (SNMP). In the first release, NetView was primarily a port of OpenView to AIX, though it did include several enhancements to the end-user interface, publications and installation process. Then the people at IBM went to work and produced two new versions with many IBM-unique functions. They also continued to incorporate additional enhancements Hewlett-Packard developed for OpenView.

This arrangement continued up until Hewlett-Packard announced version 4 of OpenView, at which point IBM decided to develop NetView independently. Therefore, while NetView will continue to incorporate the OpenView/NetView core—including the set of programming interfaces that make it possible to port applications between the two—future enhancements will be unique to NetView.

Meanwhile, the marketeers with the enviable job of naming products put NetView through a couple of name changes, and now it is NetView for AIX. More substantially, IBM ported NetView to the SUN Solaris operating system and called it NetView for Solaris. Also, IBM and Digital made an agreement to port NetView to the Digital UNIX operating system and to work together on future versions of NetView and applications. Digital shipped its first version of NetView in early 1994 as POLYCENTER Manager on NetView, known to the initiated as POLYCENTER NetView. Since then, Digital has also produced a version of NetView that runs on Windows/NT.

All four versions of NetView are essentially the same product running on different operating systems, although shipments of new versions tend to happen at slightly different times. In writing this book, I've used the AIX version, and therefore the samples and examples have been tested there. Still, as all four versions are very similar, this book should apply equally to the other three.

At the time of writing, the current NetView is version 4. By the time you read this, we may be onto a later NetView, but since functions are rarely removed from software products, and since the core of NetView is now well established, this book should serve as a useful guide to future NetViews as well.

1.2 POSITIONING AND TERMINOLOGY

There are at least two distinct things people mean when they say 'network management'—of which we're only interested in one. Further complicating things is the overlap between our kind of network management and systems management. Let's look at these areas briefly to get our terminology straight and understand how NetView fits into the worlds of network and systems management.

1.2.1 The two kinds of network management

It's certain that the inventors of network management were the telephone companies. They had networks long before there were computers, and were managing them for years before any one in the data world had even heard of network management. The telephone companies are, of course, in the business of providing connections of various sorts between their customers, and are interested in managing the exchanges, switches and trunk lines that make these possible.

We data-networking types on the other hand are concerned with using these connections to send data between computers, routers, bridges and the like. We are interested in the connections themselves, but only in a simple way: how fast they are, whether they are working properly and how much they cost. We also might activate and deactivate them as bandwidth demand changes, but we certainly don't worry much about whether they are implemented with fibre, copper or microwave, or how many switches and repeaters are involved. These are issues for the telephone companies.

Indeed, the connections supplied by the telephone companies are only one of several kinds in which we are interested. We also have LANs and MANs of various sorts, and in some cases private WAN links. In addition, we're concerned with the various sorts of multiplexors and compression devices designed to make efficient use of expensive WAN connections. We're also interested in the hosts and workstations attached to our networks.

The kind of networking we're interested in can be delineated in two ways. One is based on a layered model of networks, where the telephone company is providing what we call the physical or lowest layer and the equipment and protocols using it are collectively termed logical or higher layers. This distinction is not completely satisfactory since in the case of LANs and MANs we must handle the physical layer as well. In addition, telephone companies and other carriers offer services such as X.25 packet switching and Frame Relay in which they provide and manage the higher-layer services as well.

A better distinction is ownership. We are interested in the private portion of the network, the part owned by the organization for which we work, and we leave the rest to the telephone company. This is much closer to the mark. There are, of course, data networking services available in which the provider owns the network but lets the customer perform some management. There, however, the management pertains only to the service and not to the network delivering it. Thus, the ownership distinction more or less holds.

Having thus distinguished between the two kinds of network management, and made it clear that ours is far more difficult and sophisticated than the other, we shall now completely forget about the telephone companies and use the phrase network management only as it applies to the data world. The next question is how network management relates to systems management.

1.2.2 Systems and enterprise management

It is obvious that there are only two legitimate purposes for data communications networks:

1. To give occasion for the beautifully drawn and technical-looking charts used to impress colleagues at conferences.
2. To justify the existence of network management systems.

Nonetheless, there is the annoying question of getting someone to pay for these networks, and so far the best solution anyone has found is to let people attach their computers so they can exchange meeting notices, play Doom and download viruses.

In most organizations, it is a good idea to manage these computer systems in a more or less formal way. This is especially important when the systems are large and multi-user, or when they are distributed workstations used by people who don't think it's fun to figure out which IRQ to assign an Ethernet card. Systems managers are not interested in error counters in routers, but rather in things like how busy the CPU on a workstation is, how much free disk space it has and what level of a particular application is running there. It's easy to see that these are quite different questions to the ones that get network managers up in the morning. Still, the difference can get fuzzy.

One source of fuzziness is that many computers doing applications work are also performing a communications function—sometimes switching traffic and almost always providing access to the network for its applications. Thus, the condition of the computer and its communications software is of interest to both systems and network managers. One good example of this is in traditional SNA where mainframes running VTAM (Virtual Telecommunications Access Method) play a very important role in the network.

Another source of fuzziness is the increasingly distributed nature of computing, which means the systems manager must understand something about the network stitching his distributed system together. This trend also means the tools required by systems managers are in many cases becoming very similar to those needed by network managers. For example, both need facilities to alert them to problems in remote devices, both need to be able to distribute software updates remotely and both must issue commands to remote devices.

This leads us to what is sometimes known as 'enterprise management', which incorporates both systems and networks, and in some people's minds, business processes as well. While this is an interesting topic, network management is still a distinct area, and one that in most organizations is carried out independently. For this reason, as well as to keep this book to a reasonable size, I will focus primarily on network management.

Now that we've delineated our area of investigation, let's see exactly what it involves.

1.3 NETWORK MANAGEMENT

Network management is the set of tasks that must be carried out to ensure that the network is providing the required level of service to its users at an acceptable cost. It begins with the initial planning and design of the network and continues into monitoring, maintenance, operation and accounting. It is an ongoing process carried out by network managers, operators and technicians who follow loosely or tightly defined procedures and use a set of tools. In this book, we are most concerned with one set of tools—NetView and its applications. These are a subset of the tools required for the overall process, but to position NetView's role it's worth reviewing network management in general.

The formality with which network management is performed varies considerably from one organization to another. In some cases, you will find one or two people who know something about networking and get a phone call when the LAN breaks. In others, there are large staffs with powerful computers following well defined procedures to ensure the network is available nearly all the time. Where an organization lies on the spectrum between these two extremes depends mainly on how large the network is and how important it is to provide continuous availability. Certainly large banks and retailers tend to be at the elaborate end of the spectrum while small office LANs used mainly by computer professionals tend to be at the other.

The activities of network management are a diverse lot, including such things as designing the optimal configuration of a backbone WAN, adjusting a user's bill to account for an unplanned outage and explaining to an inexperienced user that his keyboard actually has 102 Any Keys on it. There have been many attempts to organize these activities into a small number of categories and I'm sure you've seen at least some of these. It must be noted that in some cases it seems the method used to determine the categories is to select at random a small number of nouns from a recent trade journal and append 'Management' to each—and indeed that may be as good a method as any.

Still, as a means of understanding the activities of network management, a categorization can be useful, and so I humbly present mine for your possible edification:

● Configuration management
● Operations
● Problem management
● Monitoring and reporting
● Security

1.3.1 Configuration management

This is the group of activities that go into designing, building, maintaining and tracking the overall configuration of the network, including the hardware, software, communications facilities and configuration parameters of all these. Specifically it includes:

● **Network design and implementation**   This includes the initial design of the network and later upgrades and modifications. This is a very complicated area, especially when multi-protocol networks are involved and when major additions are made to existing networks. The tools required for this work are still relatively immature.
● **Software distribution**   Networking equipment is usually controlled by software and it's necessary to update it with fixes and new versions. Ideally, this is done remotely with software distribution tools, which not only transmit and install the software but also keep records of which software is running in each piece of equipment. Often, however, it is done using an older technology, SneakerNet.
● **Change control**   If the network is large and many people are involved in its maintenance, then it's necessary to have some sort of change control process to keep things straight. This might be something as simple as a single person who is consulted before any change is made and who keeps a list in his notebook or it might be a complex database or workflow management system used to co-ordinate the changes.
● **Network configuration tracking and reporting**   Many networks are large and most are complex, so it's important to have diagrams and reports showing the current and historical configuration. This information is crucial to nearly all areas of network management—handling problems, planning changes, accounting, operations and almost anything else you can imagine. The information required includes the hardware, software and media in the

network, where they are located and how they are connected together. It also includes each network component's operational status, which people are responsible for maintaining the network and reams of similar information.

Ideally, this information is collected directly from the network, but much of it must also be maintained manually, e.g. the names of people responsible for maintenance. There are many ways it can be presented, including real-time graphics displayed on expensive workstations, pictures drawn on paper and textual lists of various sorts.

It is worth noting here that a good network configuration database is fundamental to effective network management. If you don't understand the network configuration you might as well forget trying to diagnose or operate it. Nor can you have pretty GUIs (Graphical User Interfaces) that show what the network looks like. And certainly all the exotic things we love to talk about, such as like automatic operations and problem diagnosis, are impossible without a good repository.

Unfortunately, at present this area is still very troublesome. There is not a widely accepted standard for collecting and storing this information and therefore, while a large amount of configuration information is known by the equipment scattered throughout the network, there is no effective way of getting it all into a single logical repository where network management applications can use it. There have been several proposed solutions, but none has gained the acceptance required for a universal network repository. Thus, network management systems today rely on proprietary, special-purpose repositories.

● **Remote configuration and control** Any respectable piece of networking equipment will require that you set at least two hundred configuration parameters. Of course, it could figure them out by itself, but they are provided as a gesture of professional courtesy to network managers, and given forbidding names like 'Time Period Between BPDUs' to ensure that networking forever remains a dark mystery. Therefore, unless your organization has a large fuel budget, it's a good idea to have tools that make it easy to configure equipment remotely throughout the network.

1.3.2 Operations

These are the frequent tasks that must be performed by people or the network management system to control the network. Operations include such things as activating lines when more bandwidth is required, switching to backup lines in response to failures, stopping a process when it is consuming too much bandwidth and bringing parts of the network up or down for maintenance. Some of this is necessary because the networking equipment is not capable of doing it by itself. In other cases, people need to be involved because the operation must be co-ordinated across several components in the network or is too important to trust to computers.

Effective operations require co-ordination among the people carrying them out. They also require good tools for remotely issuing commands or in some other way controlling remote equipment. It is also nice to have some automation capabilities in the network management system so that complex or repetitive operations can be programmed.

1.3.3 Problem management

This is the most classical aspect of network management—reacting to problems in the network. We love to talk about 'proactive network management' and indeed it is an excellent idea to design networks to minimize failures. Still, as complex as networks are, there are going to be plenty of problems to handle. Doing so involves:

- **Notification** Ideally, the network management system notifies you when there are problems, but sometimes you learn through other methods such as phone calls or e-mail messages from users. Networks are good at telling you when there are problems by sending alarms to the management system. The difficulty, though, is they are often too good at this and may send hundreds of alarms in response to a single failure or send alarms for events that are not interesting. Thus, it's important to have filtering and even automatic correlation to eliminate redundant alarms.
- **Diagnosis** This is obviously the trickiest part of problem management and requires experts and sophisticated tools in many cases. There have been some attempts to build expert systems or other tools to automate the diagnosis process, but in reality these can solve only the simplest problems.
- **Resolution** Once they have been diagnosed, resolving problems ranges from minor operations like restarting a router to more complicated activities like applying a software fix or replacing a piece of equipment.
- **Co-ordination** Co-ordination is important if more than a few people are handling problems. The risks of there being no co-ordination range from inefficiency to catastrophe. Co-ordination can obviously be done in many ways, from simple solutions, such as having all work dispatched by a single person, to complex ones, such as full-blown problem management or workflow software.
- **Statistics** It's generally a good idea to keep a history of problems. This history can be used for all sorts of things, including calculating the reliability and availability of the network, finding network components that are particularly troublesome and, most importantly, defending yourself against the outrageous claims users make about network downtime. This historical information is produced by most problem management software.

1.3.4 Monitoring and reporting

This is the task of collecting information about the state of the network and either using it immediately or saving it in a database for future use in pretty graphics and reports. There are many different kinds of information you might want about the network:

- **Financial information** This allows you to charge users of the network—either in real money if you're a network service provider, or in 'funny money' if you're providing service within your organization. Even if you're not directly charging users, you still may want to impress them with how much benefit they're getting from the network. Information of special relevance includes user connect time, amount of information a particular user sends, the class of service they receive, e.g. high or low priority, and the types of facilities they use.

- **Availability information**   This is the amount of time that the various components and services of the network are available. Information regarding components is useful for network design and purchasing decisions, while the availability of the services, as seen by end users, is one of the most important measurements of network quality. The only foolproof way to measure service availability is to place monitors in the network which mimic users and record the availability they experience.
- **Performance information**   Network design and problem determination require a good understanding of the network's performance. This includes:
  - How heavily loaded the various network components are.
  - *Delay measurements* These include the times required for messages to cross particular switches and links, as well as end-to-end response times.

  Measurements of the first kind include:
  - CPU and memory utilization of routers, bridges and sometimes workstations and hosts
  - The amounts of traffic sent across links
  - Queue lengths and queuing delays in routers, bridges, workstations and hosts
  - Lengths of polling cycles and token cycle times
  - Errors of various kinds in network components, e.g. frames discarded by network interfaces, Ethernet collisions, Token-Ring beacons
  - Measurements of pacing mechanisms used by network protocols, for example SNA's virtual route pacing

  This sort of information is fairly easy to collect either directly from the network equipment, or from protocol analysers and other monitoring equipment. It is often useful, however, to have more complicated statistical information for each of these including variance, mean, minimum and maximum. This may be harder to obtain.

  Information of the second type—delay measurements—is much more difficult to collect since it involves issues such as clock co-ordination in the network and having the monitors understand higher-layer protocols. Arguably the most important is measurement of end-to-end response time for particular user activities, e.g. the time required for a database query submitted from a workstation to a remote server. The simplest and most effective way to collect this is putting monitors into the network which mimic users and record their findings.

In addition, programs to process the data are required, performing data reduction, summarization, analysis and report generation.

1.3.5 Security

This is quite a serious issue given the important information that flows through networks, and especially given the trend to distributed systems. Unfortunately, network security today seems to be an oxymoron. This is especially true with LANs, where every station sees all traffic and anyone can connect an inexpensive protocol analyser and see whatever they like. WAN links have their problems too. It is quite an act of faith to transmit sensitive data across the world and expect it to remain secure.

There are three main issues in network security:

1. **Privacy—ensuring sensitive information is not made public** With today's distributed systems, the only effective way to ensure privacy is to keep your sensitive data in a physically and logically secure computer, i.e. locked in secure room and protected against remote access with passwords, and never let data leave the computer unless it is encrypted.

   Another important technique, both here and in other areas of network security, is the use of 'firewalls'. As more organizations connect their networks to the Internet, these provide an important means of supplementing other forms of security.

2. **Authentication—ensuring potential users of network and system services really are who they claim to be** Passwords suffice but handling them in a distributed environment is tricky since, for example, it is definitely not a good idea to send unencrypted passwords across a network. Public and private key encryption algorithms can solve this problem. Another issue with the use of passwords is that users may need to authenticate themselves to many applications and services, with all the inconvenience that implies. It is a waste of time to log into several mainframes and servers when all could use the same password and get it from a single source. Technologies such as Kerberos and IBM's KryptoKnight are designed to handle these sorts of issues.

3. **Authorization—determining which services and resources particular users are allowed to access** This can also be done with password-based schemes in which different users are assigned particular sets of privileges.

With the growth of the networks and electronic commerce, security is becoming an increasingly important issue. The required technologies exist, but standardization and implementation of these are still underway.

1.4 MULTIPLE VENDORS AND MULTIPLE PROTOCOLS

Not only do we require sophisticated mechanisms for the five areas we have outlined—each quite complicated by itself—but these must work with the multiplicity of protocols, media and equipment found in networks. Today, most networking equipment comes with network management built into it. This will work with a network management system, either provided by the vendor (generally a special-purpose system) or one the vendor believes is important, e.g. a general SNMP manager such as OpenView or NetView. Unfortunately, given the large number of management systems on the market, you need a control centre full of them. Each system makes itself unpleasantly manifest with a user interface bearing no resemblance to the others and is often built on the assumption that the staff can devote several weeks to mastering its intricacies.

Of course, what you really want is a management system that treats your multiprotocol network in a consistent way as far as possible. Several network management systems today provide this capability to one extent or another. Certainly at the level of handling alarms this can be done, although depending on the kinds of equipment in your network, customization and coding may be required to get different alarm formats into a single management system. Also, management systems today can usually show network topology for a wide, though not universal, set of protocols. Similarly, operations and network monitoring can usually be carried out for a good range of protocols. Other more complicated and protocol-dependent tasks such as problem diagnosis, network design, software distribution and security are more difficult to perform in a truly multiprotocol manner.

1.5 CENTRALIZED AND DISTRIBUTED NETWORK MANAGEMENT

An issue that cuts across the various activities of network management is whether it is to be done from a single central location or from several different locations. To a large extent, completely centralized management gets harder to do and less appropriate as distributed computing grows. Clearly, in the days when all the intelligence was in the mainframes and the network centred around these, it was easy to accomplish centralized management. Today, it is much more difficult, since much of the computing and data transmission occurs far from the central data processing centre (assuming there even is one). Also, it is much easier to build a network today than it once was, and many organizations are doing this without the involvement of a central network management organization.

For these reasons, there is a real requirement in most networks for distributed management. Still, some groups within an organization may not want any involvement in networking or managing their own computing infrastructure. Also, having a large number of management sites can lead to redundancy and increased costs. For these reasons, centralized management is still relevant, though in most cases it will be mixed with distributed management.

In distributed management environments, the network is usually divided into several sections or management domains, with one management site responsible for each of them. The division is usually carried out along geographic or organizational lines. For example, one very common division is to have the backbone WAN under the control of a dedicated network management group, while some of the attached LANs are under control of the users themselves, or one or two specialists responsible to them.

Another common division of network management responsibility occurs when the backbone WAN is very large—perhaps spanning the world—and is broken into domains, e.g. countries, continents. This is done for practical reasons, such as reducing complexity, keeping the management centre in a time zone similar to the users' and making it possible for the network managers to speak the same language as the users.

In addition, management responsibility is often divided by network protocol. For example, the SNA and TCP/IP networks may be managed separately.

When the network is divided into management domains, there is often the requirement that the domains change over time. This is sometimes required because during the day a local group wants to manage their section of the network, but at night they prefer to turn it over to the central staff. This also occurs in world-wide networks as the working day moves across the globe. For example, during the day in the USA, the New York management centre will run the network, but when the staff there go home the London management centre takes over. Another reason that domains change over time is for reliability. If one location's network management system goes down, another will take over.

In cases where there is distributed management, the management system must support it by:

- **Allowing more than one management system to exist in the network**   This is usually possible, although multiple managers can place an unacceptable performance burden on the network. This can be true especially in network protocols such as TCP/IP that require active status monitoring (i.e. polling systems to ensure they are running). Schemes are required to reduce this burden.

● **Restricting the information presented to each network management centre**   In some cases this is a security issue and in nearly all it is important for reducing the load on the network, management systems and the staff. Sending irrelevant information to a management centre that's not interested will waste bandwidth and cycles, and give the staff headaches.
● **Restricting control of the management domains**   The most important requirement here is to ensure that each management site can issue commands and otherwise affect only their own domain. This is important for security reasons and also for co-ordination among the different centres.
● **Providing functions to change the network management domains**   This is so that one group can take over management of a domain on a shift change or when a failure occurs.

1.6 DISTRIBUTING THE MANAGEMENT SYSTEM ITSELF

There is something resembling what I've termed distributed network management that often confuses the issue. That is the question of whether to distribute the components of the network management system itself. There is no doubt that whether this is done depends to a certain extent on the style of network management. Nonetheless, there are two separate issues here:

1. Is the network management staff in one place or in several locations?
2. Is the network management system largely concentrated in one place or is it implemented as a collection of distributed systems?

It is entirely possible (as shown in Figure 1.1) to have a completely centralized network management style with all network managers in one location while the management system has many components distributed throughout the network.
   There are several reasons to distribute the management system itself:

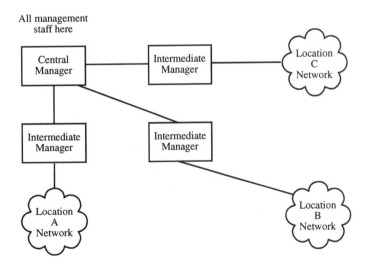

Figure 1.1 Centralized management using distributed management system

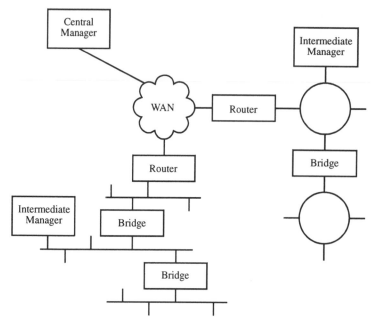

Figure 1.2 Strategically placing intermediate managers

- **Improve performance**   Network management traffic can be quite voluminous and it is a good idea to put intermediate management systems at strategic points. For example, in Figure 1.2, one is placed near each group of bridged LANs. Intermediate managers can:
  - Perform all status monitoring for local devices and inform the central manager only when there are changes.
  - Filter alarms, so that only significant ones use WAN bandwidth to get to the central manager.
  - Collect performance and accounting information from local devices and store it locally. Distributed managers can inform the central manager of anything requiring immediate attention (e.g. utilization in a router just hit 95 per cent). Later, when the network is not busy, the information can be uploaded. More cleverly, data reduction programs can process the information locally before sending it to the central manager.
  - Serve as a concentrator for multicast of voluminous data. This is especially interesting for software distribution, when the same software is to be distributed to many systems. Rather than wasting bandwidth sending 1 000 copies across the WAN, one copy can be sent to each of several intermediaries, which will then distribute it to nearby systems.
- **Improve reliability**   Clearly, since the intermediate manager is closer to its managed devices, there is a greater likelihood that communication will work properly. This means that the accuracy of the intermediate manager's data will be better. For example, status polls will be less likely to time out or get lost. In addition, any automatic operations performed by the intermediate manager will be more reliable. These considerations become more important when you consider that network management systems are most needed when the network is in the worst shape.

● **Use network management techniques that a central manager cannot use** A good example is IBM's Systems Monitor. When deployed on a LAN, it can use techniques such as broadcasting echo messages to discover new IP systems. This would be prohibitively expensive across a WAN, but can work quite nicely on a LAN. Similarly a local manager— especially one on a LAN—is privy to information a central manager is not, for example Ethernet frames that reveal the existence and statuses of systems.

1.7 NETWORK MANAGEMENT SYSTEMS

There are hundreds if not thousands of network management systems of various sorts on the market:

● Most are relatively simple systems designed to administer, operate and trouble-shoot specific kinds of networking equipment, for example, a particular vendor's bridges.
● Others are designed to tackle a small set of management tasks for a wide range of equipment and protocols, for example IBM's Trouble Ticket for problem and change management or Legent's Distribulink products for software distribution.
● Still others attempt to handle all the important management tasks, but for a particular kind of environment. For example, Microsoft's Systems Management Server, Intel's LANDesk Manager and IBM's NetView for OS/2 are general purpose management systems designed primarily for PC/LAN environments.
● Finally, there are products positioned as enterprise management systems, attempting to provide complete management support for all networking and system environments. In general—because of the huge scope of network and systems management—these products provide a framework and then leave the particulars of different environments to applications.

Enterprise management systems are implemented on IBM mainframes, UNIX systems, Intel-based systems and others. The most popular systems are on UNIX and mainframes.

The two most widely used mainframe enterprise managers are IBM's NetView/390 and Sterling Software's NetMaster. These focus on IBM SNA networks and IBM mainframe management, but also have facilities for managing non-SNA and non-mainframe environments.

Important UNIX-based enterprise managers include:

● *NetView for AIX*, and its other UNIX versions
● Hewlett-Packard's *OpenView*
● SunConnect's *SunNet Manager*
● Cabletron Systems' *Spectrum*
● Ungermann-Bass' *NetDirector*
● NetLabs' *NetLabs/Manager*

Most of these are strongest in IP network management, but provide programming interfaces for applications that manage other environments. In addition, most also provide systems management functions.

1.8 NETVIEW'S SCOPE

That brings us to the particular management system of interest to us. NetView provides a general platform on which management applications using the SNMP management protocol can be written.[1] In addition, NetView includes a set of applications for managing IP networks. Then there are many applications available from IBM and other vendors to manage additional networking environments.

I won't waste time now with an overview of NetView since we will cover it in depth later. It is worth reviewing, though, how NetView fits into the overall world of network management:

- **Configuration management** NetView is quite strong in IP network configuration management. It can automatically discover IP network topology, graphically display it and store the information in a relational database. NetView depends on applications for non-IP configuration management. It includes a facility known as the General Topology Manager, which applications can use to describe any protocol's topology. NetView then displays this information graphically.

  NetView does not address network design, planning or change control in a significant way—there are products from IBM and others to address these requirements. Many NetView applications, especially those designed to manage particular devices, do address remote configuration. Many of these also support distribution of software from NetView, although there is another IBM product family—NetView Distribution Manager—which handles this in a more general way.

- **Operations** For general operations, NetView supports SNMP and several other protocols primarily from the IP and UNIX worlds. These allow automatic operations in response to alarms and messages, or on a scheduled basis. Also, most NetView applications include operational capabilities for the environments they manage.

- **Problem management** NetView and its application have strong function in this area. NetView supports the notification and history aspects of problem management. It logs all incoming alarms, i.e. SNMP traps, and displays them to operators under the control of filters in its Events application. For other aspects of problem management, NetView relies on its applications and IBM's Trouble Ticket product. Trouble Ticket provides problem tracking, co-ordination and history, as well as an alternative notification scheme to NetView's.

  NetView itself helps in the diagnosis process in two main ways—first, by graphically depicting the configuration and condition of networks and, second, through its MIB Browser which lets you look in detail at network components. NetView applications for specific environments generally provide detailed information useful in diagnosis. Many also allow you to run diagnostic routines and to retrieve dumps and traces.

  NetView also has programming interfaces that provide access to incoming alarms. These allow custom problem management functions to be written.

- **Monitoring and reporting** Because of its support for SNMP, NetView is a good monitoring tool, allowing periodic collection of fault, performance and other information from network components. NetView can check the collected data against installation-defined thresholds and can also log it to flat files or to any of several vendors' relational databases.

---

[1] It also supports applications that use the OSI Common Management Information Protocol (CMIP), though in this book we're not concerned with this area.

Reporting is an area NetView does not address. However, its data can easily be used by the many report-generation tools on the market. You can also write your own reporting programs relatively easily—especially if you have NetView log its data to a relational database.

● **Security** NetView does not address this area, except that it controls access to its own functions.

Thus, the areas for which NetView has significant support are:

● Problem management
● Graphical network display
● Operations
● Monitoring and reporting

Because NetView addresses these areas, and because each is an interesting and important issue in network management, these are the four areas we will explore in depth in this book.

TWO

PROTOCOLS

Protocols are an important piece of the network management puzzle—they define the interactions between management systems and the network components they manage. There are several management protocols around, but in this book we're concerned primarily with one, the Simple Network Management Protocol (SNMP). SNMP was originally designed for the Internet and other TCP/IP (Transmission Control Protocol/Internet Protocol) networks, but it has since been implemented in many other environments. Today, most networking equipment includes SNMP capabilities and usually with good function. SNMP does have its weaknesses, as we will see. To address these, the SNMP Version 2 protocol has been developed and is being proposed as a new standard. Still, with SNMPv1 a great deal of useful management can be done, and at the time of writing, network equipment supporting SNMPv2 is rare.

There is another set of management protocols relevant to multiprotocol networking. These have their origins in the OSI world, and the most famous is the Common Management Information Protocol (CMIP). Many people believed that these would be widely implemented, and would even become universal standards. However, their use has so far been limited to a few special environments, for example equipment used in telecommunications. It is true the OSI management protocols are functionally richer than SNMP, but that has been outweighed by the difficulty of implementation and the machine resources required in the managed systems.

Thus, of the major protocols for managing multiprotocol networks, SNMPv1 is today the most significant. It is also the protocol NetView and its applications use to get most of their work done.

In this chapter, we will focus on SNMPv1. We will also briefly review the TCP/IP protocols, since these are closely related to it. A complete discussion of either of these topics would be quite lengthy. Here my aim is to provide enough background information to make it possible to understand NetView. If you would like to understand TCP/IP more deeply, I suggest you read Douglas Comer's (1991) book. For a complete discussion of SNMPv1, I suggest the first edition of *The Simple Book* by Marshall Rose (1991).[1]

---

[1] The second edition (1994) primarily addresses the SNMPv2 protocol. SNMPv2 is also covered by William Stallings (1993). However, since these books were published, there has been considerable activity in revising the protocol.

2.1 THE INTERNET PROTOCOL

The heart of TCP/IP is the Internet Protocol (IP). NetView is a manager of IP networks and also uses them to get much of its work done. It is therefore important to review the basics of IP and some related protocols.

IP, like other data networking protocols, is used to allow the exchange of information between computers, which in the present context are called 'hosts'. IP's name comes from the fact that it was designed as a way to tie together groups of networks—all potentially using different protocols—into an overall 'internetwork' providing end-to-end services to hosts. For example (as shown in Figure 2.1) an internetwork might be used to tie together three networks: an Ethernet, a Token-Ring and a Frame Relay network.

Clearly, since each of these three networks uses a different protocol, something additional is required to allow, for example, a host in the Ethernet to communicate with one in the Token-Ring. This can be done by running IP as a common protocol throughout the internetwork and using the local protocol within each network to carry the IP messages. Routers connect the networks together and switch messages from one network to another.

Suppose a host connected to the Ethernet needs to send a message to one on the Token-Ring. To do this, it would send the message across the Ethernet to the router. This would send the message across the Frame Relay network to the second router, which would then send it across the Token-Ring to the destination host. At each stage of the trip, the protocol of the particular network would be used.

We can think of an internetwork's protocols as being organized into three layers (see Figure 2.2). Each layer provides a service to the layer above and, to do so, uses the services of the layer below. The top layer provides services to application programs.

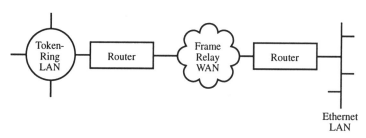

Figure 2.1 An internetwork

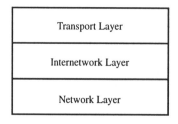

Figure 2.2 Layered model of IP

The three layers are:

- **Network layer**   The protocols used to carry messages from one host to another in the same network. (This has nothing to do with the network layer in the OSI reference model.)
- **Internetwork layer**   The protocols used to carry messages from one host to another in a different network. For consistency, these protocols are used to carry messages within the same network as well.
- **Transport layer**   The protocols providing additional services to users of the internetwork, for example guaranteeing the delivery of messages and controlling the rate at which they flow.

The hosts in an internetwork will implement all three layers to support their application programs. Routers also implement all three layers, though they use only the bottom two for the actual switching of messages through the internetwork. They use the top layer for 'applications' required to support routing, e.g. network management programs.

Let's look at each of these layers in more detail.

2.1.1 Network layer

The network layer accepts messages from its users and delivers them to users elsewhere in the network. These users are normally instances of the internetwork layer. Examples of network protocols are Ethernet, Token-Ring, Fiber Distributed Data Interface (FDDI) and Frame Relay, There are many others.

As shown in Figure 2.3, a user of the network layer passes it a message along with instructions such as where it should be sent. The network layer places the message inside a 'frame', which consists of the message itself and a 'header'. The header contains control information required by the protocol. The frame is then sent across the network to the destination host. There, the network layer removes the header and delivers the message to a user (which user is determined by information in the header).

The network protocol performs its work in either a reliable or an unreliable manner. Thus, it may simply give up when it cannot easily send a frame across the network or it may try over and over until it succeeds. In TCP/IP, either approach is acceptable.

Most network protocols send the entire message in a single frame, that is, they do not perform segmentation. Since there will be a limit to a frame's size, large messages must be broken into pieces before they are given to the network layer.

2.1.2 Internetwork layer

Now let's consider an important user of the network layer—the internetwork layer.

The protocol here—IP proper—accepts messages from users and delivers them to other users residing anywhere else in the internetwork. These users are most often transport protocols. The internetwork layer works similarly to the network layer, accepting data up to a certain limit, adding control information as a header, and sending this across the internetwork. The data and header are collectively referred to as a 'packet'. It's possible that the packet will be too large to

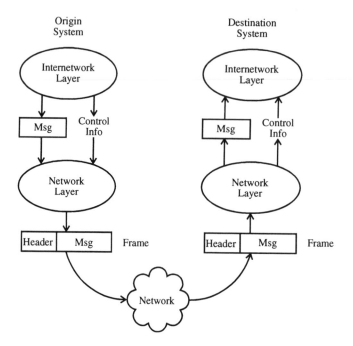

Figure 2.3 Sending data with the network protocol

fit into a single network-layer frame, in which case the data will be sent in mutliple packets and reassembled at the destination.

One of the most important pieces of information in the IP header is the destination address. This 32-bit address is divided into two parts:

● The address of the network in which the destination host lies.
● The address of the destination host within that network.

As shown in Figure 2.4, the first stage in a packet's trip across the internetwork is from the origin host to a router on the same network. It is also possible that the ultimate destination of the packet will be in the same network. In this case, no router will be involved and the packet will be sent directly to this destination. Assuming at least one router will be involved, the following steps will occur in the transmission of the packet:

● A user in the origin host passes the internetwork layer some data and instructions such as where to send it. The IP layer creates the packet, and determines the router to which it should be sent. It passes the packet to the network layer.
● The network layer, as usual, attaches its own header to form a frame, and sends it across the network to the destination router.
● At the router, the network layer receives the frame, removes its header and delivers the embedded packet to the IP layer.
● The IP layer in the router looks at the packet's header to determine the ultimate destination. The destination may be in a network to which the router is attached or may be in a remote

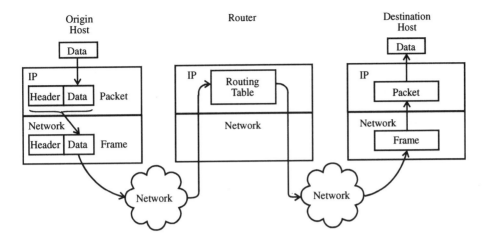

Figure 2.4 Sending an IP packet

network. If local, the router sends the packet directly to the host, using the network protocol. If remote, it chooses the next router is the packet's journey, and sends the packet using the network protocol. This next router must of course be in a local network and it is desirable that it be closer to the destination. We'll see how this choice is made in a moment.

● This process is repeated in each router along the packet's path, until the packet is delivered to the destination host.

The IP protocol carries out its work in an unreliable manner. Thus, in each step along the packet's path, the protocol simply sends the packet along and forgets about it. If the packet is lost or corrupted, there is no attempt to re-send it.

The main complexity in the IP protocol is the question of 'routing', that is, determining the next router to which a packet should be sent. In the simple internetwork we're considering here, there is only one path a packet can take between the origin and destination hosts. However, in most internetworks, there are many such paths and therefore at least some of the routers will have to make choices. Clearly, it would be good if the routers did this so that the packet takes the shortest and fastest path through the internetwork.

The basic mechanism used for making these choices is the 'routing table'. Each router maintains such a table, which indicates, for each possible destination network, the next router to which a packet should be sent. Routing tables are built in a variety of ways. In the simplest case, the network administrators simply define them, a method known as 'static routing'. More flexibly, the routers will chat among themselves and automatically build their routing tables from their collective knowledge of the internetwork. This is called 'dynamic routing' and there are several protocols used to perform it. Examples include Routing Information Protocol (RIP) and Open Shortest Path First (OSPF).

By allowing packets to be sent across a multiprotocol internetwork—albeit in an unreliable manner—IP is clearly an improvement over network layer protocols. Still, more is needed.

2.1.3 Transport protocols

Transport protocols enhance the service provided by IP, making it easier for application programs to use the internetwork. They provide one or more of the following enhancements:

- **Unique access points**   There are potentially many applications in a single host that need to use the internetwork and a mechanism is therefore required to coordinate their access to it. For example, it's necessary to determine which application should receive the data in each incoming packet.
- **Reliable delivery**   While IP doesn't care if packets get lost, many applications programs cannot afford to lose their data. Transport protocols can add reliable delivery by tracking which data has been successfully received at the destination, and re-sending that which has not been.
- **Sequencing of data**   IP does not guarantee that packets are delivered to the destination in the order sent. When order is important, transport protocols can attach sequence numbers to outgoing data, and re-sequence as necessary at the destination.
- **Flow control**   A program may send data much more quickly than the destination can receive it. To avoid jamming the internetwork or losing data, flow control mechanisms can slow the sender to a pace the receiver can handle.

While several transport protocols have been defined for IP, two are most widely used:

- **Transmission Control Protocol**   TCP provides all the enhancements listed above. It is a 'connection-oriented' protocol so that, when two programs wish to communicate, they create a virtual connection between themselves. This connection provides the basis for reliability, flow control and sequencing. When using TCP, programs send their data in 'streams'. Thus, rather than breaking outgoing data into segments, a program simply sends a sequence of bytes which is reliably delivered to the destination. The TCP service performs any segmentation required by the internetwork.
- **User Datagram Protocol (UDP)**   This is a very simple transport protocol for programs that do not require all the services (and complexities) of TCP. UDP simply provides a way for one program to send limited length messages to another. UDP sends these 'datagrams' to the destination on a 'best effort' basis. If datagrams get lost or corrupted, UDP forgets about them. Multiple datagrams may be delivered out of sequence. However, UDP does ensure that any datagrams actually delivered to the destination are not corrupt.

    In UDP, there are no connections between programs, but instead programs simply 'listen' for incoming datagrams.

A program uses either TCP or UDP through an abstraction known as a 'port', each of which is identified with a number. These provide the basis for multiplexing the incoming data to the correct applications. Thus, when a program wishes to use TCP, it connects to a particular TCP port and also specifies the port on the remote host of its intended partner. In UDP, an application simply connects to a port and waits for data.

    By convention, some port numbers are 'well known', that is, they are used by common utility programs such as time servers, login servers and file transfer servers. These utilities generally have the same port numbers on all hosts to ensure easy interoperability.

A concept related to ports is that of 'sockets'. These are programming abstractions from the UNIX world which applications use to interact with TCP and UDP. Sockets are similar to file handles and they represent a program's connection to a particular port in a particular transport protocol.

2.1.4 Applications

To make all this machinery useful, we of course need application programs. These may be applications dedicated to a particular purpose (e.g. payroll processing) or they may be the standard utility programs found on hosts supporting IP.

One common utility is *telnet*, with which a user can log into a remote host. Another is the File Transfer Protocol (FTP). This allows a user on one host to connect to another and transfer files. For security a user ID and password must be given. A related utility is the Trivial File Transfer Protocol (TFTP), which is FTP *sans* security.

There are also the Network File System (NFS) and the more recent Andrew File System (AFS). These allow one host's disks or directories to be remotely mounted by another, so that they appear to be local.

Most important to us is the 'application' known as SNMP.

2.1.5 Address resolution

There are a few other aspects of IP we should review before we go on. One is the Address Resolution Protocol (ARP). A few pages back, we discussed the fact that each host and router has an address used in the IP protocol. What we skimmed over is that there are also addresses in the network protocols. These allow systems on the same network to identify one another.

For example, in an Ethernet using IP, each system will have an IP address. It will also have an Ethernet address which uniquely identifies it within the LAN. When one system wishes to send a frame to another, it must know the destination's Ethernet address. The question is, how does it know this network address? The routing tables do not help since they contain IP addresses only.

ARP solves this problem. It relies on the fact that network-layer protocols generally provide a broadcast facility which allows a frame to be sent to all systems in the particular network. When a system needs to know the network address corresponding to a given IP address, it broadcasts a special message in the network. The message requests that the system with the given IP address respond by sending its network address. Assuming that system is present and active, it will do so.

This much clearly solves the problem, but not very efficiently. If this had to be done each time a host or router sent a packet, it would clog the network with broadcasts and delay transmission. Thus, systems maintain 'ARP caches' in which they remember the mappings they have learned. Generally, an ageing scheme is incorporated so that each entry is retained in the cache for only a limited period of time. This allows for systems that change their network or IP addresses.

2.1.6 Addresses and names

We have seen that IP uses 32-bit addresses in which one portion identifies the network and the other identifies the system. To be picky, it is actually the network interfaces on systems that have IP addresses. If a system has only one network interface, e.g. a single Ethernet card, then this distinction is essentially irrelevant. If it has two or more interfaces, e.g. an Ethernet card and a modem, then each will have a distinct address and in fact each will usually reside in a separate network. Routers generally have multiple IP addresses.

Let's look at bit more closely at the network portion of the address. A network normally corresponds to an organization. Thus, one company will have a single network address, identifying it uniquely in the Internet. The company then assigns the host addresses within its network. Of course, that network may have many protocols running within, such as Token-Ring, Ethernet and PPP (Point-to-Point Protocol), and therefore will be structured as its own (smaller) internetwork. To accommodate this, a scheme known as 'subnetting' is used. This allows the company's network to look like a single network to the outside world, while it has its internetwork structure within.

IP addresses come in three flavours, Class A, B and C. Figure 2.5 shows the formats of each. In a Class A address, each network may contain approximately 16 million host addresses, in Class B 65 534 and in Class C 254 addresses.[2] Although the total number of possible addresses is large, the Class A and B addresses are nearly used up. Since Class C addresses have limited usefulness, this has become a serious issue for the Internet.

Normally, when people write IP addresses, they use the 'dotted decimal' notation, in which each byte of the address is represented by its decimal equivalent and the four resulting numbers are concatenated together with dots. For example, 9.180.181.7 denotes an IP address in which the most significant byte is 9, the second most significant 180 and so on.

IP addresses—whether represented as 32-bit binary quantities or in dotted decimal—are not particularly handy for people to use. Thus, it is possible to assign one or more names to each IP address. For example, my system has the name 'bennett.hursley.ibm.com', which corresponds to the address 9.20.26.9. When someone wants to *telnet* to my system, they can simply refer to it by its name.

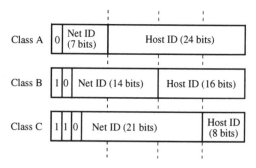

Figure 2.5 IP address formats

---

[2] The host address of all zeros is reserved to represent 'this host'. The address of all ones is reserved as the 'broadcast' address.

The mapping from name to address can be defined in several ways. The simplest is to provide each host with a file explicitly listing names and corresponding addresses. There are of course several disadvantages to this approach, including the hassle of manually defining these files, the disk space required, and the problem of updating them when the mappings change. Thus, the Domain Name System (DNS) has been devised.

In the DNS, names have a hierarchical structure which avoids the need for a central authority that assigns all names. This is accomplished by having multi-part names in which each part is potentially owned by a different naming authority. For example, in my system's name ('bennett.hursley.ibm.com') the string 'com' indicates that the name is in the domain of those administered for commercial organizations, and the 'ibm' indicates the domain of names administered by IBM. The IBM site in Hursley, UK administers those with the string 'hursley' and the administrators there assigned my system the string 'bennett'. They also defined the mapping from my system's name to its IP address.

This much solves the problem of assigning unique names to IP addresses. To provide systems with easy access to the mappings when they wish to communicate, name servers are positioned throughout the internetwork. These name servers use a rather elaborate protocol to exchange information among themselves and to avoid the need for all servers to know all mappings. They use a scheme in which there is a hierarchy of servers. Those at the lowest levels know only a subset of the internetwork's names. If they are asked to map a name they don't know, they can consult a higher level server. This scheme is explained in detail in Comer's (1991) book.

2.1.7 ICMP

A very important protocol in the IP world is the Internet Control Message Protocol (ICMP). It includes a series of messages that IP hosts can send to one another to perform low-level monitoring and control of an IP internetwork. These are sent using the services of the IP layer.

The most famous ICMP messages are Echo and Echo Reply. They are used by an IP system to determine whether another is reachable and alive. To do this, an IP system sends an Echo message to the other, which responds with an Echo Reply.

ICMP Echo and Echo Reply are the basis of the widely used PING (Packet Internet Groper) command available in nearly all IP implementations. With PING, you specify the address of an IP system and then ICMP Echoes are repeatedly sent to it. Any replies are reported back to you. This is extremely useful for diagnosing problems in IP internetworks. As we will see, NetView makes extensive use of this facility, mainly to monitor whether IP systems are active.

There is also a broadcast version of this, in which a system can send Echoes to the broadcast address in a network. All systems on the network that receive the Echo will respond with an Echo Reply. This can be used to determine the addresses of all active systems on a particular network.

2.1.8 The X protocol

An important tool in the IP world is the X protocol. This is part of the X Window System used in UNIX and elsewhere to implement graphical user interfaces (GUIs). X Windows provides the basic infrastructure for GUIs, but does not implement 'details' such as window frames, button boxes and menus. These are handled instead by a 'window manager', the most famous of which is the Open Software Foundation's Motif.

X Windows allows applications to implement their user interfaces in a location-independent manner. As shown in Figure 2.6, the application runs in a host such as a UNIX system. The user accesses the application from a remote system known as an X station. This may be a special purpose device (with screen, keyboard and mouse) or it may be a workstation that supports X Windows, for example one running UNIX, OS/2 or Windows. Communication between the X station and the host is done according to the X protocol, which is carried over TCP .

The application interacts with the GUI through software known as an X Client. On the X Station, software called an X server runs to present the GUI to the user. Client and server here are the opposite of what we would expect, but if you think of the X station as analogous to a print server, it's not that strange.

The important point here is that the application is unaware of the user's location. Thus, the user could be on the same LAN or could be on the other side of the world. He could also be directly using the application's host, in which case the X client and server would run on the same system. Normally, X is not used across WANs. Although the protocol is oblivious to the user's location, the large amounts of information exchanged make WANs impractical.

As we will see, NetView uses X Windows and Motif for its GUI, and the X protocol is one of the methods through which it supports remote users.

2.2 SNMP VERSION 1

Let's now look at the SNMPv1 protocol, which for brevity we will call SNMP.

SNMP is a very simple protocol, and yet it includes much of what's required for network management. SNMP is primarily used to make information in networking equipment available to the management system, especially performance, error and configuration information. There are also many implementations in which the management system uses SNMP to control network equipment. In theory, you could implement almost any kind of management you like using SNMP, although there are two significant issues that limit this in practice. One is that SNMP security is not especially strong and the other is that SNMP is not very good at bulk data transfers.

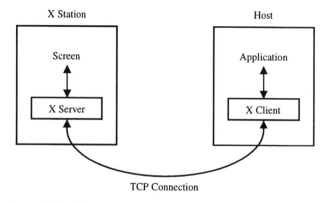

Figure 2.6 The X protocol

The security issue has caused reluctance to implement significant control mechanisms with SNMP. For example, allowing the management system to reconfigure a router with SNMP would be unwise if you believe it's easy for a hacker to break its security. However, as we will discuss below, this security exposure has been overstated, at least in relation to other protocols that are trusted.

The bulk data issue is that SNMP cannot effectively utilize network bandwidth during large data transfers. This has meant that management tasks such as software distribution have not been widely implemented with SNMP.

Both these problems have been addressed in SNMPv2, although its slow take-up makes one wonder how serious they really are. Meanwhile, SNMPv1 has been implemented widely for network monitoring, and to a lesser extent for network control.

2.2.1 Standards

Like the other IP-based protocols, SNMP has been developed and standardized under the auspices of the Internet Engineering Task Force. The SNMP standards reside in a set of documents called Requests for Comments (RFCs). RFCs are used in the Internet world to disseminate many kinds of information, including standards. Their name comes from the fact that they are circulated for review among those interested in the Internet and its technology. There are RFCs on all sorts of topics, from IP itself to its applications.

Four RFCs document the core of SNMPv1:

- RFC 1155—'Structure of Management Information'
- RFC 1157—'Simple Network Management Protocol'
- RFC 1212—'Concise MIB Definitions'
- RFC 1213—'Management Information Base II'

There are also many other RFCs that document extensions to standard SNMP for particular purposes, especially for specific networking protocols.[3]

2.2.2 Managers and agents

In SNMP, all interactions occur between 'managers' and 'agents'. This is shown in Figure 2.7. Usually, the manager is the network management system and the agent is a piece of software running in a network component, for example a router. The agent is the logic that is required to interact with the manager, and also to interact with the component itself to carry out management tasks. The manager and agent exchange messages according to rules specified by SNMP.

---

[3] All RFCs are widely available on the Internet, for example by FTPing to the node nis.nsf.net. You can log in as user 'anonymous' and the RFCs are in the directory documents/rfc. Unless you know specifically the RFC you want, you would do well to first get the index which is in the file INDEX.rfc. Another interesting document to get is the latest version of the 'Internet Official Protocol Standards' which documents the standards status of the various RFCs. At this writing, the latest version is in RFC 1780. This will no doubt have changed by the time you read this so the best thing to do is search the index. I've also put all RFCs mentioned in this book into the set of softcopy materials available from the Internet at www.mcgraw-hill.co.uk (check on editorial information for professional computing).

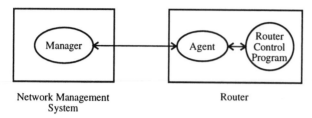

Network Management
System

Router

Figure 2.7 Manager and agent

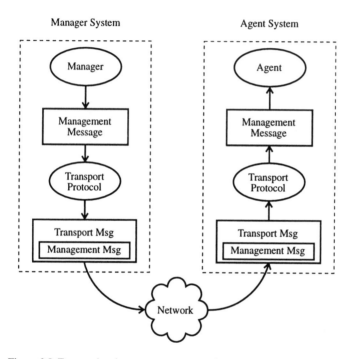

Figure 2.8 Transporting the management protocol

For example, if the manager wants to tell the router to reset an interface card, it will place its instructions in a message, and send it to the router's agent. The agent will then pass these instructions to the router control program. Similarly, if the router control program encounters a serious problem, it will instruct its agent to send a message to the manager.

Management protocols such as SNMP rely on 'transport protocols' to carry their messages. SNMP usually relies on the IP-based transport protocols, in particular UDP. Thus, as shown in Figure 2.8, the management protocol 'runs over' or 'on top of' the transport protocol.

It is therefore important that the manager and agent use the same management and transport protocols. These days, arranging the former is easy if you're using SNMP, but in some cases it can be tricky to provide the required transport protocol. We will consider these issues later.

So far we've been discussing the manager–agent model in its most simple context. More elaborate arrangements are also possible:

- One is where the agent communicates with an intermediate manager, which in turn communicates with a higher-level manager. Here simple and routine management tasks are performed by the intermediate manager, while more complex or important tasks are performed by the higher-level manager.

    In some management protocols, there is a special sub-protocol defined for use between the higher-level manager and the intermediate. In SNMP, it is the same as the normal manager-agent protocol. Thus, the manager believes the intermediate is an agent, while the real agent believes it's a manager. (In SNMPv2, there is a special manager-agent protocol.)

- Another arrangement is shown in Figure 2.9, where the agent does not reside in the network component to be managed, but instead is in a separate piece of equipment. Here the agent is referred to as a 'proxy agent'. There are several reasons for this arrangement, but they all boil down to the real agent not being able to talk to the manager. This may be because the agent does not support SNMP or because it does not support the transport protocol used by the manager. Proxy agents serve as translators of one kind or another between managers and network components.

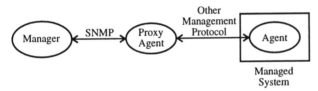

Figure 2.9 Proxy agent

2.2.3 Protocol and MIBs

To understand SNMP, it will be useful to think of its two important parts:

- **The protocol proper**   This defines the messages exchanged between managers and agents, the message formats and the rules for exchanging them.
- **The information contained in the messages**   Most of this information is formulated in terms of abstractions called 'managed objects'.

We can think of a managed object as a variable that contains a piece of information. Collections of these are maintained by agents. For example, the agent in a router might have an object that contains some text describing its location and another object that gives the number of frames it has sent on a particular interface. Managers can then send requests to agents to obtain the values of these objects.

    Managers can also send requests to agents to change objects and this provides the basis for operations. For example, the agent in a router could have an object that, when set to 1, causes the router to activate a particular interface and when 0 to deactivate it.

    The collection of managed objects maintained by an agent is called its Management Information Base (MIB). People sometimes think of this as a database, but an agent's MIB will normally be implemented in RAM or virtual memory, or will be created on the fly. The important point is that the MIB is structured according to SNMP rules and the manager can access it in a standard way, regardless of how the agent implements it.

In SNMP, there is a grand total of five messages. Three of them—Get, GetNext and Set—are directly concerned with the manager reading and manipulating managed objects. The fourth is the response agents send to any of these. The fifth, Trap, allows for asynchronous notification from the agent to the manager when an exceptional condition occurs.

2.2.4 MIBs

As shown in Figure 2.10, an agent's MIB has two major parts. One is the base set of objects that all agents are required to have. The other is the set of additional objects the agent may have to support management of particular facilities in its system. For example, a router will have the base MIB to hold general information and then may have additional objects for special hardware it contains.

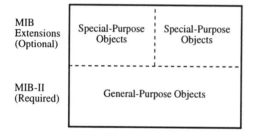

Figure 2.10 MIB extensions

The base MIB that all agents must implement is known as MIB-II. As its names suggests, it is the successor to an earlier base MIB. MIB-II defines a few hundred objects, which are structured into several groups. Each group pertains to an aspect of the agent or its system. For example, there is the Interfaces Group which consists of objects related to communications interfaces. Some of these groups must be implemented by all agents, while others are required only by agents whose system supports a particular function. For example, all agents must implement the Interfaces Group, while only those agents whose systems support TCP must implement the TCP Group.

The sets of additional objects that agents implement are termed 'MIB extensions'. Some MIB extensions are standardized in RFCs, especially when their objects pertain to widely implemented functions. For example, there are standard MIB extensions for the management of Frame Relay networks. In other cases, the MIB extension will be defined privately, usually by companies developing networking software and equipment. For example, most router manufacturers define private MIB extensions for special features in their products.

Before we look at the information contained in MIBs, let's understand their structure.

Naming Clearly, if the manager is to access managed objects, each must have a name. In SNMP, this name is called the 'object identifier'. We could of course name objects after our friends and pets, but the designers of SNMP felt a more organized approach was required. This approach is based on the idea of a 'naming tree'. The goal is to structure names so that different organizations can create their own without conflicting with one another, much like the IP Domain Name System we discussed a few pages back.

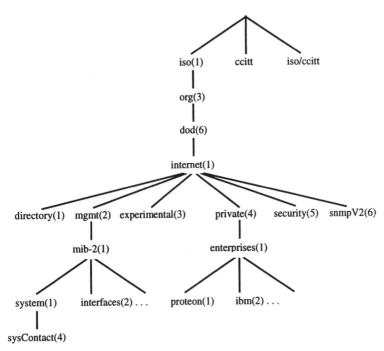

Figure 2.11 The naming tree

The naming tree, part of which is shown in Figure 2.11, is structured in a hierarchical manner. Different parts of the tree are 'delegated' to particular organizations who can then assign names by constructing a sub-tree of their own. The top node in the tree is owned by some unspecified but all-powerful being. This node then has three child nodes. These delegate naming spaces to the two international standards organizations, the ISO and the CCITT,[4] and also to the two collectively. Then, as shown in the diagram, the ISO's sub-tree is further delegated until we come to the first node of interest to us, the node *internet*. This is owned by an organization known as the Internet Assigned Numbers Authority. Under this, we find two nodes relevant to us, the node *mgmt* under which names for standardized management are found, and the node *private* for privately assigned names.

The actual names (the object IDs) are derived directly from this tree. Each node has a number assigned to it as shown in the diagram, and this number is unique among all nodes on the same level of the tree. A particular object's ID is derived by starting at the top of the tree and following the nodes down to it. The ID is then the list of numbers corresponding to the nodes encountered along the way. By convention this object ID has dots to separate each of the numbers.

For example, the *sysContact* object in the System Group of MIB-II has object ID 1.3.6.1.2.1.1.4.

There are two portions of the naming tree which are particularly interesting to us: the *mib-2* portion under *mgmt* and the *enterprises* portion under *private*.

---

[4] ISO is the International Standards Organization and CCITT the International Telegraph and Telephone Consultative Committee (CCITT is from its French name).

The *mib-2* portion of the tree contains the names for MIB-II. It also includes several additional groups of objects defined by RFCs for specific purposes. For example, under the node *transmission* there are several media-specific groups, including those for FDDI and Token-Ring. The objects named in this portion of the tree must be sufficiently general that they apply to a wide range of implementations.

The *enterprises* sub-tree contains all object IDs that are defined in private MIB extensions. It is further divided into sub-trees assigned to vendors and other organizations. For example, node 1 under *private* is assigned to Proteon, while 2 is assigned to IBM. In this sub-tree, the objects have a narrower applicability than those under *mib-2* and will usually apply to equipment from particular vendors.

Objects and instance So far I've been talking about managed objects and variables as if they were the same thing, but the time has come for us to pull our socks up and be clear about terminology.

Objects—in the strictest sense of the word—are prototypes or templates. Their 'instances' are the things the manager actually accesses. The object itself simply has attributes such as data type which the instances inherit.

A managed object can have zero, one or many instances. Objects that are limited to one instance are called 'scalar objects'. An example is the *sysContact* object from MIB-II. This has one instance which contains the name of the person responsible for the system. Other objects may have multiple instances. An example is the *ifSpeed* object from MIB-II, where each instance holds the speed of one of the interfaces in the system.

An instance of an object is often called a 'variable' since it contains the actual management information.

Each instance of an object has an 'instance identifier'. By convention, the identifier for a scalar object is 0. The identifiers for multiple instance objects have other values. These might, for example, be 1, 2, 3 and so on or can be more complicated, for example 1.2 or 3.4.5.6. In general, the syntax of instance identifiers is the same as that for object identifiers—a series of numbers concatenated together with dots.

The instances of objects are themselves considered to be objects, though they are of a special type and do not for example have their own instances. Thus, instances are named with object IDs. An instance's object ID is formed by simply appending its instance ID to its parent's object ID. For example, if the object 1.2.3 has an instance 4, then the instance will have the object ID 1.2.3.4.

Tables Let's look a bit more at objects that have multiple instances. These are used to build tables, as can be found for example in the Interfaces Group of MIB-II. It is natural to represent a system's interfaces and their attributes with a table. As shown in Figure 2.12, each row of the table is used to describe an interface and each column to hold an attribute. To keep things simple, let's assume that all we want to know about an interface is its type (i.e. Ethernet, Token-Ring, Serial), speed and a brief text description. (As we will see, MIB-II contains much more information about interfaces.)

In SNMP, this table would be represented as shown in Figure 2.13. We would first create three multiple instance objects. Let's call them *ifSpeed*, *ifType* and *ifDescr* as they are in MIB-II. Then, for each interface in the host, we would create an instance of each object. Thus, instance 1

	ifType	*ifSpeed*	*ifDescr*
Interface 1	Ethernet	10 000 000	"3COM Ethernet Adapter"
Interface 2	Token-Ring	16 000 000	"IBM Token-Ring Adapter"
Interface 3	Serial	14 400	"SLIP Modem Interface"

Figure 2.12 Host's interface in table

```
ifType.1   Ethernet
ifType.2   Token-Ring
ifType.3   Serial

ifSpeed.1 10,000,000
ifSpeed.2 16,000,000
ifspeed.3 14,400

ifDescr.1 "3COM Ethernet Adapter"
ifDescr.2 "IBM Token-Ring Adapter"
ifDescr.3 "SLIP Modem Interface"
```

Figure 2.13 Tabular MIB objects representing host's interfaces

of *ifSpeed* would hold the speed of interface 1, instance 1 of *ifDescr* its description and instance 1 of *ifType* its type. Instance 2 of the objects would describe interface 2 and so forth.

We can think of the objects as the columns of the table, and the instances as the rows. For this reason, multiple instance objects are sometimes called 'columnar objects'. The instance ID of a columnar object is often referred to as its 'index'. Note that in a table there is no rule that says the indices must be sequential or begin with one.

Tables are not particularly exotic data structures, but they're as complicated as SNMP gets. They are enough for most purposes, but if you need to model something more complicated, you can use instance IDs with multiple parts. For example, suppose the interfaces in our example each had two ports, and that we wanted to have a different description, speed and type for each port. To do this we could assign:

- instance ID 1.1 to interface 1, port 1
- instance ID 1.2 to interface 1, port 2
- instance ID 2.1 to interface 2, port 1

and so on. In effect, we would have a three-dimensional data structure. In SNMP, this is treated as a table which just happens to have more complicated instance IDs.

Ordering There is an ordering defined on all the objects and instances in a particular MIB. This ordering is the obvious one—determined by the numbers in the object IDs. Numbers to the left have the greatest significance. For example:

```
1.1.1 < 1.1.2 < 1.1.2.0 < 1.2.1 < 1.3
```

This ordering turns out to be useful for several purposes, for example 'walking' through all the variables in a MIB. We will look at this in the section on the GetNext request.

MIB-II Before continuing with the general principles of MIBs, let's look at a concrete example, MIB-II. This MIB contains information that is common to most systems you might want to manage with SNMP. It is defined in RFC 1213 and contains a great deal of information. With just MIB-II, a considerable amount of useful network management can be done.

MIB-II is divided into ten groups, most of which are mandatory for all SNMP agents conforming to the standard. Here we will look at it briefly; you can get the full details from RFC 1213.

System group This group is mandatory. It contains general information about the agent's system and has the following seven scalar objects:

- *sysDescr*—text description of the system.
- *sysObjectID*—an object ID describing the agent. This will normally be an object ID from under the enterprises node of the naming tree. In most cases, the *sysObjectID* will identify the particular make and model of networking equipment or the particular software it is running.
- *sysUpTime*—hundredths of seconds since the agent started.
- *sysContact*—text giving the contact person for the system.
- *sysName*—administratively assigned name for the system. By convention, this is the system's full domain name (from the DNS).
- *sysLocation*—text giving the location of the system.
- *sysServices*—an integer sum describing the services offered by the system. (The details of how this is done are in RFC 1213.)

For example, my system has the following System Group variables:

```
sysDescr:   OS/2 SNMP AGENT version 1.2
sysObjectID: 1.3.6.1.4.1.2.6.46
sysUpTime:   4206
sysContact: Larry Bennett
sysName:    bennett.hursley.ibm.com
sysLocation: Chalfont St Giles, England
sysServices: 76
```

Interfaces group This group is mandatory and contains information about each of the system's interfaces. This includes a scalar object (*ifNumber*) giving the number of interfaces and then a table in which there is one row for each interface.

The table (*ifTable*) contains the following columnar objects:
- *ifIndex*—this contains the instance ID, i.e. index, for the row. For example, the index will be 1 for interface 1.
- *ifDescr*—text describing the interface.
- *ifType*—an integer indicating the type of the interface, e.g. 6 = ethernet-csmacd, 17 = sdlc.
- *ifSpeed*—the speed of the interface.

- *ifPhysAddress*—the 'physical address' or, in this chapter's earlier terminology, the 'network address' of the interface.
- *ifOutOctets* and *ifInOctets*—number of bytes sent and received on the interface.
- Several other objects giving further details for the interface, including its status and some error counters.

From this example, we can see the general principle that the index is also a columnar object within the table and can be accessed just as any other object can.

Address translation group While this group is mandatory it is also 'deprecated', which is to say it may be removed in a future version of the MIB. The information here is also contained in the IP Group (described in the next section). It consists of a set of mappings between the physical (i.e. network) addresses of systems and their IP addresses. This generally reflects the system's Address Resolution Protocol (ARP) cache.
  This group consists of a table with the following columnar objects:

- *atIfIndex*—the index of the interface (from *ifTable*) through which this address is accessible.
- *atPhysAddress*—the physical (network) address.
- *atNetAddress*—the IP address.

IP group This group is mandatory and contains information about the IP protocol running in the system. It contains 20 scalar objects and three tables.
  The scalar objects are mainly counters of various events in the IP protocol on this system, but also include a few other bits of information. The more interesting scalar objects are:

- *ipForwarding*—whether this system forwards IP packets, i.e. whether it can serve as a router.
- *ipOutRequests* and *ipInReceives*—counters of IP packets sent and received.
- *ipForwDatagrams*—number of IP packets this system has forwarded.
- Several counters of various sorts of errors that have occurred in the IP protocol on this system.

The three tables in this group are:

- *ipAddrTable*—this gives information about the interfaces on the system. For each, it gives the IP address, the subnet mask (used in the IP subnetting mechanism we discussed earlier), the largest IP packet it can handle and its index in the Interfaces Table.
- *ipRouteTable*—this describes the IP routing table in this system.
- *ipNetToMediaTable*—this contains essentially the same information as is found in the Address Translation Group.

ICMP group This group is mandatory. It contains information about the operation of the ICMP protocol in the system and has only scalar objects:

- There are four scalar objects that apply to all ICMP messages handled by this system: *icmpInMsgs*, *icmpOutMsgs*, *icmpInErrors* and *icmpOutErrors*.
- The rest of the scalars form 11 pairs. In each pair, one scalar counts the number of times a particular ICMP message type has been sent and the other counts the number of times it has been received. For example, *icmpOutEchos* counts the number of times an ICMP Echo request has been sent, while *icmpInEchos* counts the number of times it has been received.

TCP group This group is mandatory for systems that implement TCP. There are 14 scalar objects and a table.

Among the more interesting scalars are:

- Three objects describing the TCP re-transmission process used by this system, specifically an identifier of the algorithm used and the maximum and minimum time-out values.
- Two objects giving the current and maximum number of TCP connections for the system.
- Several counters of TCP errors on this system.

The table is called *tcpConnTable* and it has one entry for each of the system's TCP connections. For each connection, it gives the:

- State
- Origin address and port
- Destination address and port

UDP group This group is mandatory for systems that implement UDP and describes the operation of the protocol on the system. This group is analogous to the TCP group, but as you would expect is much simpler. There are four scalar objects and one table.

The scalars are:

- *udpOutDatagrams* and *udpInDatagrams*—total number of UDP datagrams sent and received
- *udpNoPorts*—total number of UDP datagrams received for which there was no application at the destination port
- *udpInErrors*—total number of UDP datagrams received in error (excluding those counted in *udpNoPorts*)

The table, *udpTable*, is quite simple since in UDP there is no notion of connections to other systems. Thus, each row of the table simply describes a port on which an application is listening. This is done with two columnar objects, *udpLocalAddress* and *udpLocalPort*.[5]

EGP group This group is mandatory for systems that implement the Exterior Gateway Protocol (EGP). EGP is one of the protocols routers use to obtain information for their routing tables. An explanation of EGP is beyond the scope of this book, so let's simply observe that this group exists.

---

[5] In systems with multiple interfaces, *udpLocalAddress* is relevant since when an application listens, it does so on a particular interface.

Transmission group As we have seen, this group is a place-holder, under which media-specific extensions to MIB-II reside, such as those for FDDI and Token-Ring.

SNMP group This group is mandatory and contains 28 scalar objects describing the SNMP protocol on the system. These objects include:

- *snmpOutPkts* and *snmpInPkts*—number of SNMP messages sent and received.
- Several counters of the different types of SNMP requests sent and received.
- Several counters of SNMP protocol errors.
- Two counters giving the number of managed objects that have been read by a manager, and that have been set.
- *snmpEnableAuthenTraps*—controls whether the agent will send traps when it receives requests from a manager that cannot be authenticated.

ASN.1 and MIB definition MIB-II and its extensions are defined in a standard way, according to rules specified by SNMP's Structure of Management Information (SMI). The SMI specifies how to define 'MIB modules'. Each of these defines a particular collection of managed objects. MIB-II is defined in a single MIB module, and similarly most extensions are each defined in a single module.

The language used to define MIB modules is a subset of the Abstract Syntax Notation 1 language (ASN.1). This language has its origins in the OSI world and was chosen by SNMP's designers at least partly for compatibility between SNMP and the OSI network management standards. In addition to using ASN.1 as the language for defining MIB modules, SNMP also uses it to specify the syntax of the messages in the manager-to-agent protocol (e.g. Get and Set).

A complete description of ASN.1 or even the subset used in SNMP is beyond the scope of this book.[6] Instead, we will cover enough to make it easy to understand MIB modules defined with ASN.1.

There are two styles of modules. The first, documented in RFC 1155, is the SNMPv1 style. The second, documented in RFC 1442, is for SNMPv2. The two styles are very similar, and it is easy to forget the difference when reading a module. The major improvements in the SNMPv2 style are:

- More tightly defined data types for objects
- A formal method of describing what agents must do to conform to a module
- A formal method of defining traps

Here I'll describe the SNMPv1 style, since it is the most widely used and is also the only style supported by NetView.[7]

Module structure The basic structure of a MIB module is as follows:

```
<module name> DEFINITIONS ::= BEGIN
<linkage>
```

---

[6] The two editions of *The Simple Book* (Rose, 1991, 1994) are good sources for understanding the use of ASN.1 in SNMPv1 and SNMPv2 respectively.

[7] When SNMPv2 capabilities are added to NetView, it will also support the SNMPv2 style MIB modules.

```
<declarations>
END
```

The first part is obvious, serving to begin the module and give it a name. The next part, linkage, includes IMPORTS and EXPORTS statements which describe in turn the definitions this module will use from other modules and those it will make available to others. Next come the declarations which do the real work of the module. The module closes with 'END'.

Let's now look at these parts in more detail, using MIB-II as an example.

Linkage Most MIB modules import but do not export since nearly all the basic definitions of general interest are contained in RFCs 1155 and 1212. Modules can import the following:

- **Values** Usually these are object IDs defined in other modules. For example, a module that defines objects under the *mgmt* node of the naming tree will import the value *mgmt* from RFC 1155.
- **Data types** Usually these are commonly used data types, for example the *IpAddress* type defined in RFC 1155.
- **Macros** These allow the ASN.1 language itself to be extended. A very widely used macro is OBJECT-TYPE which is defined in RFC 1212. This is used in MIB modules to define objects.

Figure 2.14 is an example use of the IMPORTS statement (from MIB-II). It imports:

- The value *mgmt* from RFC 1155.
- The types NetworkAddress, IpAddress, Counter, Gauge and TimeTicks from RFC 1155.
- The OBJECT-TYPE macro from RFC 1212.

```
IMPORTS
    mgmt, NetworkAddress, IpAddress, Counter, Gauge,
       TimeTicks
    FROM RFC1155-SMI
    OBJECT-TYPE
       FROM RFC-1212;
```

Figure 2.14 Example IMPORTS statement

As can be seen from this example, values always start with a lower-case letter. Types start with an upper-case letter. Macros and ASN.1 keywords are all upper case.

Declarations Next in a MIB module comes a series of declarations in which values, types and potentially macros are defined. In most cases, you will find only values and types.

The first of these declarations will generally define data types and object IDs used later in the module. For example, the MIB-II module has the initial declarations shown in Figure 2.15:

- *mib-2* is defined in terms of the ID for *mgmt*, by appending 1 to *mgmt*'s ID.
- Two types are defined, *DisplayString* and *PhysAddress*, both in terms of the ASN.1 primitive type OCTET STRING. An OCTET STRING is a string of bytes that may or may not be printable characters. *DisplayString* and *PhysAddress* have more restrictive syntax,

though this is not formally defined here; it's just carried out in practice. Often there will be accompanying commentary in the MIB module explaining any such restrictions as well as the purpose of the type.

● Object IDs are defined for each of the groups in MIB-II. Later in the module, the actual objects in these groups will have their IDs defined in terms of these.

```
mib-2          OBJECT IDENTIFIER ::= { mgmt 1 }

DisplayString ::=
    OCTET STRING

PhysAddress ::=
    OCTET STRING

system       OBJECT IDENTIFIER ::= { mib-2 1 }
interfaces   OBJECT IDENTIFIER ::= { mib-2 2 }
at           OBJECT IDENTIFIER ::= { mib-2 3 }
ip           OBJECT IDENTIFIER ::= { mib-2 4 }
icmp         OBJECT IDENTIFIER ::= { mib-2 5 }
tcp          OBJECT IDENTIFIER ::= { mib-2 6 }
udp          OBJECT IDENTIFIER ::= { mib-2 7 }
egp          OBJECT IDENTIFIER ::= { mib-2 8 }
transmission OBJECT IDENTIFIER ::= { mib-2 10 }
snmp         OBJECT IDENTIFIER ::= { mib-2 11 }
```

Figure 2.15 RFC 1213 initial declarations

After these initial definitions come the definitions of the managed objects themselves. These are defined using the OBJECT-TYPE macro. A simple example of defining an object with this macro is shown in Figure 2.16.

```
sysDescr OBJECT-TYPE
   SYNTAX DisplayString (SIZE (0..255))
   ACCESS read-only
   STATUS mandatory
   DESCRIPTION
       "A textual description of the entity. This value
       should include the full name and version
       identification of the system's hardware type,
       software operating-system, and networking
       software. It is mandatory that this only contain
       printable ASCII characters."
   ::= { system 1 }
```

Figure 2.16 Defining *sysDescr* with the OBJECT-TYPE macro

Here the *sysDescr* object of MIB-II is defined. The 'syntax', i.e. data type, is *DisplayString* of length between 0 and 255. The object has read-only access and a status of mandatory. A text description of the object is given, and is followed by the definition of *sysDescr*'s object ID.

This definition is like 99 per cent of the definitions you will find in MIB modules.

Attributes of managed objects The OBJECT-TYPE macro can assign various attributes to the objects it defines. Let's look at some of these.

DATA TYPE One attribute is the type of data the object's instances may contain. This attribute is known as 'syntax'. There are three ways syntax can be assigned:

- With one of the ASN.1 'primitive types'. These are INTEGER, OCTET STRING, OBJECT IDENTIFIER and NULL. These types are defined in the ASN.1 language itself. The mysterious type NULL is used in cases where a place-holder object is required, for example in Get requests, as we will see.
- With a defined type. This may be defined within the module or imported. RFC 1155 defines several types for general use, including:
  - *IpAddress*—an OCTET STRING encoding of an IP address, e.g. 9.180.180.207.
  - *Counter*—an INTEGER that ranges between 0 and some maximum value and wraps to zero when it reaches the maximum.
  - *Gauge*—an INTEGER that must be non-negative, may increase and decrease, but latches at a maximum value.
  - *TimeTicks*—an INTEGER counting the number of hundredths of seconds since a particular epoch, for example since the beginning of 1970.
- With one of the two 'constructor types'. These are used to define tables, as we will see in a moment.

One data type you see frequently used in MIB modules is a refinement of the INTEGER type known as 'Enumerated INTEGER'. This uses the ASN.1 facility of specifying the particular values a type may have. In the case of Enumerated INTEGERs, symbols with particular meanings are associated with these values. An example is *ifOperStatus* from MIB-II. It is used to indicate the operational status of an interface. It is an Enumerated INTEGER which may have the symbolic values *up* (1), *down* (2), and *testing* (3). In the agent, the object will actually contain one of these three integers, but managers interpret them to have the symbolic meanings.

ACCESS Another attribute the OBJECT-TYPE macro assigns to objects is 'access'. This determines what a manager may do to the object and may be one of:

- Read-only
- Read-write
- Write-only
- Not-accessible

The last is generally used in table definitions, where some objects are defined only to provide a table's structure and are not intended for access by the manager.

STATUS The OBJECT-TYPE macro also assigns the 'status' attribute to objects. This may be one of:

- **Mandatory** All conforming agents must implement the object.
- **Optional**
- **Obsolete** No longer necessary to implement this object.
- **Deprecated** Required but notice is given that it may go away in future.

TABLES The only real wrinkle in all this is table definition and even this is not very complicated. An example should make it clear.

Consider the *ipAddrTable* from MIB-II. This table lists IP addresses known by the system and gives some information about them. An example *ipAddrTable* is shown in Figure 2.17. The ASN.1 definition of the table is in Figure 2.18.

	... Addr	... IfIndex	... NetMask	... BcastAddr	... ReasmMaxSize
Instance 9.180.180.207	9.180.180.207	2	255.255.255.0	1	32767
Instance 9.180.180.175	9.180.180.175	1	255.255.255.0	1	32767
Instance 9.20.44.2	9.20.44.2	3	255.255.254.0	1	32767

Figure 2.17 Example *ipAddrTable*

```
ipAddrTable OBJECT-TYPE
   SYNTAX SEQUENCE OF IpAddrEntry
   ACCESS not-accessible
   STATUS mandatory
   DESCRIPTION
       "The table of addressing information relevant to
       this entity's IP addresses."
   ::= { ip 20 }

ipAddrEntry OBJECT-TYPE
   SYNTAX IpAddrEntry
   ACCESS not-accessible
   STATUS mandatory
   DESCRIPTION
       "The addressing information for one of this
       entity's IP addresses."
   INDEX   { ipAdEntAddr }
   ::= { ipAddrTable 1 }

IpAddrEntry ::=
   SEQUENCE {
      ipAdEntAddr
        IpAddress,
      ipAdEntIfIndex
        INTEGER,
      ipAdEntNetMask
        IpAddress,
      ipAdEntBcastAddr
        INTEGER,
      ipAdEntReasmMaxSize
        INTEGER (0..65535)
```

Figure 2.18 Definition of *ipAddrTable*

The first statement in the ASN.1 defines the table itself with the SEQUENCE OF constructor type. Thus, the *ipAddrTable* is a sequence of objects which have the type *IpAddrEntry*.

The second statement defines the value *ipAddrEntry* (not the type). It is an object ID derived from *ipAddrTable*. The columnar objects in the table will have object IDs derived from this. This statement also defines the table's indexing, which we'll discuss in a moment.

The third statement then defines the type *IpAddrEntry*. Here the constructor type SEQUENCE is used to indicate that each *IpAddrEntry* (i.e. each row of the table) is a sequence of five columnar objects. These five objects are themselves defined later in the MIB module. I've omitted them since they are defined the same way scalar objects are.

The index for the table, as defined in the second statement, will be based on the columnar object *ipAdEntAddr*. This object contains the IP address for each row of the table, and therefore the ID for each instance in a given row will be that IP address. For example, if a row pertains to IP address 9.180.180.207, then the instances of the five objects in that row will have instance identifier 9.180.180.207.

Unless you're planning to write a MIB module, I suggest you do not worry too much about the fine points of these definitions. Just note that this is the pattern of definitions used to define tables in SNMPv1. Since there is nothing more complicated than a table, there is no need to worry about how you could generalize this definition.

2.2.5 Protocol

In covering the MIB side of this business we have finished the hard part. What remains—the protocol itself—is easy.

There are five messages in SNMP which may be sent between manager and agent:

- *GetRequest*—A manager sends this to an agent to get the values of one or more managed object instances.
- *GetNextRequest*—A manager sends this to an agent to get values in a more devious way than with GetRequest. We'll see how below.
- *SetRequest*—A manager sends this to an agent to change the values of one or more instances. This request can also implicitly create instances.
- *GetResponse*—Contrary to what its name implies, agents send this message as the response to all three of the requests.
- *Trap*—An agent sends this to the manager when an exceptional condition occurs, for example when it wishes to inform the manager of a problem in its system.

As shown in Figure 2.19, all five of these are defined in terms of a structure called 'Message'. A Message contains the following information:

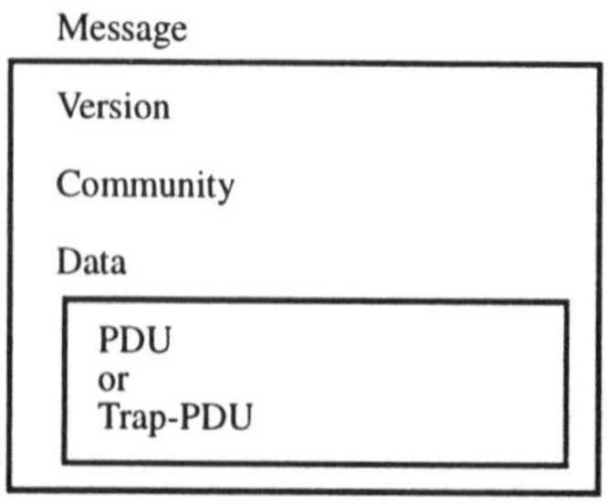

Message
```
Version

Community

Data
  ┌─────────────┐
  │ PDU         │
  │ or          │
  │ Trap-PDU    │
  └─────────────┘
```

Figure 2.19 SNMP message

- **Version** An INTEGER that is 1 in SNMPv1.
- **Community** An OCTET STRING that contains the 'community name'. This is a string used for authentication and other purposes, as we'll see below.
- **Data** This contains a structure that further defines each of the five messages. In the four messages other than Trap, this is a common structure known as 'PDU' (Protocol Data Unit). In Trap, this is a special structure known as 'Trap-PDU'.

The PDU structure contains the following information:

- **request-id** An INTEGER value used for correlating requests with responses. The same request-id is used in the request from the manager and the response from the agent.
- **error-status** An enumerated INTEGER which may be one of: *noError* (0), *tooBig* (1), *noSuchName* (2), *badValue* (3) and *genErr* (5).
- **error-index** An INTEGER used when the error is with a 'variable binding' passed in a request. This points to the erroneous binding.
- **Variable-bindings** Zero or more variable bindings.

Each variable binding consists of the object ID of a MIB variable (i.e. an instance) and a value to which it is 'bound'. These bindings are used to pass the values of MIB variables between manager and agent. Their particular use depends on which message contains them, as we'll see below.

Traps are also defined with the Message structure, but they do not use the PDU sub-structure. We will consider their contents below.

Let's now look at each of the five SNMP messages.

GetRequest A manager sends this to an agent in order to get the values of one or more MIB objects. These must not be aggregate objects (e.g. tables) but actual instances. Figure 2.20 shows the overall flow a manager uses to get the values.

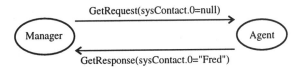

Figure 2.20 GetRequest and GetResponse

The manager places into the request one or more variable bindings, each of which has the object ID of an instance to be retrieved. The value to which the instance is bound is irrelevant, but by convention is set to an instance of the type NULL.

When the agent receives the GetRequest, it attempts to find all the requested instances and, if successful, sends a GetResponse back to the manager. This will have variable bindings identical to the GetRequest except that each instance will be bound to its value in the agent's MIB.

There are several possible errors the agent may encounter in carrying out the GetRequest. For example, a requested instance may not exist in its MIB. In any such error case, the agent sends a GetResponse to the manager, but with the error-status set to indicate the particular error condition.

GetNextRequest This is similar to GetRequest, but the instances to be retrieved are specified indirectly in order to achieve some nice effects, as we will see in a moment. In this section, it's important to remember the ordering discussed earlier for object IDs. You will recall, for example, that the ID 1.2.3 comes before 1.2.3.0 and 1.2.4.

Let's consider the mechanics of GetNextRequest. The manager places into the variable bindings one or more object IDs, just as with GetRequest. However, the object IDs need not be for actual instances, but can be for objects anywhere in the naming tree. For each such object ID, the agent finds the instance in its MIB that immediately follows it. To be precise, it finds the instance whose object ID follows it in the ordering defined on object IDs. The agent then returns to the manager a GetResponse whose variable bindings contain the objects it found and their values.

For example, a manager might send a GetNextRequest with the object ID 1.3.6.1.2.1.1.1. This is the ID of the *sysDescr* object in MIB-II (not its instance). The agent would look in its MIB for the next instance after this ID. Normally, this would be the instance of *sysDescr*, since this instance's object ID is 1.3.6.1.2.1.1.1. If this instance did not exist, then the agent would look farther. It might find, for example, the instance of *sysObjectID*, since it follows *sysDescr* in MIB-II.

The most obvious use of GetNextRequest is when the manager wishes to 'walk' some portion of the agent's MIB. NetView provides the command *snmpwalk* which will return all the instances and values under a particular node of the naming tree. It does this by sequentially performing Get-NextRequests, starting with the object ID of the node you specify. It stops once it gets back an instance whose ID is not under the starting node. If you want to see the entire contents of an agent's MIB, you can ask *snmpwalk* to return everything under the node *mgmt*. If you want to see just the System Group variables, then you can ask it to return all under the node *system*.

Another use of GetNextRequest is to get several instances at once without having a single failure abort the whole operation. For example, suppose the manager wants to get instances *a*, *b* and *c* from an agent, but isn't sure if the agent has them all. If the manager simply used GetRequest for the three and *b* didn't exist, then the entire operation would fail. Instead, the manager could use GetNextRequest and specify the IDs of the objects just before *a*, *b* and *c*. Then, even if *b* didn't exist, the operation would succeed and return *a* and *c* along with their values. The manager could then inspect the returned variable bindings to ensure it had the instances it expected.

There are several other uses for GetNextRequest. It provides an easy way for a manager to traverse a table. Here the manager would specify the object ID of the table itself on the first request and would get back the first instance in the table. The manager would then perform another request using that instance's object ID to get the next one and so on until it reached the end of the table. This is especially useful (and efficient) when the table's row indices are unknown or complex. For example, the indices may not form a nice sequence like 1, 2, 3, etc. Or there may be missing instances in the table.

SetRequest A manager uses SetRequest when it wants to create or change instances in agents' MIBs. In its mechanics, SetRequest is much like GetRequest except that the manager supplies non-null variable bindings. The agent sets each corresponding instance in its MIB to the value supplied. If an instance doesn't exist, the agent creates it. If the Set operation is successful, the agent responds to the manager by sending a GetResponse in which the variable bindings are identical to those in the SetRequest.

Traps Traps provide a means for the agent to inform the manager of an exceptional condition, e.g. the CPU just burst into flame. The agent sends a trap to the manager in an unsolicited manner, that is, without being polled.

There are two types of traps, 'generic' and 'enterprise specific'. Generic traps are those whose meaning is defined by the SNMP standards and express situations common to many types of SNMP agents. There are six of these defined.

Enterprise specific traps cover all other situations. Their definition is not standardized, but rather is left to anyone who cares to define them, most usually equipment manufacturers and software developers.

As you might expect, traps are designed so that their definition can be delegated in an orderly manner. Three fields together specify the exceptional condition being communicated by the trap. These are:

- **Generic code** This is an integer in the range 0 to 6. Codes 0 to 5 are used for 'generic' traps and have the following meanings defined by SNMP:
  - 0—*Cold start* The agent has just initialized itself and its configuration (e.g. MIB variables) may be altered.
  - 1—*Warm start* The agent has just initialized itself without altering its configuration.
  - 2—*Link down* An attached link has gone down. The first variable in the bindings identifies the link.
  - 3—*Link up* A link has come up. The first variable in the bindings identifies the link.
  - 4—*Authentication failure* The agent has received a message from a manager that cannot be authenticated. (We will discuss authentication below.)
  - 5—*EGP neighbor loss* Communication with an EGP neighbour has been lost.
  If the generic code is 6, then the trap is enterprise specific and its exact meaning is determined by the next two fields.
- **Enterprise ID** This field is set to the value of the agent's *sysObjectID* and serves to identify the type of the agent. When the trap is enterprise specific, we can think of this field as selecting the particular 'space' of codes to which the third field pertains.
- **Specific code** This code identifies the exceptional condition. This specific code is unique only for a given enterprise ID and has its meaning defined by the owning organization.

Let's consider an example. Suppose that Dodgy Dental Ltd have a new product, the Home Fissure Filler, which for safety reasons they have decided to equip with an SNMP agent. Further suppose they have assigned it the *sysObjectID* 1.3.6.1.4.1.999.1.

One evening, an unsuspecting young man is repairing a cavity and the Fissure Filler malfunctions, spilling several grams of mercury into his mouth. Naturally, Dodgy will need to know about this so that their attorneys can begin preparing their defence. The SNMP agent therefore sends an enterprise-specific trap to the manager back at Dodgy. This trap has a generic code of 6, an enterprise ID of 1.3.6.1.3.1.999.1 and the specific code of 13 that the Fissure Filler's designers assigned to this condition.

A trap also includes a time stamp and the address of the agent to clarify further what has happened. Still, when an agent is reporting a problem, it would be nice to convey some supplemental information to enlighten the manager further. In the case of the Fissure Filler, for example, it might be useful to include the name and address of the victim and the amount of mercury spilled.

This can be accomplished by including variable bindings in the trap. These are syntactically the same as those used, for example, in GetRequests, but here they are used to pass along to the manager any sort of information the agent desires. The manager is then free to do what it likes with these. In the best case the manager will have been programmed to interpret them correctly and in the worst case it can simply ignore them.

The object IDs used in the variable bindings can be anything at all. To be tidy, they should be either object IDs of variables in the MIB (if MIB variables are being included) or they should be object IDs from a part of the naming tree owned by the enterprise, e.g. under the enterprises tree.

This flexibility in the use of variable bindings is a fairly significant weakness of the trap mechanism. In some management protocols, for example SNA Management Services, supplemental information is provided in a structured and standard way. This means that the manager can interpret it without requiring special programming for each case. With traps, however, there is no standardization and this can make them awkward for the manager to interpret.

Authentication and communities And now we come to what is arguably the messiest part of SNMP, the community name. This bit of information is the crux and the Achilles' heel of SNMP security. Before we look at the problems with it, let's first see how it works.

A community name is a string of octets, each of which is normally a printable ASCII character, but in theory could be anything between 0 and 255. By far the most commonly used community name is 'public'.

As we have seen, community names are contained in all SNMP messages. They are relevant primarily for messages sent from the manager to the agent, and here they are meant to indicate two things:

- The 'MIB view'. This is the set of objects in the agent's MIB that are accessible by the manager. For example, a manager sending a request with community 'basic' might have access only to the objects in the agent's System Group, while a request with community 'privileged' might have access to everything.
- The level of access that the manager is allowed for these objects. This may be read-only or read-write.

In practice, the agent must have one or more community names defined to it, and the manager must know these.

When an agent receives a request from a manager, it:

1. Compares the community name to its list of defined communities.
2. If it doesn't find a match, then it discards the request. It may optionally send an authentication trap to one or more managers.
3. If the agent finds a match, then it determines whether the objects to be operated on are within the MIB view defined for the community. How this is done is up to the implementation. For example, there might be a file the agents reads which lists the groups of objects accessible for each community.
4. The agent must then determine whether the access levels permit the requested operation. The first consideration is whether the community allows read-only or read-write access to the objects. (How this is done is again implementation-specific, most likely based on a file.)

The second consideration is whether the level of access defined for the object itself will permit the operation.

As you would expect:

- A SetRequest succeeds only if the community permits read-write access and each object's access level is write-only or read-write.
- A GetRequest or GetNextRequest will work regardless of the community's access level as long as each object's access level is read-only or read-write.

It is clear from all this that a community name is much like a password. The problem is that community names flow in clear text in SNMP messages. Therefore, anyone with an inexpensive line tracing tool and physical access to the network can easily get the community names and spend a happy evening reconfiguring the network.

Some agents throw in an additional feature to enhance security. They accept requests only from certain IP addresses. They may also restrict the community names they accept from particular addresses. Generally, there is a file listing the addresses of managers and (sometimes) the community names each is allowed to use. The agent then checks each incoming request to ensure that these restrictions are not violated. This embellishment does not improve things as much as it might seem, since it is fairly easy in IP to 'impersonate' addresses.

The question, therefore, is how much you want to trust to community names. In many cases, vendors are reluctant to provide important management functions based on Sets because of this issue. However, some people have argued that community names have been unfairly singled out. Many systems, for example, allow utilities such as *telnet* and FTP to control, reconfigure and download code to them. These utilities use passwords that flow in clear text, as do an untold number of other sensitive applications. If you think about the number of important computing resources protected merely by clear text passwords, it makes you wonder at how relatively few incidents of larceny and sabotage occur.

In SNMPv2, the security problem has been addressed with an elaborate set of mechanisms.

Encoding As mentioned earlier, ASN.1 definitions specify the syntax of SNMP's messages. However, in their ASN.1 form, the messages are not suitable for transmission across the network. Instead, a process (from the OSI world) must be applied to transform them into what will actually be sent. This process is performed according to the Basic Encoding Rules (BER). These provide a flexible and efficient way of encoding the messages into strings of bytes. Here we won't explore this process since the chances are very good that you will never see a BER-encoded message in your life. Still, it is important to know this step exists.

The overall process of actually building and sending an SNMP message is shown in Figure 2.21. The message defined by ASN.1 is transformed into a string of bytes by the BER process. Then (assuming UDP is being used) the BER-encoded string is passed to the UDP service on the local system. The service places the string into a datagram and sends it to the destination system. There, the reverse process is used to recover the SNMP message.

Mapping onto transport protocols SNMP is most often used in IP environments and usually relies on UDP to carry its messages. UDP's simplicity makes it a good protocol for SNMP to use. There are cases where it would be better to use a richer protocol like TCP, partly because such protocols retry failed transmissions and more importantly because they ensure that mes-

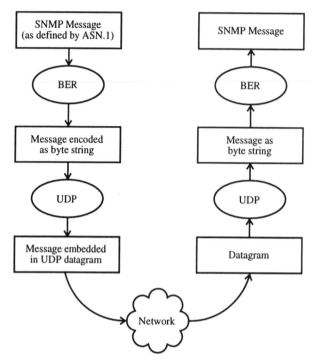

Figure 2.21 Sending an SNMP message

sages are delivered in order. This latter point is important, for example, when traps are being used to convey state information. If an agent uses traps to indicate the state of a link, sending them when the link goes up or down, it is important to prevent traps from arriving out of order.

Still, there are two strong arguments for using UDP. The first is that network management should work well when the network is on its knees and yet this is when more complicated protocols such as TCP tend to behave strangely. UDP on the other hand may throw things away in such cases, but won't worry about the state of the network. It will just keep plodding along.

The second argument is that network management should place as little load on agents as possible. UDP is easier to implement and requires fewer resources, e.g. memory, than do protocols such as TCP.

The mapping of SNMP onto UDP, depicted in Figure 2.22, is quite simple:

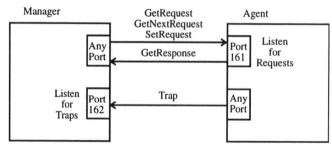

Figure 2.22 Mapping SNMP onto UDP

- Managers send GetRequests, GetNextRequests and SetRequests from any port they choose to port 161 on the agent. Agents therefore must listen on this port.
- Agents send GetResponses to the port on the manager from which the corresponding request was sent.
- Agents send traps to port 162 on the manager who must therefore listen on this port.

Let's consider an example:

- A technician who is trying to configure a router becomes frustrated and smashes it with a 19-inch monitor.
- The router's disk crashes and therefore its agent sends a trap to a management station. The agent sends this to port 162.
- An operator sees the trap and wishes to know the location of the router. She instructs the management station to poll the router's agent for its *sysLocation* variable. The management station sends a GetRequest from port 1100 to port 161 on the agent.
- The agent then replies with a GetResponse to supply the location information, sending this back to port 1100 on the management station.

SNMP has also been mapped onto other protocols, including TCP, IPX, AppleTalk and the OSI Connectionless-mode Transport Service.

2.3 SMUX AND THE DPI

There are two additional protocols in the SNMP realm we should briefly consider. Both are concerned with the case (depicted in Figure 2.23) that a single system has several different process that must be managed through a single SNMP agent. For example, a system may run several different communications protocols and need to provide objects in its MIB for each. Or a system may run several applications, each of which needs to provide some objects in the MIB. In addition, these processes may need to send traps to a manager.

There are two protocols that address this problem. The first to do so was SMUX (the SNMP Multiplexing protocol). It has been widely implemented, but because of problems discovered in

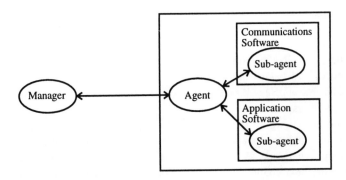

Figure 2.23 SNMP multiplexing

implementations, a successor protocol has been developed. This is known as the DPI (the SNMP Distributed Protocol Interface). Both SMUX and the DPI provide a means for processes in a system to communicate with the manager through the system's agent. They allow the processes to implement MIB objects that the manager can access, and also allow them to send traps to the manager. Unless you're developing SNMP applications, it is not really important to understand how these two protocols work and therefore I'll spare you a description. It is important, however, to know they exist since many agents use these to provide orderly management of the functions in their hosts.

SMUX is documented in RFC 1227 and the DPI in RFC 1592.

2.4 PROXY AGENTS

Earlier in this chapter, we touched on the concept of proxy agents. This is an important subject and therefore worth a little more discussion. As we saw, a proxy agent serves as a management gateway between an SNMP manager and something which must be managed but doesn't speak SNMP. This *something* may be a piece of networking equipment, a computer or an entire network. Although SNMP is widely implemented, there are still many computers and networks that don't support it. To incorporate the management of these under a single SNMP manager like NetView, it's possible to use proxy agents.

In general, we can assume that in the non-SNMP environment there is some other sort of management protocol available. For example, if it's an SNA network, then there will be the SNA Management Services protocol.

Thus, as shown in Figure 2.24, the proxy agent translates between SNMP and the non-SNMP management protocol. The proxy agent must support SNMP, UDP and IP. It must also support the non-SNMP management protocol, as well as any transport protocol required to carry it (e.g. SNA).

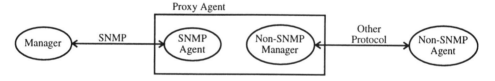

Figure 2.24 Proxy agent as protocol translator

The proxy agent then translates all SNMP requests (e.g. Get, Set) from the manager into requests in the non-SNMP protocol and passes these into the non-SNMP environment. The reply must then be translated back into an SNMP GetResponse. Alarms from the non-SNMP environment must be translated into traps.

There are a few issues raised by having an intermediary. If the proxy agent is acting on behalf of a single piece of equipment, then things are relatively straightforward. If, on the other hand, it is acting on behalf of an entire network, identifying non-SNMP systems in requests and responses can be complicated. In the next chapter we'll look at solutions to this problem and how NetView supports them.

2.5 PERSPECTIVE

Despite its simplicity and limitations, SNMP Version 1 allows a great deal of useful management to be done. It is the most widely implemented protocol and the first to become a real working standard. The reason, no doubt, is its simplicity. One can quickly learn it and implementations are relatively easy and lightweight. Of course, the fact that it was developed at a time when TCP/IP became highly fashionable didn't hurt.

There are three significant problems with SNMP Version 1:

- Security, as we have seen.
- Bulk data transmission. Transporting a large number of MIB variables from agent to manager can be very slow even on high speed lines.
- Lack of a manager-to-manager protocol. Medium and large organizations usually employ several management stations, and it is important these be able to co-operate.

All three of these deficiencies are addressed in SNMPv2. It seems unfortunate though that, in addressing the deficiencies, the protocol has become a good deal more complicated and difficult to understand. At present, the take-up of SNMPv2 appears to be very slow and it is an open question whether it will ever achieve the sort of universality its predecessor has. Meanwhile, the world is happily managing networks with SNMPv1.

THREE

NETVIEW AND COMPANY

NetView is first and foremost an SNMP manager and thus is quite good at managing IP networks. NetView also provides a platform for managing non-IP networks and there are many applications available that take advantage of this. These provide management for DECnet, SNA and many other environments. In addition, there are two other management products from IBM, Systems Monitor and Trouble Ticket, which work closely with NetView to extend its capabilities in several important ways. In this chapter we will first look at the use of NetView in both IP and non-IP networks, and then we will see how Systems Monitor and Trouble Ticket fit in.

For IP network management, NetView includes several ready-built functions, the most important of which are:

- Automatically collecting the topology of IP networks, and displaying it graphically
- Receiving SNMP traps from the network and displaying, logging and automatically reacting to these
- Polling SNMP agents for MIB information and storing, displaying and processing this information in several ways

NetView also includes a set of programming interfaces that can be used to build other IP management applications. For example, several router manufacturers have taken advantage of these to build applications that manage the specific features of their equipment. NetView's programming interfaces allow such applications to issue all the SNMP requests to agents and access the data they send to NetView. These interfaces also allow applications to interact with the user through the NetView GUI and to access and modify the data NetView maintains for IP networks.

Thus, for IP networks you can use NetView as it is and do quite a lot or you can go beyond this by purchasing an application or extending it yourself.

For non-IP networks, NetView relies on proxy agents and applications. As we have seen, proxy agents extend NetView's SNMP management into non-IP environments, translating

SNMP into other management protocols. With proxy agents alone, you can perform basic management of these non-IP environments since many of NetView's SNMP functions will work there as well. For example, if the proxy agent allows you to collect data from a MIB that describes the non-IP network, then NetView tools can be used to collect and display this information. In addition, traps from a proxy agent can be displayed and otherwise handled by NetView.

To go beyond these basic SNMP capabilities for non-IP networks, NetView applications can be built. For example, NetView on its own could collect and display the data that a proxy agent provides for a DECnet network. However, it would be much more useful to have a NetView application that interpreted this data and displayed it to you in a way suitable for DECnet. Such an application might also provide you with command dialogues that make it easy to control DECnet, and would probably also provide a graphical display of the DECnet topology.

Displaying topology is a particularly important function that is common to many NetView applications for non-IP environments. NetView therefore includes facilities that make it easy for applications to implement the displays and help ensure they do so in a consistent and integrated way. These facilities are provided by two NetView components—the General Topology Manager (GTM) and *xxMap*. Applications can send information describing networks to GTM, which stores it in its database. *xxMap* then uses the information to display graphical views of the networks.

As we will see, there are many NetView applications and proxy agents available for managing non-IP networks. For cases where these are not available, it is possible to build your own. NetView's facilities will support your applications and there are several toolkits on the market to help build proxy agents.

In this chapter we will look at the capabilities of NetView in more detail, specifically:

- **NetView's architecture**
- **NetView as an IP manager**
- **NetView as a non-IP manager**
- **Highlights of NetView's internal structure**
- **Using Systems Monitor and Trouble Ticket to extend NetView's capabilities**

3.1 NETVIEW'S ARCHITECTURE

Let's look at the overall architecture of NetView and how it fits into the management centre, referring throughout to Figure 3.1.

In general, there will be one or more NetViews in a particular management centre, each interacting with the network to carry out the required management tasks. The interactions will be primarily based on SNMP, but may employ other protocols as well. NetView will run, as we have seen, under AIX or one of the other operating systems it supports.

We can think of NetView as having two major parts. First, there is a group of 'daemons', which are processes that run in the background of NetView's system. These perform the actual interaction with the networks and also maintain several collections of information about them. For example, there are daemons that collect network topology and others that maintain databases of several sorts.

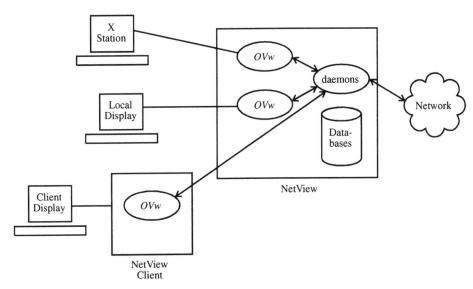

Figure 3.1 NetView architecture

Second, there is the set of processes that implement the NetView Graphical User Interface (GUI) and related functions. These run under the control of a process called *OVw*. They present the user interface using X Windows and Motif.

A NetView system will always run one set of the background daemons. The number of GUIs it runs depends on how many people are using it and whether NetView's client/server structure is being used:

- In the simplest case, one person uses NetView and does so directly from NetView's system. Here, one instance of the background daemons and one instance of *OVw* run on the system.
- One or more people use NetView remotely. They access the GUI using X stations that communicate with NetView using the X protocol. It's also possible that rather than using X stations they use systems such as UNIX, OS/2 or Windows that support the X protocol. In any case, NetView treats the users as if they were local since the X protocol makes their location transparent. Thus, one instance of *OVw* will run on NetView's system for each user.
- One or more operators use NetView, again remotely, but using NetView's client/server structure. Here each user accesses NetView from a client system and an instance of *OVw* runs there instead of on NetView's system. Rather than the X protocol, a NetView-specific protocol is used between the client and the server. This approach can be more efficient for two reasons. First, the *OVw* processes are off-loaded from the NetView server. Second, the NetView-specific protocol uses less network bandwidth. Thus, the X protocol is usually appropriate only within a LAN, but the NetView-specific protocol can be used across a WAN and still provide reasonable response time.

Combinations of these three ways of accessing NetView are also possible. For example, one person might use NetView directly while others access it using the X protocol.

NetView's user interface consists of three major parts:

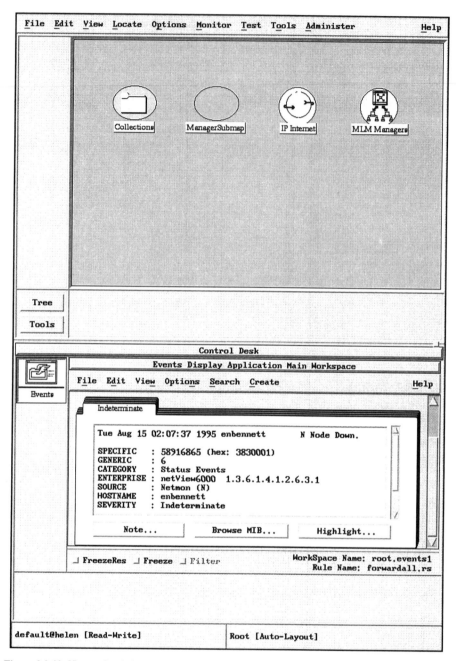

Figure 3.2 NetView main window

- A main window (shown in Figure 3.2) which is divided into two sections. In the top half, graphical views of networks are shown. Above these, there is a menu bar from which users can invoke NetView tools and applications. Users can also invoke them using the Context Menu, which pops up when you place the cursor over, for example, a system shown in a view and you press the right mouse button. The selected action is then executed against the system.

In the bottom half of the window there is the Control Desk. Here the user may run various NetView tools. Most often, a tool known as 'Events' is there. This maintains a real-time display of the traps coming into NetView. Many tools can run simultaneously in the Control Desk and you can easily switch among them by clicking icons.

- Another window called the Tool Palette. This window contains several icons, each representing a NetView tool. You can invoke these in convenient ways, for example by dragging one into the Control Desk.
- A window called the Navigation Tree. An example is shown in Figure 3.3. NetView's network graphics consist of a set of views that are arranged in a hierarchy. In large networks it can be difficult remembering where you may be in this hierarchy. The Navigation Tree shows a diagram of how these various views are related and makes it easier to navigate among them.

Finally, there is facility found on AIX systems which is very helpful for using NetView. This is the Systems Management Interface Tool (SMIT) which provides a convenient, menu-driven method of controlling and configuring the AIX system. There is a special set of SMIT screens that make it easy to control, configure and maintain NetView. All the functions available through these screens can also be performed using NetView commands, but SMIT makes it much easier.

3.2 IP MANAGEMENT WITH NETVIEW

Let's now look at the ways NetView helps manage IP networks, including:

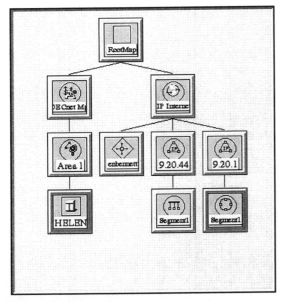

Figure 3.3 Navigation Tree

- Network topology discovery and display
- Receiving and processing traps
- Working with agents' MIBs

3.2.1 IP network topology discovery

An important feature of NetView is its ability to discover automatically the topology of IP networks. When you connect NetView to an IP internetwork, it starts looking around to see which systems are there and how the internetwork is structured. This process is known as 'discovery'. The information NetView learns from discovery is stored in its internal databases. The NetView GUI then uses it to create graphical views of the internetwork.

The method NetView uses to carry out discovery is not something we can investigate here, since it is a trade secret. Thus, we will focus instead on what discovery accomplishes and what can be done when you have difficulties with it.

By default, NetView will discover as much as possible in the networks to which it is directly connected. NetView may be in a huge internetwork, but until you instruct it otherwise, it will discover up to and including the routers leading to other networks and no farther. This is what we would normally want, since otherwise NetView could inundate an entire internetwork with the traffic required to discover and monitor it. Also, it's likely you don't want your views clogged with information about everything in the internetwork. These considerations are especially important now that many organizations are connecting to the Internet.

There are several ways you can tell NetView to discover more than its local networks. The methods of doing this are discussed in 'Using NetView for distributed management' (Section 5.2.4). In any of them, you in essence list the networks in which you want NetView to perform discovery.

Once NetView has performed discovery for a network, it will have several kinds of information about it, including:

- All systems in the network and what their IP addresses are. It will have this for workstations, mainframes, routers and anything else that has an interface in the network.
- The names of the systems. It obtains these by querying a name server.
- The protocol used in the network. For example, it will know whether the network is a Token-Ring or an Ethernet.
- Several facts about the systems in the network. It will know, for example, the description, location and contact for each. It obtains these from the systems' MIBs, specifically the MIB-II System Group.
- The network interfaces each system has and some information about each of these.
- The local routers that connect this network to other networks.
- The identities of those other networks, though not the details of what is inside them.

Once NetView has this information, it monitors the discovered systems to determine whether they are running. It does this by periodically sending ICMP Echoes to them and waiting to see if they respond within a given time period. This process can consume a significant amount of network bandwidth. On the other hand, it needs to be performed frequently enough to ensure accuracy. You don't want to wait an hour to find out that a system has gone down. If NetView is monitoring a large network, it can be difficult to find the right trade-off between accuracy and economy. Later we'll see that one solution is to off-load the status monitoring process to an intermediate manager.

In some cases discovery may happen too slowly or may not find everything it should. An example of this is shown in Figure 3.4. One reason is that NetView does not know the community names of systems in the internetwork. This can especially be a problem with key systems such as routers. Some aspects of the discovery process rely on SNMP, and therefore NetView should have community names for as many systems as possible. Another reason for discovery problems is that some systems do not communicate very frequently with the rest of the network. Since these keep quiet, it's difficult for NetView to know they exist. Implementation Tip 3.1 discusses some solutions to these problems.

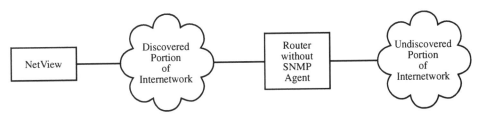

Figure 3.4 Problems in NetView discovery

Implementation Tip 3.1

You can solve NetView discovery problems by using a 'seed file'. In it you list systems you want NetView to know about for purposes of discovery. This not only makes NetView aware of these particular systems, but also helps it find nearby systems and can speed the discovery process. One case where a seed file will help is when there is a region of the NetView does not discover. If you put one or more of the systems there into the seed file, the problem will probably be solved. In general, the best systems to list in seed files are routers, name servers and others that communicate with a large number of other systems.

There is another method for handling discovery problems. That is to instruct NetView to enable additional techniques it has for discovery. Again, we cannot investigate what these are, but we can note that they generally increase the bandwidth demands of discovery. To use this method, you select 'Speed network discovery' in the SMIT screen for the NetView *netmon* daemon.

3.2.2 Graphical topology display

Using all the information it obtains, NetView builds a set of graphical views depicting the IP internetwork. Each such view is called a 'submap' (we will see below why 'submap' instead of the more likely term 'map'). NetView organizes these submaps into a hierarchy in which the level of detail increases as you descend.

The top submap in this hierarchy (the one you see when you start the GUI) is called the Root Submap. It contains one symbol for each protocol being managed by NetView. An example is shown in Figure 3.5. Among the symbols in this submap, there will be one that represents the IP

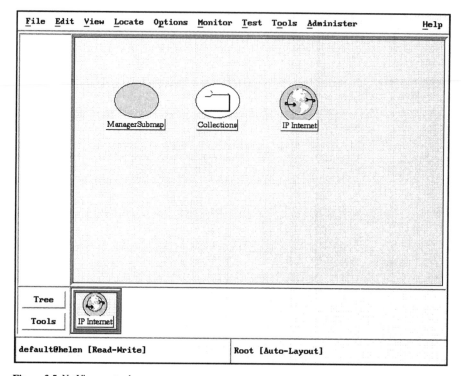

Figure 3.5 NetView root submap

Root
|
Internet
|
Network
|
Segment
|
Node

Figure 3.6 IP submap hierarchy

internetwork. This symbol is the top of the submap hierarchy for IP and is labelled 'IP Net'. Under it are a set of submaps depicting the various parts of the internetwork (see Figure 3.6).

The IP Net symbol will have a colour, generally green or yellow if things are working reasonably well. Green indicates that everything or nearly everything in the network has normal status. Yellow indicates that much of the network is normal, but there are also a significant number of systems that are 'critical', i.e. down or unreachable. If the network is in very bad shape, the symbol will be red.

From the Root Submap you can move to other submaps in the NetView hierarchy. Moving among the submaps is termed 'navigation' and relies on the fact that, in the hierarchy, each submap is represented by a symbol in the one immediately above. Normally, you open a submap by placing the cursor over its symbol and 'double-clicking' the left-hand mouse button. For example, double-clicking the IP Net symbol will open the Internet Submap that shows further details of the internetwork.

An example Internet Submap is shown in Figure 3.7. This shows all the networks making up the overall internetwork, as well as the links and routers connecting them. If the internetwork is complicated, this submap can get messy. It's possible to edit it to make it more readable, for example, by moving symbols. As we will see in Chapter 8, there are many other ways to edit submaps.

Selecting a symbol in the Internet Submap will move you to a submap showing more detail about it:

- If the symbol is a router, then NetView opens a Node Submap showing its interfaces.
- If the symbol is a connection and it represents more than one link, then NetView opens a Metaconnection Submap showing the links.
- If the symbol is a network, then a Network Submap is opened showing its details (see Figure 3.8). This will have one symbol for each router in the network, one symbol for each 'segment', and symbols for the links between these. A segment here represents, for example, an Ethernet or Token-Ring LAN.

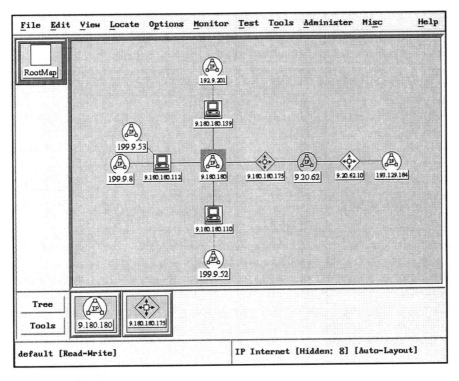

Figure 3.7 NetView Internet Submap

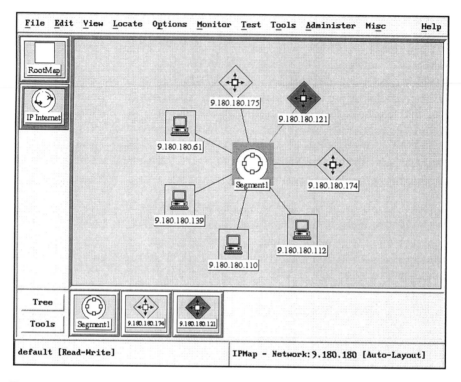

Figure 3.8 NetView Network Submap

For each segment shown in a Network Submap, there is a Segment Submap showing its details. Here, as shown in Figure 3.9, the systems in the segment will be shown in a way that reflects the type of protocol the segment uses. For example, if it's an Ethernet, the systems will be arranged around a bus; if it's a Token-Ring, they will be arranged in the ring pattern shown in Figure 3.9.

In the Segment Submap you can select one of the systems and see a Node Submap showing its interfaces. An example is shown in Figure 3.10.

In all the submaps, colour is used to indicate the statuses of the depicted resources. As with the IP Net symbol, this may be green (normal), yellow (marginal) or red (critical). There are several other possibilities as we will see in Chapter 8.

The status of any symbol in a submap is determined as follows:

- If the symbol represents a link or an interface in a system, then its status is determined from NetView's status monitoring process. As we just saw, NetView monitors status using ICMP Echoes, i.e. PINGs. Note that when NetView sends ICMP Echoes to check status, it is actually PINGing interfaces and not the systems in which they reside.
- If the symbol represents a 'compound resource', then its status is determined according to a 'status propagation scheme'. Compound resources are those which contain others, examples being segments, networks and internetworks. Also, hosts and routers are compound, because they contain interfaces.

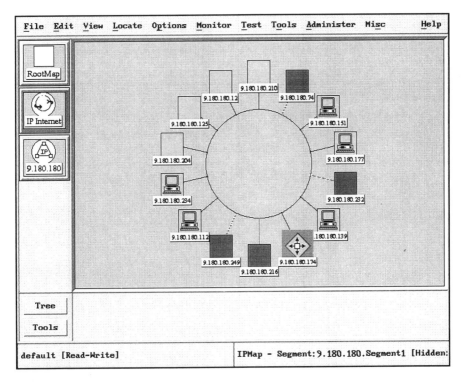

Figure 3.9 NetView Segment Submap

The status propagation scheme may be one of three possibilities, as selected by the user. The following is a rough characterization—the details are in Section 8.3.3.

- A default scheme in which the status of the compound resource is the same as its most critical underlying (i.e. contained) resource. There is, however, some provision for balancing statuses. For example, a resource that is normal will cancel the effect of one that is critical.
- A pure 'propagate most critical' scheme. Here, the status of the compound resource is that of its most critical underlying resource.
- A threshold scheme in which you define the numbers of underlying resources with non-normal status required to make a compound symbol marginal or critical.

Each of these three schemes is really quite simple and some might wish for other variations. I have known many people who want to use graphical views of networks as a kind of problem reporting system, where they watch the views and check if anything has changed to an undesirable colour. The problem with this approach is that it is difficult to have a reasonably simple picture reflect something as complicated as the statuses of thousands of network resources. If you use anything other than a 'propagate most critical' scheme, then you risk missing a resource going down. But with 'propagate most critical' your compound resources will almost always be red, since something is bound to be broken at any given moment.

A much better way to do problem reporting is to use a tool that simply informs you each time a problem occurs in the network. Many such tools exist—NetView has one, the Events

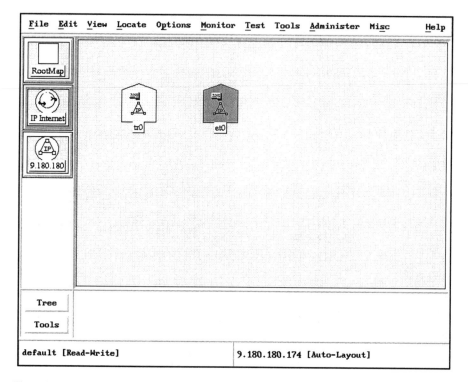

Figure 3.10 NetView Node Submap

Application—and they do not suffer from all the complexities of network graphics. If you approach things this way, you won't need to worry about status propagation schemes.

3.2.3 Launch pad

In addition to conveying the topology and status of the internetwork, NetView's submaps also serve as a 'launch pad' for other functions. Thus, a resource can be selected from a submap and then a function chosen to perform against it. For example, if you want to examine a system's MIB using NetView's MIB Browser, you can select it in a submap and choose the browser from the menu.

3.2.4 Databases for topology information

There are three databases NetView uses to maintain network topology information—the Topology, Map and Object Databases. These are not relational databases, but are collections of normal files maintained on NetView's system.[1]

---

[1] They are kept in the directory /usr/OV/databases/openview.

Topology Database The Topology Database contains the detailed topology of the IP internetwork as determined by the NetView discovery process. Discovery is carried out by the NetView *netmon* daemon, and the database also contains several flags and other information *netmon* needs. To see the contents of this database, you can use the NetView command *ovtopodump*. For example, issuing 'ovtopodump' gives a concise listing, while 'ovtopodump -rl' dumps the whole thing. Figure 3.11 shows the output from *ovtopodump* for a particular host.

```
HOSTNAME: helen
NODE ID: 721
CREATE TIME: Fri 3 Mar 17:52:59 1995
MODIFIED TIME: Fri 3 Mar 22:32:30 1995
SYMBOL CHANGE TIME: Fri 3 Mar 17:52:59 1995
STATUS: Up
FLAGS: IS_MIDLMNG IS_SIA
DESCRIPTION: IBM RISC System/6000
DESCRIPTION: Machine Type: 0x0801 Processor id: 000063624600
DESCRIPTION: The Base Operating System AIX version: 03.02.0000.0000
DESCRIPTION: TCPIP Applications version: 03.02.0000.0000
LOCATION:
CONTACT:
SNMP OBJECT ID: 1.3.6.1.4.1.2.3.1.2.1.1.2
DOES IP FORWARDING: NO
SUPPORTS SNMP: YES
NETMON FLAGS: 0x1ff
SNMP ADDRESS: 9.20.44.2
SNMP TIMEOUT: 2 seconds
CYCLE TIME: 28 minutes
INIT CONFIG POLL: MAXIMUM TIME
CONFIG POLL: Sat 4 Mar 18:47:30 1995
NEW NODE POLL: Fri 3 Mar 23:00:30 1995
TOPOLOGY POLL: MAXIMUM TIME
OTHER POLLING INTERVALS/TIMES:
            2147483647 (MAXIMUM TIME)
            2147483647 (MAXIMUM TIME)
            2147483647 (MAXIMUM TIME)
            2147483647 (MAXIMUM TIME)
            2147483647 (MAXIMUM TIME)
NODE VENDOR: IBM
NODE AGENT: IBM RS/6000
NUMBER OF INTERFACES:1
```

Figure 3.11 *ovtopodump* output (to keep this to a reasonable length, it includes the output only for the host itself, and excludes the output for the host's interfaces)

It is possible to have NetView use a relational database, rather than flat files, for the topology information. This is useful for management applications that require easy access to it. The relational databases supported by NetView are:

- Ingres Server
- Oracle7 Server
- IBM's DB2 AIX/6000
- Informix-OnLine
- Sybase SQL Server

Object Database The Object Database is a general-purpose data repository used by NetView and its applications. It is not object-oriented in the formal sense, but is structured as a collection of what are called objects; hence the name. Each object has a numeric identifier and a set of fields containing information about it. NetView uses objects to represent IP resources such as the internetwork, networks, links, systems and interfaces. NetView applications also use the Object Database to maintain information about the resources they are managing. The *ovobjprint* command prints the contents of this database.

Unlike the Topology Database, there is a programming interface to the Object Database. This is implemented as a series of C language calls, all of which have the prefix *OVwDb*. The calls are documented in IBM (1995d, e). They allow applications to read and manipulate objects and their fields.

Figure 3.12 shows the *ovobjprint* output for the same host as in the previous example.

```
OBJECT: 721

FIELD   ID    FIELD NAME                 FIELD VALUE
10            Selection Name             "helen"
11            IP Hostname                "helen"
14            OVW Maps Exists            1
15            OVW Maps Managed           1
570           IP Status                  Normal(2)
573           isIPRouter                 FALSE
584           vendor                     IBM(1)
594           isNode                     TRUE
596           isComputer                 TRUE
597           isConnector                FALSE
598           isBridge                   FALSE
599           isRouter                   FALSE
600           isHub                      FALSE
603           isWorkstation              TRUE
618           isIP                       TRUE
619           isSNMPSupported            TRUE
621           SNMP sysDescr              "IBM RISC System/6000"
622           SNMP sysLocation           " "
623           SNMP sysContact            " "
624           SNMP sysObjectID           "1.3.6.1.4.1.2.3.1.2.1.1.2"
625           SNMPAgent                  IBM RS/6000(1)
629           isMLM                      TRUE
630           isSYSMON                   FALSE
631           isSIA                      TRUE
635           TopM Interface Count       1
641           TopM Interface List        "et0 Up 9.20.44.2
                                         255.255.255.0
                                         0xAA0004000604
                                         ieee 802.3 csmacd"
657           XXMAP Protocol List        "IP"
724           IP Name                    "helen"
727           default IP Symbol List     5
```

Figure 3.12 *ovobjprint* output (this output has been slightly edited to improve presentation)

Map Database The Map Database contains information about NetView 'maps', submaps and 'symbols'. We will discuss maps and symbols in Chapter 8. For now, we can note that:

- A symbol is the representation of a resource as it appears in a particular submap. Thus, a particular router might have a symbol in the Internet Submap and another in the Network Submap.
- A map is a collection of submaps and symbols, along with information controlling their use.

The Map Database is used by NetView and its applications. The information pertains to IP and other protocols and is used by NetView processes such as *ipMap* and *xxMap,* which display network graphics. The information here overlaps with that kept in the Object and Topology Databases, but also includes information about the structure and contents of maps and submaps. It also includes details not maintained elsewhere about the symbols used to represent network resources.

The contents of the database can be written to standard output with the command *ovmapdump.* For example, issuing 'ovmapdump' gives a concise listing, while 'ovmapdump -v' gives the gory details.

Figure 3.13 shows the *ovmapdump* output for the same host used in previous examples. Note that there are normally multiple entries in the Map Database for a single host. This is because a host can be a symbol when it appears in submaps but can also be a submap itself. In particular, it can be a Node Submap. In the example here we have the host as a symbol.

```
Symbol ID: 5
Symbol State: Placed
Symbol Label: helen
Symbol Object ID: 721
Symbol Submap ID: 4
Symbol Variety: Icon
Symbol Symbol Type: Computer:Workstation
Symbol Plane: Application
Symbol Status: Normal
Symbol Status Source: Symbol
Symbol Placement Type: Sequence
Symbol X Coord: 100
Symbol Y Coord: 99
Symbol Predecessor Symbol ID: 0
Symbol Connection Endpoint 1 Symbol ID: 0
Symbol Connection Endpoint 2 Symbol ID: 0
Symbol Applications: 1
        IP Map
Symbol Behavior: Explodable
Symbol Executable Application:
Symbol Executable Action:
Symbol Executable Target Policy: 0
Symbol Executable Targets:
```

Figure 3.13 *ovmapdump* output

3.2.5 Event detection and handling

In the last chapter, we looked at the SNMP trap and we saw that this is the mechanism SNMP agents use to let the manager know there is a problem. Traps are an extremely important aspect of SNMP network management, and in this section we'll review NetView's mechanisms for receiving and processing them.

As we have seen, traps are quite simple, conveying a description of the problem condition with an Enterprise ID and two codes. Sometimes they also contain variable bindings. In spite of this simplicity, there are several things you can do within NetView to make traps the basis of a useful problem management system. Later we'll see that by using Trouble Ticket still more can be done.

Here we should note that NetView can send trap-like messages to itself when it detects an interesting condition. For example, NetView generates these when it discovers a new IP system or discovers that a system is down. These are referred to as 'events' in NetView parlance, but I'll call them traps hereafter since they are handled in essentially the same manner as traps proper.

NetView logs all traps it receives in two places:

- The file trapd.log.[2] This is an ASCII file in a readable format. By default, each entry in trapd.log will have a complete dump of the trap's information—generic and specific codes, enterprise ID, source, time stamp and variable bindings. It is also possible to change this for particular traps, so that custom information is logged instead. This is done using 'Event Configuration' as we'll soon see.
- The files ovevent.log and ovevent.log.BAK. These two files are not in directly readable format since they are intended for use only by NetView's Events and Event History applications.

It is possible to copy the trapd.log entries into one of the relational databases supported by NetView. This can be useful for installation-written programs that perform problem analysis.

After logging them, NetView displays traps to its users with the Events application. This displays traps in one of two styles:

- In a line-oriented display, in which each trap is represented by a single line of text.
- In a graphical display, where each trap is represented by an 'event card'. This style is the default and is shown in Figure 3.14.

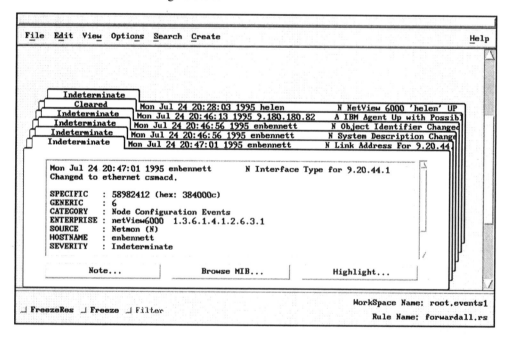

Figure 3.14 NetView Events application

---

[2] The files trapd.log, ovevent.log and ovevent.log.BAK are kept in the directory /usr/OV/log.

In addition to Events, there is also the Event History display. This is very similar to Events, but is intended for reviewing older traps and thus is not updated as new traps arrive in NetView. I'll defer detailed discussion of Event History to Chapter 7.

In either of its two display styles, Events normally shows all the information in each trap. However, as with the trapd.log, this can be changed through Event Configuration.[3] Let's look at Event Configuration and some of the other facilities for controlling NetView's handling of traps.

Event Configuration Event Configuration lets you specify a custom display format for particular traps. This format will then be used in Events, Event History and trapd.log. To customize a trap, you provide a text string that will be used for its display. There are variables you can use to include any of the fields or variable bindings from the trap.

For example, the following text string would create a two-line display with some basic information about a trap:

```
Generic=$G, Enterprise=$E, Specific=$S\nFirst variable=$1
```

Each generic and enterprise-specific trap can be customized uniquely, and you can also create customization that applies only to traps from particular agents.

There are several other ways you can use Event Configuration to customize NetView's handling of traps:

- You can specify a message that will be displayed in a pop-up window when a particular trap is received. This is useful for attracting attention to catastrophic situations.
- You can specify a category and severity to assign to particular traps. The category indicates the kind of information the trap is conveying, for example *topology*, *status* or *error*. The severity describes how serious a trap is, for example *critical*, *major* or *minor*. These can be displayed in Events, Event History and trapd.log.
- You can indicate that a particular trap should change a resource's status in NetView submaps. For example, a trap from a router that indicates its hard disk has crashed could be configured to cause the router's status to change to marginal.

Event Configuration is normally performed by using an little set of windows in the NetView GUI. It's also possible to use the *addtrap* command, which is useful when you want to configure many traps. Alternatively, you can just edit the file trapd.conf,[4] which is what the windows and *addtrap* do.

Conflicts can arise from the fact that the same customization is used in Events, Event History and trapd.log. For example, you might want trapd.log to have detailed information, but Events just a summary. In this case, the best solution is to use the NetView SNMP programming interface to create a custom log. In Appendix II there is an example of how to use this interface, and from this it would be quite easy to make your own logging program.

---

[3] To be precise, Events will show all fields and variables in a trap if there is no Event Configuration for it. However, by default, NetView has Event Configuration for many common traps, and thus will show customized information for them, e.g. some text describing the problem condition.

[4] The file trapd.conf is in directory /usr/OV/conf/C. In this book I'll mention the names of several directories which have in their paths a 'C' directory. In non-English language versions of NetView this directory may have a different name, which is taken from the $LANG environment variable used in the system.

Filters NetView also includes a trap filtering mechanism. This is vital of course because many traps are not significant enough to bother the management staff. NetView therefore applies installation-defined filters to all traps before showing them in Events and Event History. Each user may have different filters. They do not affect what is logged in trapd.log.

Filters are usually built using a tool known as the Filter Editor. Alternatively, you can build them directly by creating your own filter definition files. We will look at this in Chapter 7.

Rulesets There is also the NetView ruleset facility which allows you to define sophisticated rules for handling incoming traps. This provides the capabilities of trap filters, but in a more general and flexible way. It can also perform trap correlation, automation and many other functions. There is a very nice visual programming interface for this, known as the Ruleset Editor, which lets you create logical diagrams determining how incoming traps are to be handled. We will look at this function in detail in Chapter 7.

Automatic reaction In addition to displaying and logging traps, NetView can automatically react to them. For this, you can use either Event Configuration or rulesets to define commands that execute when particular kinds of traps are received. The commands can be anything valid in the AIX Korn shell, including AIX and NetView commands, shell scripts and C programs. There are variables that can be used to pass them information from the traps.

Thus, you can have programs that go out and try to resolve problems or perform other custom handling of traps. We will look at this area in detail in Chapter 9.

3.2.6 Working with MIBs

The heart of SNMP is the ability of the manager to access agents' MIBs, either reading or changing information in them. This provides a potentially unlimited set of capabilities ranging from simple things such as getting the system contact name to complex functions such as reconfiguring a bridge.

Much of NetView is therefore concerned with managing MIBs. By default, NetView understands the basic MIB-II and several MIB extensions. For others you must provide definition files conforming to SNMP's Structure of Management Information. These files are processed by the NetView MIB Loader function. This allows NetView functions such as the MIB Browser and MIB Application Builder to use them. In many cases these MIB extensions are included with NetView.[5] Others will be provided by vendors of NetView applications and equipment NetView manages.

Simple things You can work with MIBs in several ways. In the simplest case there are tools included with NetView, for example the *snmpget*, *snmpnext* and *snmpset* commands that carry out the three requests managers send to agents. These commands are useful if you want to write shell scripts that read or manipulate MIBs. Also, as we've seen, there is the NetView *snmpwalk* command that lets you dump all or part of an agent's MIB. This is very useful for understanding what a particular agent's MIB contains. It is also helpful in debugging SNMP-related problems.

---

[5] They are in the directory /usr/OV/snmp_mibs.

MIB Browser Getting away from command lines and into the realm of GUIs, there is the NetView MIB Browser, a very useful tool that allows you to browse through the objects in an agent's MIB. You can also use it to query and set variables. An example window is shown in Figure 3.15.

When you first come into the MIB Browser, you are just below the *internet* node of the naming tree we discussed in the previous chapter. You then descend through the tree until you reach the objects or variables of interest.

Probably the most common use of the MIB Browser is querying an agent's MIB variables. With just this function you can perform a significant amount of management since most agents' MIBs are packed with information. Another use of the MIB Browser is just to understand the structure of an agent's MIB. You might also use it to change a few variables or even perform a minor reconfiguration. In most cases, however, setting MIB variables would be something done by applications.

The MIB Browser operates in real time, that is, it only gives you information about the MIB at the time it is used. This is enough in many cases, but it is also important to understand how

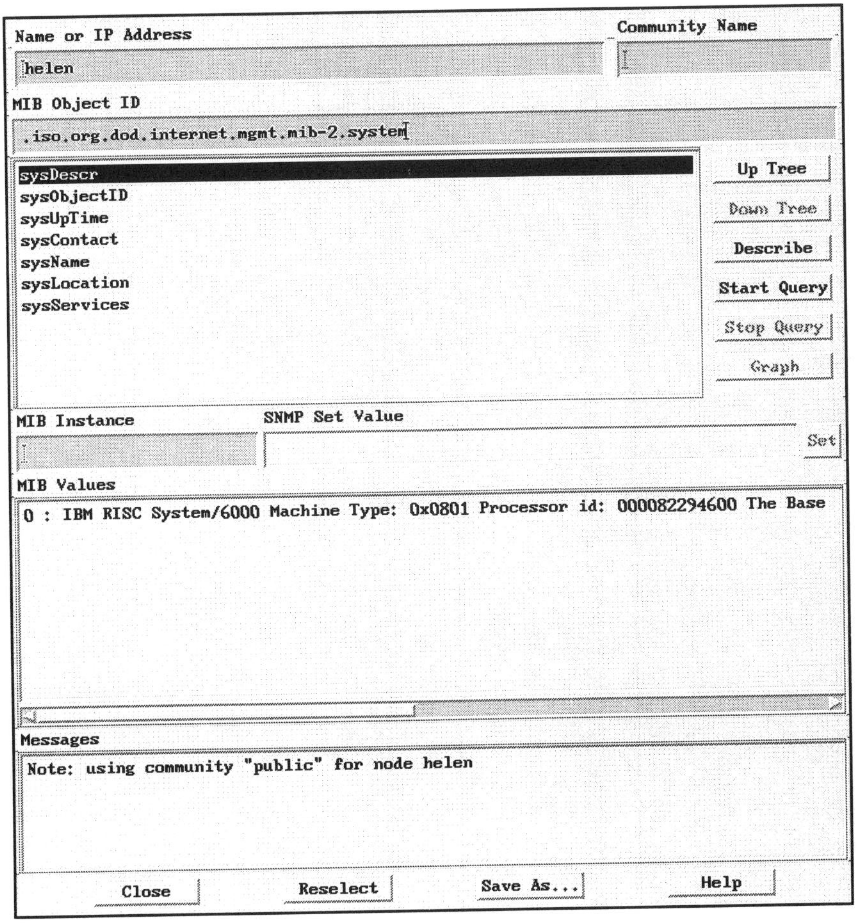

```
Name or IP Address                                    Community Name
 helen                                                 |

MIB Object ID
 .iso.org.dod.internet.mgmt.mib-2.system|

┌──────────────────────────────────────────────────┐   ┌──────────────┐
│ sysDescr                                           │   │   Up Tree    │
│ sysObjectID                                        │   ├──────────────┤
│ sysUpTime                                          │   │  Down Tree   │
│ sysContact                                         │   ├──────────────┤
│ sysName                                            │   │   Describe   │
│ sysLocation                                        │   ├──────────────┤
│ sysServices                                        │   │ Start Query  │
│                                                    │   ├──────────────┤
│                                                    │   │  Stop Query  │
│                                                    │   ├──────────────┤
│                                                    │   │    Graph     │
└──────────────────────────────────────────────────┘   └──────────────┘

MIB Instance            SNMP Set Value
|                                                                    Set|

MIB Values
 0 : IBM RISC System/6000 Machine Type: 0x0801 Processor id: 000082294600 The Base




Messages
 Note: using community "public" for node helen



    Close          Reselect         Save As...          Help
```

Figure 3.15 NetView MIB Browser

variables in the MIB behave over time, for example when monitoring a network's performance. This capability is provided by the next tool.

MIB Data Collection The NetView MIB Data Collector is a tool for periodically collecting the values of agents' MIB variables. It can then save these in files or check to see if they indicate abnormal conditions.

You might use the Data Collector if you wanted the monitor the CPU utilization of some bridges over time. If the bridges' agents had MIB variables indicating CPU utilization, you could configure the Data Collector to get and save them every 10 minutes. Later you could review these values or perhaps write a simple program to compute some statistics from them.

You might also use the Data Collector if you wanted to be informed immediately when the CPU utilization of a bridge exceeded a threshold such as 90 per cent. You would configure the Data Collector to collect the relevant MIB variables periodically and apply this threshold to their values. If it found a value exceeding the threshold, the Data Collector would then generate a trap which could be displayed by the Events application.

Control over MIB Data Collection is most easily done using a NetView GUI application called 'Data Collection & Thresholds: SNMP'. Alternatively, you can use the *setthresh* command and give all the collection specifications without ever seeing a window. In either case, you specify a MIB object, some instances of it and a list of SNMP agents from which it should be collected. In addition, you define the frequency of collection and a collection mode.

The collection mode can be one of:

- store only
- threshold only
- store and threshold

When storing is selected, the MIB values are saved in a set of files.[6] When thresholding is selected, you define a numeric threshold. You also define a 'rearm' value which is less than the threshold and is used to provide hysteresis for the process. Then (as shown in Figure 3.16) when a collected value crosses the threshold, a trap is generated. As long as subsequently collected values of the variable stay above the rearm value, no further traps are generated. When the value does go below the rearm value, the thresholding process will reset so that a trap will be generated if the value exceeds the threshold again. The rearm value thus serves to avoid generating zillions of traps when the variable hovers around the threshold.

For example, if you wanted to monitor the CPU utilizations of some bridges, you might define a threshold of 95 per cent and a rearm value of 85 per cent. The first time a bridge's CPU utilization exceeded 95 per cent a trap would be generated. Then, suppose CPU utilization hovered between 90 per cent and 100 per cent for a while. No traps would be generated because of the rearm value. Later, suppose utilization drops below 85 per cent. The threshold would be rearmed and the process would start over. Note that a trap is generated when the measurement drops below the rearm value. This is useful for knowing when the problem condition has ended.

One nice feature of the Data Collector is its use of 'MIB expressions'. These are arithmetic expressions involving MIB variables. For example, suppose you want to collect MIB information indicating how busy a particular link is. In MIB-II there is no single MIB object that gives

---

[6] In the /usr/OV/databases/snmpCollect directory.

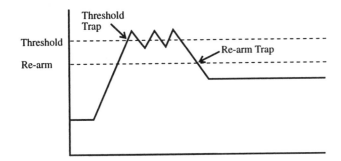

Figure 3.16 Threshold and re-arm process

this measurement, but it is possible to calculate it from several objects that are available there. Thus, you can define an expression for calculating the desired measurement from the objects and then treat the expression as if it were an object itself. Specifically, you could instruct NetView to collect the expression, and NetView would get all the required objects and compute the desired value. This could be stored or used in a threshold, just as with real objects.

There is also a sneaky use for MIB expressions. This is to get past the restriction that you can have only positive thresholds, that is, thresholds in which the variable crosses the threshold in the upward direction. If you want to watch a variable to make sure it does not go below a particular value, then you can create a MIB expression which is the negative of the variable.

Once you've collected data, you can do several things with it, for example create graphs, generate reports and perform analysis. We will look at this area in Chapter 10.

MIB Application Builder You can use the MIB Application Builder to quickly create applications that display data collected from MIBs. The applications can be hooked into the NetView menu structure and can be one of the following types:

- **Form** This can be used to display the current values of one or more scalar objects. For example, you might want to make a form that shows the incoming and outgoing IP traffic for a given system. To do this, you would select the variables to be displayed, give your application a name (and other identifying information) and indicate which NetView menu pull-down you would like to include it in.

  An operator could then select a system in a submap and invoke your application from the menu. NetView would collect the required variables from the system and display them in a window.

  You can provide a selection rule, which is a logical expression that indicates the kinds of systems for which the application is valid. This makes it possible, for example, to make your application available for only a particular router model.

  An example form is shown in Figure 3.17. It displays the variables in the System Group.
- **Table** This works the same as form except that it is for MIB objects arranged in a table. The columns in the window correspond to the columnar objects of the table, and the rows correspond to the instances of these. An example is shown in Figure 3.18, where four

```
 File   View                                                    Help
─────────────────────────────────────────────────────────────────────
 Name or IP Address
┌─────────────────────────────────────────────────────────────────┐
│ enbennett                                                         │
└─────────────────────────────────────────────────────────────────┘

┌─────────────────────────────────────────────────────────────────┐
│ sysDescr    :  OS/2 SNMP AGENT version 1.2, with DPI version 1.1.09 (Jul│
│ sysObjectID :  .iso.org.dod.internet.private.enterprises.ibm.ibmProd.46 │
│ sysUpTime   :  (7362) 0:01:13.62                                        │
│ sysContact  :  Larry Bennett                                            │
│ sysName     :  bennett                                                  │
│ sysLocation :  Chalfont St Giles                                        │
│ sysServices :  76                                                       │
│                                                                         │
│                                                                         │
└─────────────────────────────────────────────────────────────────┘
 Messages
┌─────────────────────────────────────────────────────────────────┐
│                                                                   │
│                                                                   │
│                                                                   │
└─────────────────────────────────────────────────────────────────┘

        Close              Stop              Restart
```

Figure 3.17 Form created with MIB Application Builder

```
 File   View                                                    Help
─────────────────────────────────────────────────────────────────────
 Name or IP Address
┌─────────────────────────────────────────────────────────────────┐
│ enbennett                                                         │
└─────────────────────────────────────────────────────────────────┘
 ifType                 ifSpeed   ifPhysAddress        ifOperStatus
┌─────────────────────────────────────────────────────────────────┐
│ iso88025-tokenRing     4000000   40 00 77 3E 45 8D    up          │
│ ethernet-csmacd       10000000   08 00 5A 6B FC FB    up          │
│                                                                   │
│                                                                   │
│                                                                   │
│                                                                   │
│                                                                   │
└─────────────────────────────────────────────────────────────────┘
 Messages
┌─────────────────────────────────────────────────────────────────┐
│                                                                   │
│                                                                   │
│                                                                   │
└─────────────────────────────────────────────────────────────────┘

        Close              Stop              Restart
```

Figure 3.18 Table created with MIB Application Builder

objects from the MIB-II Interfaces Table are displayed for two interfaces on a particular host.

● **Graph** Here you choose one or more MIB objects that may each have one or several instances. NetView's *xnmgraph* tool is then driven to produce a graph with one line for each instance. There are colour-coded labels to identify the lines. The graph can show data that has been previously collected, as well as data collected in real time according to parameters you specify. An example is shown in Figure 3.19. Here two objects from the Interfaces Table—*ifInOctets* and *ifOutOctets*—are graphed for two interfaces on a host.

Other applications The best way to work with a MIB is through an application that interacts with the agent and interprets its information. For example, several vendors of routers supply NetView applications that work with the specific objects maintained in their equipment. These display tables and diagrams and provide operational tools. NetView's SNMP programming interface provides the base for these applications.

3.2.7 Other functions in NetView

NetView includes several other functions that are useful in managing IP networks. One is a tool with which you can select a system from a submap and have NetView PING it, displaying the results in a window. PING is invaluable when you are trying to figure out if a system is up or whether there is any sort of connectivity to it. This tool makes PING a bit more convenient to use. Related to this is a remote PING tool with which you select two resources, and NetView then PINGs from one to the other.

A similar hook is provided for convenient use of *telnet*. This is quite useful when you want to log into a host and run some commands. There is also an analogous method for invoking SMIT on a remote AIX system.

There is also the Demand Poll function which causes NetView to PING a system and send it SNMP Gets for basic information. The results are shown in a window and are also used to update NetView's databases. This function is useful for ensuring the system is properly functioning at that precise moment, and also to force NetView to synchronize its databases with reality. Normally, NetView checks systems only periodically, so sometimes this is necessary.

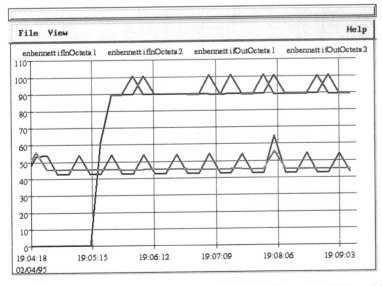

Figure 3.19 Graph created with MIB Application Builder (NetView produced this graph in colour, but it's been converted to greyscale here)

Another handy tool is the Locate Route function. You select two systems and NetView displays the route that would be taken by an IP packet going from the first to the second. NetView uses SNMP Gets to obtain this information from the relevant routers and thus it works only if you have SNMP access to them. There is also a command line version of this, *findroute*.

3.3 MANAGING NON-IP WITH NETVIEW

Let's now consider how NetView can manage protocols other than IP. Some of the tools we've just reviewed will apply here as well. In particular, those for working with MIBs and for handling traps can also work in non-IP networks with the help of proxy agents. There are also NetView facilities designed specifically for the non-IP world. The following subsections give an overview of these.

3.3.1 Using SNMP proxy agents

NetView's support for SNMP allows it to manage non-IP networks through proxy agents. To a large extent, the fact that a proxy agent is involved is transparent. The main exception is that NetView must send SNMP requests to the proxy agent rather than to the managed systems themselves.

Each request sent to the proxy agent needs to include identification of the target system in the non-IP network. However, in SNMP requests there is no specific place to put this. It is not practical to use the variable bindings because, for example, in a Get request this would mean that the manager is asking for the value of the variable. Thus, the community name is used instead to select the target system. This is not as hokey as it might seem since one of the things a community name does is select a MIB view. Here we simply need to think of each MIB view as corresponding to a particular managed system or, more precisely, as being the set of objects in the proxy agent's MIB that pertain to the managed system.

NetView supports this scheme by allowing you to give a name and corresponding community to each non-IP system and then specify the proxy agent through which it can be reached. Then, whenever the name of the non-IP system is used in the NetView GUI or programming interface, the request is sent to the proxy agent using the appropriate community name.

The definitions required for this facility are placed in Local Registration Files (LRFs) and processed by the *ovaddobj* command. Alternatively, you can use the NetView SNMP programming interface to create the definitions.

3.3.2 Pre-built proxy agents

In many cases, there will be a pre-built proxy agent available for the type of equipment or network you want to manage. For example, IBM provides the following proxy agents:

● *The Proxy Agent/2* for managing FDDI LANs
● *LAN Network Manager for OS/2* for managing Token-Ring LANs
● *LAN NetView Management Utilities for OS/2* for managing PC/LAN workstations and servers

In addition, there are several proxy agents from other vendors, including:

- *DNM* from ki Research for managing DECnet
- Novell's *NetWare Management System*, which in addition, to being a manager in its own right, can also serve as a proxy agent for NetWare environments

If there is not a proxy agent available, then you will probably want to get one of the several toolkits available for building them. Examples of these include:

- *EventIX* from Bridgeway Corporation
- *Emanate* from SNMP Research
- A set of toolkits from PEER Networks
- *NetScript/6000* from Diederich and Associates
- *NAP for AIX* from Automated Network Management

The usefulness of a proxy agent depends on the kinds of functions it implements. The fact that a particular one supports an environment you need to manage doesn't mean it will meet all your requirements. The kinds of functions to consider when looking at a proxy agent include:

- Conversion of alarms to traps
- Provision of a MIB that lets you view and collect important information about the non-IP environment
- Commands or SNMP Sets to control and configure the non-IP environment
- Provision of topology information that can be used by NetView's GTM or a NetView application to produce graphical views of the environment

In addition, it's quite useful if there is a NetView application that works with the proxy agent to interpret its information, e.g. show it in windows, and make it easy to control the non-IP environment.

If the proxy agent is sufficiently capable, it can provide a powerful way to extend NetView's management into non-IP networks.

3.3.3 NetView programming interfaces

NetView applications are an important aspect of non-IP management. To support these, NetView includes an extensive set of programming interfaces that can be used by C language programs. These can be used to build full-blown applications and can also be used to extend NetView's capabilities in less ambitious ways.

There are many NetView programming interfaces. The ones relevant to this book are:

- **SNMP interface** This allows programs to exchange SNMP messages with agents. The calls allow programs to:
  - Build SNMP messages.
  - Send and receive SNMP messages.

- Register to receive traps coming into NetView. There are filtered and unfiltered versions of this. In the former case, the program specifies a 'filter string' that determines the subset of incoming traps it wishes to receive. These use the same filtering mechanism we discussed earlier for use with Events and Event History.
- Access and manipulate the NetView SNMP configuration database, which contains information controlling NetView's SNMP interactions with agents. It includes community names, status polling intervals and proxy agent characteristics.

- **CMIP interface**   This allows programs to exchange OSI CMIP messages with agents.
- **GTM interface**   This allows programs to describe non-IP topology to NetView's General Topology Manager.
- *OVw interface*   So named because it is implemented by the NetView *OVw* process. This interface is quite extensive, providing access to:
  - The NetView user interface. Programs can create and manipulate maps, submaps and symbols. They can also add commands to the NetView menus and create customized help.
  - The NetView Object database. Programs can read and manipulate objects and their attributes.
- **Security interface**   This allows programs to ensure users are authorized to use their functions. It also allows programs to access other aspects of NetView's security mechanisms.

3.3.4 General Topology Manager and *xxMap*

GTM and *xxMap* allow programs to define non-IP topology for graphical display in NetView. We will cover GTM and *xxMap* in much more detail in Chapter 8, but for now I'll just give an overview of the process. This is also diagrammed in Figure 3.20:

- Non-IP topology information is obtained by a special kind of proxy agent called a 'topology agent'. It is special because it can supply this information to NetView in the particular form required by GTM. This agent may run in NetView's system or it may run elsewhere in the network.

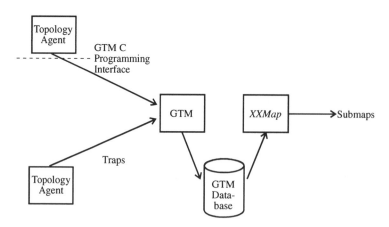

Figure 3.20 Non-IP topology collection and display

- The topology agent communicates its information to GTM in one of two ways:
  - By sending to NetView special enterprise-specific traps that are diverted to the GTM process. These traps define which components exist in the network and how they are connected to each other. The traps also indicate the status of the components.
  - By using the several C calls in the GTM programming interface. These support the same functions available through the trap interface.
- GTM then stores this information in its database (this is maintained in the directory /usr/OV/databases/openview/gtmdb).
- The NetView *xxMap* process then accesses the GTM Database and from it generates a collection of submaps. These submaps are similar in appearance to those used for IP networks. *xxMap* builds one hierarchy of submaps for each protocol defined in the GTM Database, and places a symbol in the Root Submap to represent each of them. This is depicted in Figure 3.21.

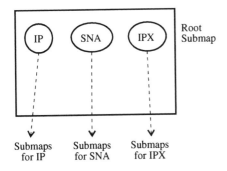

Figure 3.21 Non-IP topology collection and display

Thus, if you had two applications, one that placed SNA topology into the GTM Database and another IPX, then in the Root Submap you would have a symbol for each of the two protocols. From either of these you would be able to navigate through the set of submaps below.

There is one particularly nice feature included in the GTM mechanism. This is a means of representing the common case that a single network adapter has multiple protocols running on it. For example, on my Token-Ring adapter, I run SNA, IP and NetBIOS. Thus, the *single* interface participates in three protocols and it would be nice to have this reflected in the submaps. This can be done by defining to GTM the relationship of the adapter to the protocols. GTM would then treat my adapter as a single entity rather than three, as might otherwise be the case. It would also enable a feature known as 'protocol switching'. This allows the user to move easily between the submaps of the different protocols in a way that makes their relationships clear. We will look at all this in more detail in Chapter 8.

3.4 NETVIEW INTERNAL STRUCTURE

As we have seen, NetView is structured internally as two sets of processes. The background daemons carry out the interactions with the managed networks and maintain several databases. The *OVw* processes handle interactions with the users and related tasks. Let's look in more detail at the more interesting of these processes.

3.4.1 Background processes

Normally, the daemons are always running. They are started in one of three ways:

- By the operating system when it initializes. The script /etc/rc.tcpip which is driven at system start-up contains a line to invoke the /etc/netnmrc script which starts the NetView daemons.
- Because someone issued the *ovstart* command. This command explicitly starts the background processes but not the *OVw* processes.
- Because someone issued the *nv6000* command. This is the command normally used to start the NetView GUI. It starts one instance of the *OVw* processes (for the issuing user) and also starts the background processes if they are not already running.

You can issue the *ovstatus* command to see the status of each background process.

ovspmd—**process monitor daemon** *ovspmd* is the parent of the other background daemons. It is invoked by whichever method is used to start NetView. *ovspmd* reads the file ovsuf (this is in the directory /usr/OV/conf) to determine which other daemons it should start and in which order it should do so. It is also responsible for monitoring and stopping the daemons.

orsd—**object registration services daemon** This daemon maintains the Object Registration Database and is mainly concerned with OSI CMIP information. For us, it is interesting for two reasons. First, it supports the naming scheme we have seen for managing non-IP systems through a proxy agent. Second, it can get us into trouble. If you change the IP address of NetView's system, you will have problems because the Object Registration Database will continue to hold the old address, with unpleasant consequences. The solution to this is explained in Implementation Tip 3.2.

Implementation Tip 3.2

If you change the IP address of NetView's system, you will need to recreate the Object Registration Database so that it contains the new address. If you don't, you may see a pop-up message indicating that NetView had an error connecting to 'CI' (the communications infrastructure).

To fix this problem, you can either run the *reset_ci* script found in /usr/OV/service, or issue the following commands:

```
ovstop OVORS_M
rm /usr/OV/conf/ovors
ovstart OVORS_M
ovaddobj /usr/OV/lrf/ovelmd.lrf
ovaddobj /usr/OV/lrf/ovesmd.lrf
```

---

pmd—**post master daemon** *pmd* is responsible for routing messages between NetView processes and the agents managed by NetView. It implements the SNMP (and CMIP) protocol stacks. In the case of SNMP, all outgoing Gets, GetNexts and Sets are issued via *pmd*. Responses come back to *pmd*, which then routes them to the appropriate processes.

netmon—**IP network monitor daemon** *netmon* is the heart of NetView's IP management. This daemon implements IP topology discovery and also monitors the managed IP networks for status changes. In addition, *netmon* generates traps for certain events, for example, when a system is discovered or when its status changes. The information *netmon* discovers is put into the Topology and Object Databases.

ovtopmd—**Topology Database daemon** This daemon manages the NetView Topology Database under the direction of the *netmon* daemon.

ovwdb—*OVw* **Object Database daemon** This daemon maintains the NetView Object Database, handling requests from many NetView processes and applications.

snmpCollect—**SNMP collection daemon** *snmpCollect* is the daemon that carries out the NetView MIB data collection process, periodically polling agents and storing the retrieved data in the directory /usr/OV/databases/snmpCollect.

gtmd and *noniptopod* The daemons *gtmd* and *noniptopod* manage NetView's interactions with non-IP topology agents.

The real workhorse here is *gtmd*. It manages the GTM Database and processes the traps and C calls updating it. *noniptopod*'s role is only to start any programs that may be required to support a particular topology agent. For example, you may need a program running in NetView's system to transform the agent's information in some way before sending it to *gtmd*. This is explained in Chapter 8.

trapd—**trap daemon** *trapd* is one of three daemons that process incoming traps—the others are *ovesmd* and *nvcorrd*. There are three daemons for historical reasons and each performs a different aspect of trap processing. *trapd* writes the trapd.log file. It is also the source of traps for the other two daemons, as well as for applications that have connected to the unfiltered programming interface for receiving traps.

ovesmd—**event sieve daemon** This daemon implements the trap filtering mechanism. *ovesmd* distributes traps to NetView processes such as Events, as well as to applications that have connected to the filtered programming interface for receiving traps.

nvcorrd—**event correlation daemon** *nvcorrd* is the daemon that implements the ruleset mechanism. It processes each incoming trap according to the active rulesets and passes selected ones along to subscribing applications such as Events.

actionsvr—**event correlation action daemon** This daemon executes all commands driven from rulesets. *nvcorrd* passes each command to *actionsvr*, which then starts a child process to execute it.

ovelmd—**event log daemon** *ovelmd* maintains the ovevent.log and ovevent.log.BAK files. These are sources of information for both the Events and Event History applications.

trapgend—**trap generation daemon** *trapgend* is a little AIX systems management subagent that runs in either the local AIX system or a remote one. *trapgend* uses the SMUX protocol to connect to the system's SNMP agent and carries out several functions:

- It can take messages as they are written to the AIX system error log and convert them into traps, which it sends to NetView. This allows you to use the trap mechanism to detect problems on AIX systems throughout the network.
- It implements a MIB extension with objects describing the system's CPU and disk utilization. This means that NetView can collect this information from AIXs throughout the network.
- It carries out the remote PING function in NetView. This allows NetView to instruct one remote system to PING another. This is useful for testing connectivity between remote systems.

trapgend is installed on the local AIX by default. NetView is also able to distribute *trapgend* to remote AIXs, which in general you will want to do.

ovactiond—**Event Action Daemon** Like *actionsvr*, this daemon executes commands in response to traps, enabling automatic reaction to events in the network. However, here it is done under control of the Event Configuration process and not rulesets.

Before version 3 of NetView these commands were executed by an instance of the Events application. In particular, an instance of Events would run the appropriate command any time the corresponding trap passed its filters. The problem with this approach was that it made automatic command responses dependent on the GUI being active. Also, when multiple GUIs were active, it introduced the possibility of the command running multiple times even though you just wanted it to run once. Thus, in version 3 the *ovactiond* daemon was introduced to provide a single process to run these commands. Still, there may be cases where you prefer to have a command run under Events. Implementation Tip 3.3 discusses this.

Implementation Tip 3.3

There may be times you don't want to run commands under *ovactiond*, and instead want to run them under Events. For example, Events would be the right place to run a command that opens a window to display some information about a trap or one that asks the operator how to handle it. In such cases, you can disable *ovactiond* and do things the old fashioned way.
   To disable *ovactiond*:

- Deactivate *ovactiond*'s Local Registration File with the command:

   ```
   ovdelobj /usr/OV/lrf/ovactiond.lrf
   ```
- Edit the file /usr/OV/app-defaults/Nvevents so that *executeCommands* is set to *True*.

---

tralertd—**trap to alert daemon** In some installations, there will also be a NetView/390 carrying out network management. Here it is often useful to have NetView notify NetView/390 of certain traps or other events it receives. We will look at this in more detail in the next chapter, but here let's notice *tralertd*'s role in the process.

tralertd is responsible for converting traps into SNA's equivalent, alerts. *tralertd* receives traps using filters you specify and converts those passing the filters into alerts that are sent to NetView/390.

spappld—**service point application daemon** It is also useful when you have a NetView/390 to be able to issue commands from the mainframe and have them executed in NetView's system. *spappld*, the companion to *tralertd*, supports this process.

NetView/390 operators can use its RUNCMD facility to execute commands on remote systems. When the remote system is NetView, *spappld* receives the command and executes it in the AIX environment. It then returns the response to NetView/390.

3.4.2 Foreground processes

There are quite a few foreground processes. It would take too much space to cover them all, so let's just review a few of the really important ones.

OVw This is the parent process for the NetView GUI, started by the *nv6000* script. *OVw* performs the basic management of the user interface and is responsible for starting other GUI applications. It also implements the *OVw* programming interface through which GUI applications interact with the user.

ipMap **and** *xxMap* These processes are responsible for generating the IP and non-IP submaps, respectively.

nvevents *nvevents* is the application that implements the Events window. *nvevents* obtains historical trap information from the files ovevent.log and ovevent.log.BAK. It then obtains real-time traps according to the filters and rulesets selected by the user.

nvela *nvela* implements the Event History window. It works as *nvevents* does, reading both ovevent.log and ovevent.log.BAK, but does not receive real-time traps.

3.5 SYSTEMS MONITOR

Having now reviewed NetView itself, let's look at two closely related products, Systems Monitor and Trouble Ticket.

Systems Monitor is a pair of products from IBM that have different functions but were developed together and are controlled through a common GUI. Both run on several operating systems and fill two important management roles:

● The System Information Agent (SIA) provides a great deal of information about the system on which it runs. It does this through a MIB extension that has objects describing the hardware, system software, communications, applications and users.
● The Mid-Level Manager (MLM) serves as an intermediate SNMP manager, to which NetView can delegate many management tasks. The MLM can interact with NetView in

cases requiring central or higher-level management. The MLM would be installed at several strategic locations in the network—each close to a concentration of managed systems so that information flows only locally. The MLM thus provides a way to reduce network overhead and off-load management processing from NetView.

Both these incarnations of Systems Monitor are configured by a NetView application which is known to the initiated as the *smeui* (Systems Monitor End User Interface). While at the time of writing the *smeui* runs only under AIX, the MLM and SIA run under several operating systems.[7]

Let's look at the two incarnations of Systems Monitor in more depth.

3.5.1 System Information Agent

The SIA implements a MIB extension on UNIX or OS/2 which contains all sorts of system-related information (see box). This information can be collected by NetView (or any SNMP manager) and used for monitoring and diagnosing the system.

The SIA also includes a function known as the Command Table, which allows you to add objects to its MIB extension. To do this, you define commands that run when the manager issues a Get or Set to your objects. These commands can go off and collect information or make changes, and return the results to the manager. As with nearly all Systems Monitor functions, the commands are arranged in a MIB table.

The SIA also has a useful function known as the File Monitor Table. This keeps an eye on various aspects of files on the SIA's system and sends traps to NetView when they change. The SIA can monitor a file's existence, its contents and several other characteristics. There are many uses for this facility. One is the obvious monitoring of critical files. Another is to generate traps based on messages written to a log file. We will look at this in more detail in Chapter 7.

System Information Agent MIB Extension

The SIA's MIB extension includes the following information:

- System configuration, including paging space, buffers and disk
- Installed hardware devices
- Token-Ring and Ethernet adapter information, including configuration and performance
- Paging information, including size and utilization of paging spaces
- File system statistics
- Subsystem and process status
- User information, including total number and who they are

This list pertains to the UNIX versions of the SIA. In the OS/2 version, this information is somewhat different, being based on the 'Host Resources MIB' (RFC 1514).

---

[7] These include AIX, HP-UX, Solaris and NCR UNIX. The SIA also runs under OS/2 and in the future the MLM may run there as well. At this writing the OS/2 version of the SIA is provided as part of IBM's NetView for OS/2 product.

As shown in Figure 3.22, the SIA implements its MIB extension by running as a SMUX sub-agent to the system's SNMP agent.[8] Thus, all Sets and Gets for the SIA's portion of the MIB are passed through to it by the SNMP agent.

The SIA MIB extension is quite extensive and we won't go through it here. You can see its structure in Figure 3.23. For more details, you can read about it in IBM (1995f) or look through its MIB module.[9]

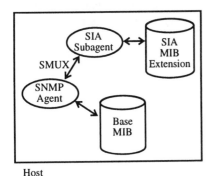

Host

Figure 3.22 SIA subagent

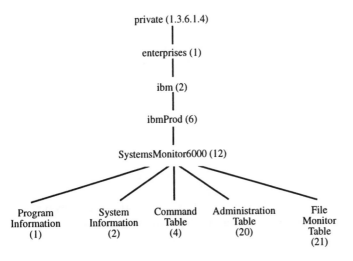

Figure 3.23 SIA MIB structure

---

[8] On OS/2 it uses the SNMP Distributed Protocol Interface (DPI) instead.

[9] On systems with the SIA installed, the MIB module is in the file /usr/lpp/smsia/original/ibm-sysinfo.mib. It is also included in the softcopy materials for this book available on the Internet at www.mcgraw-hill.co.uk (check on editorial information for professional computing).

3.5.2 Mid-Level Manager

In this role, Systems Monitor serves as an intermediate SNMP manager, filling a big hole in SNMPv1. In unembellished SNMPv1, if you want to manage an entire network from one location, the manager must interact directly with every agent. This means:

- All traps from all agents must traverse the entire network to get to the manager (in many cases only to be discarded because they are not interesting). This wastes network bandwidth and cycles in the management system.
- All SNMP data collection must be performed by the central manager. As with traps, much data collected by SNMP is not very interesting. It is often collected only to see if it indicates exceptional conditions, which it usually doesn't. It's therefore a waste of network resources to perform all collection from a central location.
- Probably worst of all, all discovery and status monitoring must be performed from the central site. This means PINGs and SNMP requests must be frequently sent across the entire network. In the case of status monitoring, this can be especially bad since accuracy requires very frequent checking.

Clearly, a better solution is to place intermediate managers throughout the network. These intermediate managers carry out most of the interactions with the agents and send data to the central manager only when it's interesting. SNMPv2 provides a basic framework for this kind of architecture, but that's not useful yet. Systems Monitor's MLM implements it using SNMPv1. To agents, the MLM appears to be a manager; to NetView, it appears to be an agent.

In most cases, you would deploy one MLM on each LAN (or group of bridged LANs). The MLM would then carry out the following functions locally:

- **Trap filtering**   Agents in the MLM's 'domain' would be configured to send their traps to the MLM. You would then define MLM filters to determine which are interesting enough to send to NetView. The others will be logged on the MLM's system for future reference, e.g. for reporting or diagnosis.

   The MLM also allows you to define commands to be executed in response to particular traps. Thus, you can perform automatic reaction locally.
- **SNMP data collection**   You can configure the MLM to collect MIB data in its domain. This data is logged locally by the MLM, and you can ship it to the central site as required. The MLM can also compare the data to thresholds and, when these are exceeded, execute commands locally or send traps to NetView.
- **IP discovery and status monitoring**   The MLM can perform these activities on behalf of NetView. We'll see how in a few moments.

Figure 3.24 shows the structure of the MLM MIB extension. You can learn more about it in IBM (1995f) or by looking through its MIB module.[10]

---

[10] On systems with the MLM installed, the MIB module is in the file /usr/lpp/smmlm/original/ibm-midlevelmgr.mib. It is also included in the softcopy materials for this book available on the Internet at www.mcgraw-hill.co.uk (check on editorial information for professional computing).

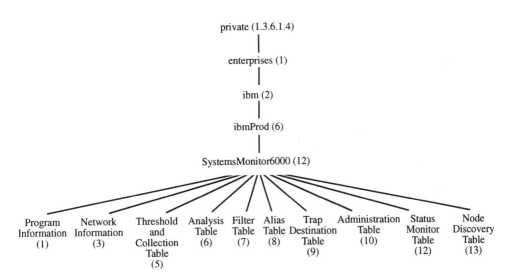

Figure 3.24 MLM MIB structure

3.5.3 System-Level Manager

In addition to the MLM and SIA, there is another Systems Monitor package, the System-Level Manager (SLM). This is intended for cases where you want to have the MLM's function, but at a lower price and in a form that manages the local system only. For example, you might have a system whose MIB variables you want to monitor using the MLM's SNMP collection function or whose traps you want to run through the MLM's filtering. In this case, you could buy an MLM and install it on the system. However, if you aren't using a distributed management structure and don't need all the capabilities of the MLM, you can buy the SLM instead and save some money.

The SLM has essentially all the facilities of the MLM, but cannot perform any management outside its own system. Thus, it cannot:

- Perform discovery and status monitoring
- Collect and threshold MIB variables on other systems
- Receive and process traps from other systems

It can, however, forward traps from the local system to NetView.

3.5.4 Defining Systems Monitor tables

In later chapters, we will look at many of Systems Monitor's capabilities in more detail. Here let's look at a general issue pertaining to both the MLM and the SIA—the tables contained in their MIB extensions. (Here I'm not mentioning the SLM since it's really just a scaled-down version of the MLM, and therefore works very similarly.)

There are many of these tables and the operation of both the MLM and SIA is controlled by them. They determine which functions will be carried out and all parameters controlling them. For example, the SIA's File Monitoring Table controls the SIA file monitoring function.

The tables can be configured in one of the following ways:

- Through the *smeui*. This is the easiest way, and is good for doing a relatively small amount of configuring. The *smeui* provides a window for each table in which you will see a list of its entries, which you can manipulate and query.
- By using a configuration file. Both the MLM and SIA have configuration files they can read to build their tables, and you can edit these. I like this technique, not only because it gives me a chance to play with the wonderful(!) *vi* editor, but also because it's easy to set up many table entries quickly (see Implementation Tip 3.4).
- From the 'resume files'. Both the SIA and MLM use these to save the table configuration from their most recent execution. By default, they build their tables from these files when they reinitialize.
- By using SNMP Sets from any SNMP manager. For example, you could use NetView's *snmpset* command.
- Through the Agent Policy Manager (APM). This is an alternative to the *smeui* which can be used for two of the Systems Monitor tables—the SIA's File Monitor Table and the MLM's Threshold Table. This GUI has the significant advantage that with it you can conveniently distribute the table definitions to multiple Systems Monitors.

Implementation Tip 3.4

If you want to use configuration files to define Systems Monitor tables, you must explicitly tell the SIA and MLM to use them. By default, both will load from their 'resume files'. To load from the configuration files instead, use the '-i' flag when starting the SIA or MLM. For example, use 'midmand -i' to start the MLM. If you use SMIT to start them, answer 'no' to 'Use resume file option'.

Let's now consider the MLM and SIA tables themselves. Their general structure is similar to other MIB tables, as we discussed under 'Objects and instance' (Section 2.2.4). Thus, within each table, there are several objects forming the columns, and instances of these forming the rows. Consider, for example, the MLM's Trap Destination Table used to define the managers to which the MLM forwards traps. The table has the columnar objects shown in Figure 3.25.

```
State
Name
Host
Mask
ParticipationState
ActivationTime
ActivationDayOfWeek
DeactivationTime
DeactivationDayOfWeek
Messages
```

Figure 3.25 Columnar objects in MLM Trap Destination Table (for readability, I have omitted their common prefix, *smMlmTrapDestination*)

Without bothering about the details, each row of the table causes the MLM to forward traps to a manager, and each column gives the forwarding details. For example, the instance of *Mask* in each row controls which traps will be forwarded.

The object of interest, though, is *Name*. Each instance of this contains a sequence of ASCII characters such as 'ForwardToBob'. This is the name of a particular row. In addition, it is the ID for each instance in the row.

Now the alert reader will wonder how a string such as 'ForwardToBob' can be used as an instance ID. After all, instance IDs are supposed to be made of numbers and dots. The answer is that Systems Monitor forms the instance ID from the sequence of ASCII values corresponding to the letters in the name. For example, if a row has the *Name* 'ed', then its object identifier will be 101.100.

This indexing technique is shown in Figure 3.26. It is used in many Systems Monitor tables.

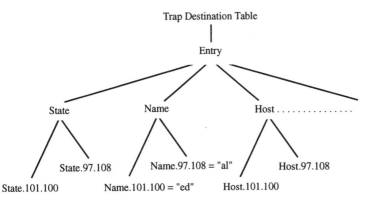

Figure 3.26 *sysmon* table indexing

There are a few other things Systems Monitor tables have in common. Most contain two general columnar objects (in addition to *Name*):[11]

- A *State* object. This controls whether a row is active or not. Sometimes it will also control other global aspects of the row.
- A *Description* object. This is a text description of the row's purpose.

Another thing many MLM tables have in common is their use of the Alias Table. This table allows a list of IP names or addresses to be given a name, the 'alias'. For example, a group of hosts could be given the name *bighosts*. Other MLM tables can then refer to the group simply as *bighosts*.

3.5.5 MLM IP discovery and status monitoring

Let's now look at how the MLM can off-load IP discovery and status monitoring from NetView. There are two possible flavours of this:

[11] The main exceptions to this are the tables in the SIA which do not control SIA functions but instead provide information about the system.

- Off-load status monitoring only
- Off-load both status monitoring and discovery

Let's consider status monitoring first. Here the MLM will monitor only those systems in its own network (being precise once again about the network versus internetwork distinction), which generally will be a LAN or a group of bridged LANs . This works out nicely because the MLM's status monitoring activities will be confined to a relatively small, high-bandwidth environment.

The MLM will go off and merrily PING away at these systems. If this process indicates that one is down, the MLM will inform NetView by sending a particular enterprise-specific trap. When received in NetView, this trap will cause the creation of an Interface Down internal event—just as if *netmon* had made the discovery. Similarly, when the system comes back up, the MLM will send another enterprise-specific trap that will cause an Interface Up internal event. Thus, the fact that status monitoring has been off-loaded is largely transparent.

The off-loading of status monitoring is driven from NetView. You instruct NetView to do this either by specifying particular options when you start the *netmon* daemon or, more likely, by specifying these options in SMIT. You can either have NetView off-load to all MLMs it knows about or you can explicitly list the MLMs.

In either case, when NetView discovers an eligible MLM, it instructs it to perform status monitoring by doing the following:

- It creates an alias in the MLM's Alias Table. The alias lists all the IP systems NetView has discovered in that MLM's network.
- NetView then creates an entry in the MLM's Status Monitor Table. The entry uses the alias to indicate the systems that should be monitored. The entry also contains monitoring parameters the MLM should use, including the frequency at which it should be performed.

Thus, NetView will off-load status monitoring for all the systems it knows about in the MLM's network. Meanwhile, NetView discovery will still be running and, as NetView finds new systems, it will update the alias to include them.

MLMs can also perform IP discovery for their networks. As noted earlier, because an MLM is doing this only for the network in which it resides, it can employ techniques that are either unavailable or unforgivable in an internetwork manager such as NetView. One technique the MLM can use is sending broadcast PINGs on its network and looking to see who answers. Another is to watch the traffic flowing in the network and extract hints about the local topology. The MLM can also use discovery techniques similar to NetView's. Thus, off-loading discovery to MLMs not only saves bandwidth, but can also improve accuracy.

To cause NetView to off-load discovery, you specify particular options when starting the *netmon* daemon. As with status monitoring, NetView will do this either for all or for only particular MLMs.

In addition, you also configure discovery in the MLMs themselves. To do this, you set some objects in the Discovery Group. The more interesting of these objects are (omitting their common prefix, *smMlmDiscovery*):

- **State**   Whether discovery is enabled in this MLM.
- **Sensor**   Controls the use of 'sensing' in discovery. There are three possibilities: passive sensing, active sensing and none at all. Either form of sensing means the MLM will monitor

packets in its network and use the information for discovery. With active sensing, it will in addition actively discover the network (using the same kinds of techniques as NetView) based on information it gleans from these packets.

- **SensorMaxReads and SensorMaxInterval** These objects control how frequently and intensively sensing is performed. Thus, you can fine tune, trading off performance against possible accuracy improvements.
- **BroadcastSearch, BroadcastSearchTime, BroadcastSearchDays and Broadcast-SearchNow** Together, these objects control the use of broadcast PINGs for discovery. This process may be:
  - – Turned off completely.
  - – Driven immediately.
  - – Scheduled to run regularly at a particular time. (As in other Systems Monitor tables, the time can be specified with much flexibility, as times of day and days of the week.)
  - – Scheduled to run once at a particular time.

  Because of the bandwidth consumed by broadcasting, these objects are designed to control its use carefully.

3.6 TROUBLE TICKET

Trouble Ticket is an IBM product that carries out many of the functions required for problem and change management. For problem management, it addresses the areas of:

- Collecting information about problems and maintaining it in a database
- Notifying appropriate people that problems have occurred
- Co-ordinating the several people and organizations who may be involved in diagnosing and resolving problems
- Maintaining historical records about problems and producing various kinds of reports from these

Thus, Trouble Ticket is a kind of workflow system optimized for problem management.

Trouble Ticket can run by itself, but is much more interesting when it works with NetView. From NetView, it can obtain two important kinds of information:

- **Traps** Based on these, Trouble Ticket can automatically start the process of managing a problem. This is obviously much preferable to relying on people for the information.
- **IP Topology Information** Doing a good job of problem management requires an understanding of the network's topology and thus Trouble Ticket must be provided with information about the network resources that may have problems. For IP networks, Trouble Ticket can obtain this directly from NetView, thus saving much typing.

A central idea in Trouble Ticket is the distinction between a problem and its symptoms. One problem may have several symptoms and, unless these are correlated, the management process can get muddled. For example, if a router goes down the management system may receive:

- Traps from each of the other routers to which it was connected

- Traps from workstations and application programs that can no longer communicate
- Phone calls from users

It is obviously desirable to tie all these symptoms together and treat them collectively as one problem. Thus, Trouble Ticket uses two kinds of logical entities in problem management. 'Incident reports' represent symptoms and 'trouble tickets' represent the problems themselves.

Trouble Ticket is implemented in two major parts. First, there is a server which runs on AIX, performing the interaction with NetView and maintaining the database. Second, there is client software which implements the user interface and can run under AIX, HP-UX, Windows and SunOS.

Trouble Ticket allows you to track problems from the time they are first detected through to their resolution, and on to later historical analysis. As shown in Figure 3.27, the basic flow of problems through Trouble Ticket is:

1. Trouble Ticket first learns of one or more symptoms of a problem. For each symptom, it creates an incident report. It may learn of each symptom in one of the following ways:
   - NetView receives a trap from the network and passes it to Trouble Ticket.
   - An operator creates an incident report using a Trouble Ticket window.
   - A program in the local AIX creates an incident report. There is a command provided with Trouble Ticket that allows programs to do this.
   - An e-mail message is sent to Trouble Ticket. This e-mail message would include special keywords containing the incident report parameters.
2. Once each incident report is created, it is added to the list of outstanding reports. This list can be viewed by operators and other members of the management staff. The incident report's creation can drive processes which, for example, add an item to the list of notifications for a particular operator or send an e-mail message to a technician. It could also drive a command to do something more exotic (and user-implemented) such as paging.
3. Next, the incidents related to a single problem would be grouped together and attached to a trouble ticket. This step is performed using Trouble Ticket windows. One created, the trouble ticket becomes the basis for all further managing and tracking of the problem.
4. The trouble ticket would then be assigned to someone who will own the problem throughout its resolution. An action plan for resolving the problem can be defined and each action item assigned to a particular person. There are also facilities to notify each such person of the actions they have been assigned. Planned completion times can be attached to the actions.
5. Trouble Ticket then provides several tools to monitor the progress of each trouble ticket. These include windows in which you can view all open or delinquent trouble tickets, or all trouble tickets assigned to a particular person. Problems can be escalated to a higher level within the organization after pre-defined delays. You can also associate service-level agreements with each trouble ticket and track the response times against them.
6. Once the problem is resolved, the ticket is closed and maintained in a database for historical analysis. Trouble ticket provides several pre-built tools to generate reports from this information.

Normally, Trouble Ticket stores its information in a database, which is included with the product and which is usually invisible to the user and administrator. It is possible, however, to run SQL queries against the database using the *rgen* utility included with Trouble Ticket.

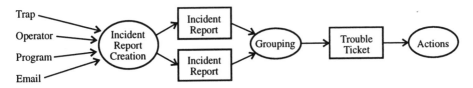

Figure 3.27 Managing a problem with Trouble Ticket

Alternatively, Trouble Ticket can store its information in an Ingres or Sybase database. In this case, the SQL and other tools provided with the database can be used to query the Trouble Ticket information.

Closely related to problem management is making changes to the network. Trouble Ticket thus has change management facilities, which are integrated with its problem management capabilities. Both can make use of the same network configuration information. It is also possible to associate a change request with the trouble ticket that has necessitated the change. Trouble Ticket also provides tools for tracking and co-ordinating the processing of change requests.

3.7 SUMMARY

Together NetView, Systems Monitor and Trouble Ticket form the core from which a multiprotocol network management can be built. By themselves, the three products form a complete solution in IP networks. For environments other than IP, NetView applications will be required and we will investigate these in Chapter 6. But first, while we're covering network management platforms, let's look at how NetView can integrate with NetView/390.

FOUR

INTEGRATING WITH NETVIEW/390

NetView/390's roots are in the world of IBM mainframes and SNA networks. It has since been extended to manage many other environments, but this is still where NetView/390 has its greatest use. Meanwhile, SNMP-based management systems have focused on the IP and UNIX world, with the result that the many organizations with both these environments will need an SNA-based manager such as NetView/390 as well as an SNMP-based one such as NetView. To provide a sensible management system, it is important that both managers can work together. This is the topic we will cover in this chapter.

NetView/390 runs under IBM's MVS, VM and VSE mainframe operating systems and includes built-in management capabilities for SNA networks. It also provides a platform for mainframe systems management and for network management of environments other than SNA. There are several applications from IBM and other vendors making use of this platform to manage, for example, NetWare LAN environments, DECnet networks and even IP networks.

NetView/390 started its life in 1986 when IBM put together four products for managing SNA networks and added some additional code to glue them together. Since then IBM has added functions for managing non-SNA networks, and positioned NetView/390 as an overall enterprise management system.

The main components of NetView/390 are:

- **Command Facility** This is the basic infrastructure under which most of the rest of NetView runs and also provides a 3270-terminal based user interface. It has facilities for:
  - Issuing commands to the network and system
  - Processing messages received from the network and system
  - Reacting automatically to messages
  - Logging information of various sorts

  It also provides a set of programming interfaces in REXX, C, PL/1 and some NetView/390-specific languages.
- **Hardware Monitor** This processes alarms from the system and network. It presents them to its users, writes them to logs and works with the Command Facility to provide a means of reacting automatically to them.

- **Session Monitor** This is a tool for monitoring SNA sessions and diagnosing problems with them. It also provides facilities for monitoring SNA network performance and availability.
- **NetView Graphic Monitor Facility (NGMF)** While the rest of NetView/390 is on the mainframe, this part runs on OS/2 and provides a graphical operator interface into many of NetView/390's functions.
- **Resource Object Data Manager (RODM)** This is an object-oriented repository for network and systems data. It is analogous in many ways to NetView's GTM and is used by some NetView/390 applications as the place they store their topology information for various kinds of networks. Much of this information is displayed in graphical network views on NGMF workstations.

4.1 WHO'S ON TOP?

Both NetView and NetView/390 are capable of being overall enterprise managers and, in installations with both, the question of which is most appropriate naturally arises. The answer depends mainly on what kind of networks and systems are to be managed and whether the built-in capabilities and applications of one manager are more suitable than the other. In some cases, it is easy to decide. For example, in environments with lots of IBM equipment, mainframes and SNA networks, NetView/390 is almost always the best choice. Similarly, if the environment is based primarily on IP and UNIX machines, NetView makes more sense. In other cases it is more difficult, for example when there is a mix of IP/UNIX and SNA/mainframe environments. In any case, there are several ways NetView and NetView/390 can co-operate in the overall management process, and in this chapter we will review the most important of these.

In most cases, NetView and NetView/390 will have one of two relationships as shown in Figure 4.1:

1. NetView/390 is the overall enterprise manager and NetView is the sub-manager. In this case, you would probably be using NetView as an IP network manager and perhaps also a UNIX systems manager. There are two software products from IBM that make this approach quite effective. These are the 'AIX NetView Service Point' and 'NetView Multi-System Manager'.
2. NetView is the overall enterprise manager and NetView/390 the sub-manager. You can use the IBM product SNA Manager/6000 to manage the SNA network from NetView, treating NetView/390 as a kind of SNA proxy agent.

   In this case, you will have some but not all SNA management functions available under NetView. Thus, as we will see, you will still probably need to rely on NetView/390 to carry out many tasks, particularly in the reporting and monitoring areas.

   There is not anything available to perform mainframe systems management from NetView. It would be possible to write applications to do this and I know of some installations that have done so, but this is quite a large project.

In this chapter we will look at each of these two approaches. One thing to bear in mind here is that both of these solutions work only when the NetView is running under AIX.

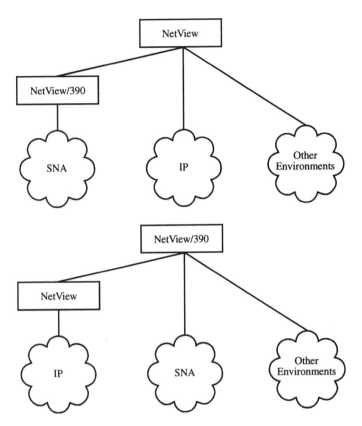

Figure 4.1 Possible relationships between NetView and NetView/390

4.2 NETVIEW AS A SUB-MANAGER FOR NETVIEW/390

Let's first consider the case that NetView/390 is the enterprise manager and NetView serves as a sub-manager for IP network and UNIX systems management.

4.2.1 AIX NetView Service Point

This product—which for simplicity we'll call 'the Service Point'—is a kind of management gateway between NetView/390 and NetView. It runs with NetView on an AIX system and allows the following types of interactions between NetView and NetView/390:

● Traps received in NetView can be made available to NetView/390. NetView/390 uses as its management protocol IBM's SNA Management Services and in this protocol the equivalent of the trap is the 'alert'. The Service Point can convert traps received by NetView into alerts and send these to NetView/390. Once in NetView/390, the operators there can see them along with the other alerts NetView/390 receives. It is also possible to use NetView/390's facilities for automatically reacting to alerts.

● NetView/390 operators can issue commands and have these executed by NetView or by NetView's AIX system. NetView/390 has a general-purpose command called RUNCMD which takes a command string and sends it to a gateway such as the Service Point. Once there the command is executed in an AIX shell—either the Bourne or Restricted shell—and the results are returned to the NetView/390 operators. These commands can be AIX commands, NetView commands, shell scripts and so on.

With these two capabilities, it is possible to perform a basic level of management from NetView/390 using NetView as a sub-manager. In particular, it is possible to be aware of problems that occur in the NetView-managed environments and also to control these environments using commands. It is possible to combine RUNCMD with *rexec* (a UNIX facility for issuing commands to other systems in the IP network) so that commands sent to the Service Point are then forwarded to other systems in NetView's network, considerably enhancing the power of this approach.

Figure 4.2 shows how the Service Point is implemented. It runs on NetView's system and relies on the services of another IBM product called AIX SNA Server/6000. The latter implements an SNA protocol stack on AIX and the Service Point uses it to maintain SNA sessions with NetView/390. For those of you who are SNA gurus, these may be either APPC or SSCP-PU sessions and the Service Point appears to NetView/390 as either a PU 2.1 or a PU 2.0. Using APPC and PU 2.1 is the preferred approach since it increases the flexibility of where the Service Point is placed in the SNA network and also improves performance.

Because the Service Point uses SNA sessions, it must obviously be connected to the SNA network. Later we will see some techniques for handling cases where this restriction causes difficulties. The Service Point conforms to the SNA Management Services architecture and in that architecture's parlance it behaves as a 'service point'. Thus, from NetView/390's viewpoint the Service Point can be handled in a generic way according to the architectural rules for all service points.

As shown in Figure 4.3, the Service Point relies on two daemons in NetView's system, *tralertd* and *spappld*. It passes commands received from NetView/390 to *spappld*, which

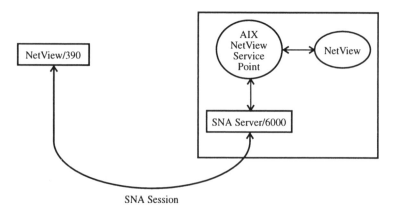

Figure 4.2 AIX NetView Service Point

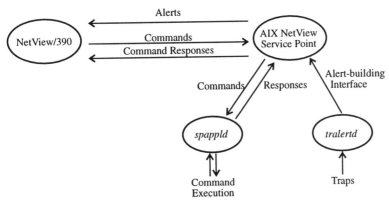

Figure 4.3 *spappld* and *tralertd*

actually executes them and returns their output back to the Service Point. Traps are handled by *tralertd,* which converts them to alerts and passes them to the Service Point for transmission to NetView/390.

Let's look at these alert and RUNCMD mechanisms a bit more closely.

4.2.2 RUNCMDs

This mechanism is easy to understand. The NetView/390 operator issues a RUNCMD whose parameters include a command string and the name of a system on which it should be executed.

NetView/390 then puts this information into one of two possible messages defined in the SNA Management Services protocol—an 'NMVT' or a 'CP-MSU'. Both these are general-purpose messages used for carrying not only commands but also alerts and anything else required in network management. The difference between them is not really important, but the NMVT is used when communication is over an SSCP-PU session and the CP-MSU when an APPC session is used.

Upon receipt of the NMVT or CP-MSU, the AIX Service Point passes the command string to the *spappld* daemon. *spappld* executes it, then collects the command's output and gives it back to the Service Point. The Service Point then places the output into another NMVT or CP-MSU and sends it back to NetView/390, where it is written to the screen of the operator who issued the command.

You can also write programs that issue RUNCMDs from NetView/390 using the REXX language. This is quite useful for making simplified commands and also for incorporating RUNCMDs into more complex functions. You could write a REXX program that issued several commands to collect information from the IP/UNIX environment via NetView, formatted the results and presented them to an operator.

Figure 4.4 shows a simple REXX program that uses RUNCMD. It lets NetView/390 users get a quick look at a system's contact by getting and displaying the value of its *sysContact* variable. The program uses the NetView *snmpget* command to obtain the variable's value, retrieves the command's standard output, and then formats this on the NetView/390 screen.

```
/* NetView/390 REXX exec to return the sysContact for
   an agent. The agent's name or address is passed
   as the single parameter. */

/* Init service point name and spappld application name. */
nvaixsp = 'AIXNVSP1'
nvappl = 'NVAIX'

/* Get system name parameter */
parse arg sysname

/* Issue RUNCMD to get the value of sysContact. */
'RUNCMD SP='nvaixsp',APPL='nvappl',CLISTVAR=YES,snmpget',
   sysname '.1.3.6.1.2.1.1.4.0'

if rc <> 0 then exit 4

/* Get output from command -- in second response line */
response = dsirun002

/* Remove label from response to get actual value. If
   nothing left after parsing then there was an error
   in the RUNCMD or snmpget. */
parse value response with ' : ' ':' sysContactValue
if sysContactValue = '' then exit 8

/* Format output */
   say 'sysContact is' sysContactValue
```

Figure 4.4 Example NetView/390 REXX program

4.2.3 Trap to alert conversion

While traps have a very simple structure, alerts are much more complex. Traps have fields defined for only the most basic information and then everything else is simply stuffed into variable bindings in a free-form way. This has the advantage of making the trap mechanism flexible and easy to understand, but the disadvantage that there is no standard way of encoding the information. Therefore the manager must know how each agent constructs the variable bindings.

Alerts on the other hand were designed so that there is a standard way of encoding nearly any kind of information you might like. As with the RUNCMD mechanism, alerts are transported in either NMVTs or CP-MSUs. In either case, the content is essentially the same, consisting of a series of little data structures called 'vectors', 'subvectors' and 'subfields'. These structures often contain 'codepoints', which are numeric codes describing various details about a problem. These codepoints are general-purpose, describing problem details in a way that many different kinds of alert senders can use. There are codepoints describing the type of the problem, its probable causes, recommended actions to resolve it and many other details. Because alerts are so highly structured, the manager can interpret them in a way that is largely independent of their source.

The AIX NetView Service Point provides a programming interface that applications can use to construct alerts and send them to NetView/390. The *tralertd* daemon uses this interface to create and send alerts based on traps received by NetView. Figure 4.5 depicts the overall process. (The particulars of alerts' contents and formats are described in IBM (1993b). The Service Point's programming interface is documented in IBM (1993a).)

Since you will probably not want all traps to be sent to NetView/390 as alerts, you can define filters to eliminate some of them. These filters are the same kind used in NetView for the

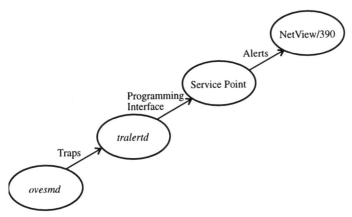

Figure 4.5 Trap to alert conversion

Events window. *tralertd* uses the filters when it connects to the NetView SNMP interface. It will receive only the traps passing the filters and convert only these into alerts. To specify the filters, you use the NetView Alert Filter Control window.

Because traps and alerts are completely different animals, the conversion process is complicated. It will be done in one of three ways:

- The trap may come from the AIX error logging facility. AIX and its applications use this facility to log error information. They do not simply log messages but instead log information structured in a special way. In fact, this information is structured very similarly to the way alerts are. *tralertd* monitors this log, watching for entries that have been marked as 'alertable'. It takes the information from these and builds traps which it sends into NetView. Into each trap, *tralertd* will put several variable bindings that contain all the information required for the alert. Thus, the conversion is simply a matter of copying this information into the appropriate alert fields.
- The trap may be one that is recognized by NetView. 'Recognized' means that a mapping from the trap to an alert is defined in the file tralertd.conf.[1] There are many mappings put there by default to handle the generic SNMP traps and some enterprise-specific traps generated by NetView itself. You can also add to these using NetView's Alert Editor. In this case, you will be able to directly control how the conversion is done.
- The trap may not be recognized by NetView and thus will be converted using a default scheme. Here the alert fields describing the problem in general terms (the type, description and probable cause codepoints) will be set to reflect the trap's generic code. The other items in the trap, including the agent's address, the specific code and the variable bindings, are copied into several other fields of the alert. Most are copied into 'Detailed Data' subvectors. These subvectors are much like variable bindings in that they provide a mechanism to include information for which no other place can be found. Here they are used not so much because the alert cannot accommodate them, but because in the default scheme it is not possible to interpret the meanings of the specific code and the variable bindings.

---

[1] This file is in the directory /usr/OV/conf.

The gory details of the process are guaranteed to give you a headache and so I'll stop with this rough characterization. If you really want to know, you can consult IBM (1993b, 1995c).

4.2.4 NetView MultiSystem Manager

With the AIX NetView Service Point, you get the ability to monitor traps and issue commands to the UNIX/IP world. This is a good start, but if you are a serious NetView/390 user you may also want to see graphical representations of the IP network and have these integrated into NetView/390's graphics for other protocols. NetView MultiSystem Manager (NMSM) provides this.

NMSM runs as an application of NetView/390 (see Figure 4.6). The basic idea is that you install its agents in the network and then it collects topology, status and alerts from these. At the time of writing, there are agents available for:

- **IP internetworks**   NetView
- **Token-Ring LANs**   LAN Network Manager for OS/2
- **Workgroups (based on OS/2 LAN Manager and NetWare)**   LAN Management Utilities for OS/2
- **Workgroups (based on NetWare)**   using an agent supplied with NMSM

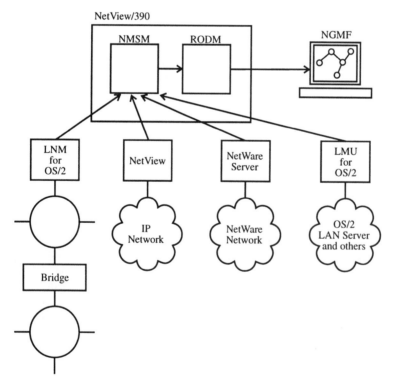

Figure 4.6 NetView MultiSystem Manager and its agents

NMSM takes the topology and status information from these agents and stores it in NetView/390's RODM. Once this data has been placed into RODM, NetView/390 is able to display graphical views of the environments on NGMF workstations.

Thus, NMSM can integrate the IP displays into the others supported by NetView/390. The way the IP topology is displayed on NGMF is very similar to the way it is done in NetView—using the same hierarchy of submaps. NMSM also provides the ability to issue commands to NetView (using the RUNCMD facility, but hidden underneath a GUI) and also to display alerts from the IP network (in a nicer format than Hardware Monitor's).

The NMSM agent for NetView uses the AIX NetView Service Point to communicate with NetView/390 and therefore you must also run SNA Server/6000. As you would expect, the connection between NetView and NetView/390 must be SNA—either SSCP-PU or APPC.

4.3 SNA MANAGER/6000

This is the other way around—where NetView manages the mainframe, or more accurately the SNA network in which the mainframe resides. SNA Manager runs as a NetView application and provides facilities to manage SNA networks from the NetView GUI.

SNA Manager collects information from NetView/390 about the topology and status of the SNA network. It then presents this information to NetView users by creating a set of SNA submaps.

SNA manager also makes it possible for NetView operators to see alerts from the SNA network. To do this, it performs the reverse of the process carried out by *tralertd* and the AIX NetView Service Point. It receives these alerts from NetView/390 and converts them into traps. These are displayed in the NetView Events window and are also processed by all the other NetView trap-handling machinery.

SNA Manager also provides a 'point and shoot' command interface so that an operator can select a resource in an SNA submap and a command to execute against it from a menu. Some of these commands are built-in, for example activating and deactivating SNA resources. In addition, you can add your own commands. SNA Manager also provides a plain command line so an operator can type in a command to be transported to NetView/390 and executed there.

4.3.1 SNA Manager structure

Figure 4.7 shows SNA Manager's structure and its relationship to NetView/390. SNA Manager implements the user interface for managing the SNA network from NetView, but relies on NetView/390 to perform all the interactions with the SNA network, including:

- Collection of topology and status information
- Receipt of alerts from the SNA network
- Execution of commands to control the SNA network

SNA Manager thus interacts heavily with the NetView/390 and to do this it always maintains two APPC sessions with it. Thus, you must have SNA connectivity between NetView and NetView/390. In addition, you will almost certainly need to have some sort of 3270 terminal

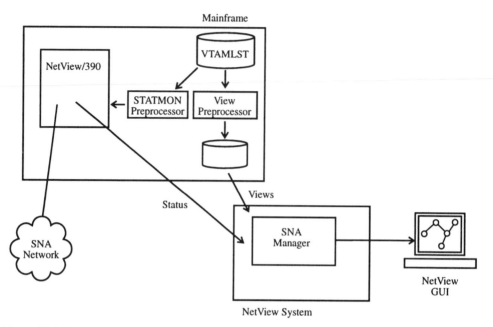

Figure 4.7 SNA Manager and NetView/390

emulator on the NetView system so that you can interact directly with NetView/390. This is necessary to perform some of the administrative functions for SNA Manager (e.g. starting the APPC sessions, which must be done from the NetView/390 side). In addition, there are many good SNA management functions available only through NetView/390's 3270 interface, for example the Session Monitor.

To get things started, there is an administrative task you must perform. This is to collect the SNA network topology information from the mainframe and download it to SNA Manager's AIX system. This involves the following steps:

1. You run a job known as the STATMON Preprocessor on the mainframe. This reads VTAM's configuration datasets (VTAMLST) to understand the SNA network. The information from this job is used by NetView when it sends status information to SNA Manager.
2. You run a second job known as the View Preprocessor against these same datasets. This job gathers information used to draw the submaps of the SNA network.
3. You then download the output from the View Preprocessor to the AIX system. You can use a terminal emulator, FTP or anything else that can perform a binary download.
4. SNA Manager will now have all the information it needs to create the submaps, except the current status of the network. This will be sent automatically from NetView/390.

One consequence of this process is that if the SNA network configuration changes, i.e. VTAMLST changes, you must rerun the preprocessors and download the views again. Also, if the configuration changes through VTAM Dynamic Reconfiguration (in which no changes are made to VTAMLST) then SNA Manager will be unaware of it.

4.3.2 Alert to trap conversion

As we have seen, NetView/390's Hardware Monitor implements the machinery for handling alerts in the mainframe. These may come into NetView/390 from several different sources including the SNA network and the mainframe itself. Wherever they come from, the Hardware Monitor handles them in several ways, filtering uninteresting ones, presenting them to NetView/390 operators in 3270 screens, logging them to its databases and providing the infrastructure for automatic reaction to them.

In addition, Hardware Monitor sends the alerts it receives to SNA Manager where they will be converted to traps. The actual forwarding is done by a special task in NetView/390 called DSIAL2WS.

As with all alarm mechanisms, SNA alerts generally flood into NetView/390 at great speed and only a subset are interesting. Rather than send uninteresting ones to SNA Manager, there are two filtering mechanisms you can use to discard some before forwarding. The first is the NetView/390 AREC filter. This controls which alerts are displayed to NetView/390 users in its screens. Any alerts not passing this filter will not be eligible for forwarding to SNA Manager. The second is a mechanism in which SNA Manager indicates to NetView/390 the kinds of alerts it should forward. All others are discarded by DSIAL2WS before forwarding.[2]

SNA Manager translates the alerts it receives into enterprise-specific traps and sends them to NetView. They are handled like other traps. The enterprise ID identifies the type of device the alert came from, and the specific code identifies the particular alert condition. SNA Manager sets these two fields as follows:

- The enterprise ID always begins with 1.3.6.1.4.2.6.27.1.[3] To this, SNA manager appends three more numbers based on the type of device the alert is from. (For those familiar with SNA, these three numbers are based on the contents of the Product Set ID subvector in the alert.)
- The specific code is copied from the Alert ID field of the alert (from the Generic Alert subvector). This is an exotically constructed 32-bit value that uniquely identifies the problem condition, and thus is appropriate as a specific code.[4]

The pair of enterprise and specific codes therefore uniquely identifies a particular problem condition from a particular kind of device. Thus, they can be the basis for selecting a custom display of the trap in NetView's Events, or for determining which automatic action to take in response.

The agent address in the trap is set to the IP address of the AIX system where SNA Manager is running. This may seem a bit strange, but there is not much choice since the real agent (whether you consider it to be NetView/390 or the device sending the alert) lives in the SNA world and does not necessarily have an IP address.

---

[2] This mechanism is controlled by the SNA Manager file /usr/OV/snamgr_alert.conf.

[3] This is an ID in IBM's subtree under *private*.

[4] The Alert ID is computed by performing a Cyclic Redundancy Check (CRC) on the parts of the alert that describe the problem and the type of the device. It therefore renders the enterprise ID somewhat redundant, though for simplicity we should regard it as describing the problem condition only.

In addition, SNA Manager includes several variable bindings in the trap. These are discussed in the box 'Variable bindings in SNA Manager traps'.

The above discussion applies only to SNA Manager's handling of 'generic alerts'—the newer kind of alerts in SNA. There are other older types and these are handled by SNA Manager with an analogous process. I won't trouble you with the details. If you want them—as well as any other information about SNA Manager—see IBM (1994).

Variable bindings in SNA Manager traps

The traps SNA Manager creates from alerts contain the following information in their variable bindings:

- The SNA name of the alert sender.
- The Product Set ID from the alert. This describes the hardware and software on the alert sender.
- The Alert Type from the alert (giving a broad categorization of the alert condition).
- The Alert Description from the alert (giving a more specific description of the alert condition).
- The Probable Cause code point from the alert.
- As much data additional data from the alert as will fit in the remaining 25 variable bindings. Specifically, this is the information that would be shown in one of Hardware Monitor's screens, the 'Event Detail' panel.

4.3.3 Commands

SNA Manager allows you to execute commands to control the SNA network. This is done in a point-and-shoot manner so that the commands are executed for resources selected in SNA Manager submaps. In most cases, these would be sent to NetView/390 for execution.

The command capabilities of SNA Manager can be divided into the following three sets:

- **Built-in commands**   SNA Manager provides a menu which by default has Activate, Deactivate and Recycle. For the Activate command, SNA Manager builds a VTAM Activate command, i.e. 'V NET, ACT ...', and sends it over the APPC session to NetView/390 for execution. The output from the command is displayed in a pop-up window. Deactivate and Recycle work similarly. Recycle is just a combination of Deactivate and Activate.
- **User-defined commands**   You can add your own commands to the SNA Manager menu. To do this, you use the Command Profile Editor and define a command string that will be passed to NetView/390 for execution. In doing this, you have the ability to include variables in the command string, such as *%resource%* for the name of the resource currently selected in a submap, *%domain%* for its SNA domain name, and *%network%* for its SNA network name. For example, you could add a command to perform a VTAM display for a resource, with the following command string:

```
D NET,ID=%resource%
```

● You can also write C programs that are invoked from the Commands pull-down. This is a generalization of the user-defined command approach just discussed. Whenever an SNA Manager command (built-in or user-defined) is invoked, it is passed to a 'command exit'. This is a program that takes the command string and does something with it. By default this will be an IBM-supplied exit that simply sends the command to NetView/390 for execution. You can, however, define your own exits. Documentation of this may be found in IBM (1994) and examples are placed in the directory /usr/snamgr/interface if you have SNA Manager installed.

4.4 SUMMARY

It's possible to have either NetView or NetView/390 as the enterprise manager with the other acting as the sub-manager. In either case, the basic network management facilities will be available, including commands, alarms and display of network topology. Which you choose to be your enterprise manager will depend on the kinds of networks you need to manage.

FIVE

MANAGEMENT SYSTEM ARCHITECTURE

Let's now turn from the details of management tools to the broader question of the overall management system's architecture. We will first look at the general characteristics of the networks to be managed and then move on to the management system itself. We will investigate issues such as the hardware and software requirements, connectivity requirements and distributed management.

5.1 THE NETWORKS TO BE MANAGED

The majority of data networks in the world surely are small stand-alone LANs in which PCs communicate with each other using Novell's IPX and other PC/LAN protocols. These networks, while certainly important, are not interesting to us here since it is unlikely they would require a UNIX-based multiprotocol manager such as NetView. There are simpler solutions available.

Similarly, WAN networks based entirely on SNA are not interesting to us here—if you have an all-SNA network, then you want NetView/390.

Having thus eliminated a huge portion of the networking business, what's left? The networks we're interested in are those typically found in medium and large organizations, and are based either on IP exclusively or on a mixture of IP and other protocols including SNA, IPX, NetBIOS and others.

As shown in Figure 5.1, these networks will generally be composed of:

- A small number of backbone WANs. These will most often use IP or SNA as their transport protocol. Typically, IP routers or SNA communications controllers will be used to switch the traffic. The connections between these will be various sorts of communications facilities such as leased lines, Frame Relay networks and, in the future, ATM networks.
- A much larger number of LANs, connected together by the WANs. These LANs will usually be implemented with Ethernet, Token-Ring and FDDI, and in the future may use ATM. The LANs will often have a networking structure of their own, for example several LANs

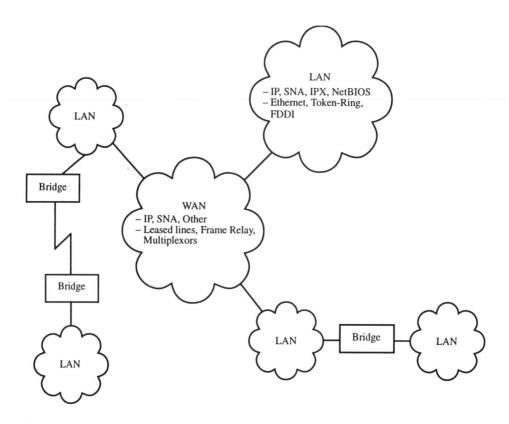

Figure 5.1 Multiprotocol networks

may be connected together with bridges or routers. These may connect LANs on different floors of the same building or LANs on different sides of the world.

In LANs, there will normally be many networking protocols in use. These include IPX, NetBIOS, SNA, IP and AppleTalk among others. When these protocols need to be sent across the WAN, they will typically be enveloped inside the WAN transport protocol.

One important point to bear in mind is that, in any LAN or WAN, it is likely there will be a layered set of protocols and facilities in use, all of which must be managed. For example, an IP WAN may be implemented as a Frame Relay network over which IP packets are sent. The network management system must be able to manage both the Frame Relay and IP layers of the network, and preferably recognize the relationship between the two. Similarly, in an Ethernet LAN, the management system must be able to manage the Ethernet layer of the LAN, e.g. the cable, concentrators and the Ethernet protocol itself, as well as the protocols that run over the Ethernet.

Finally, we should note that there will also be computers involved in these networks, and these generally need to be connected together so that useful work can be done. These computers will be of all sorts, from mainframes down to PCs, and will usually connect to the LANs. Computers play an important role in the network protocols. In the simplest case, they will contain protocol stacks allowing them to communicate across the network. In more complex cases, they will be integral to the network's operations, as is the case, for example, with mainframes running VTAM in SNA networks. Thus, the management system must also be able to monitor and control these computers, at least the parts of them that participate in the network.

5.2 HARDWARE AND SOFTWARE

With this very brief review of common multiprotocol networks in mind, let's now look at how we can build a management system for them. Of course, since this is a book about NetView, our fundamental assumption is that it will be the basis of the management system and this will lead us naturally to several choices about hardware, software, protocols and other aspects of the architecture.

5.2.1 Management system

There will be one or more locations in the organization from which network management is performed. In some organizations, the goal will be to do all management from a single location, thus pooling scarce networking expertise, simplifying co-ordination and realizing economies of scale. In others there will be several management locations—the distributed style of management. We will look in detail at distributed management with NetView later in this chapter and consider how many NetViews are appropriate in that case. For now, let's look at how NetView would be deployed in each management centre.

In each, you would run at least one copy of NetView under AIX, Solaris, Digital UNIX or Windows/NT. As we have seen, the management staff there would access NetView in one of three ways:

1.   Directly from the system on which NetView runs.
2.   From an X station which connects to NetView across a LAN.
3.   From an AIX workstation using the NetView client/server feature. Here, the user may be in the same building as NetView and connect across a LAN, or may be on a different continent and connect through a WAN.

The NetViews will carry out several kinds of management activities. They will:

●   Collect and process traps
●   Monitor and display the topology of networks
●   Collect data from agents' MIBs
●   Control the components of the network

There may also be NetView applications running to support management of multiprotocol networks and to otherwise extend NetView's capabilities.

In most cases, there will be one NetView at each management centre. There are, however, reasons why you might run several, the most important being that a single system does not have the necessary horsepower. It's a good idea to try first off-loading work to Systems Monitor MLMs. If you still need more than one NetView, you will need to decide how to split management responsibility among them.

This must be done with care so that the staff won't need to consult several NetViews to get a single task done. The most likely way to divide responsibility is by regions of the network, so that each NetView performs all management tasks for a particular region. Another possibility is to split the tasks in a functional way. For example, with two NetViews:

- One would perform real-time monitoring of the network. Thus, it would monitor the network topology and status, present this to operators in submaps and receive and process traps. Operators would log into this NetView for normal activities.
- The other NetView would gather data required for more long-term monitoring and analysis. It would periodically collect data from agents' MIBs and log it away. Later, programs would digest it to create reports.

A discussion of how to size the machine required for NetView and its applications is beyond the scope of this book, but Implementation Tip 5.1 gives some guidelines. The power and memory requirements for a NetView system surprise some people. They wonder why a 'peripheral' activity like network management requires such a large system. Network management, though, is vital to effective networking and always seems to need large computers. Consider, for example, that there are some networks in which one or two very powerful mainframes are completely dedicated to network management.

When selecting the machine, you need to think in terms of fast processors and large amounts of RAM. Note that the figures suggested by Implementation Tip 5.1 are for NetView alone, and some of NetView's applications also have substantial machine requirements. Even

---

Implementation Tip 5.1

To get a rough idea of NetView's memory requirements, consider the following guidelines. These are for NetView alone, i.e. not its applications, and they assume that the operators use NetView either directly from its machine or from X stations:

- The two main considerations are the number of objects in the NetView Object Database and the number of concurrent NetView users. The number of objects is usually between two and three times the number of IP addresses in the network. Applications may add additional objects.
- The base amount of memory for NetView and its supporting AIX is then determined from the following table:

```
   Objects                      RAM
-------------------------      -----
    0     to     4999          64MB
  5000    to     9999          80MB
 10000    to    14999          96MB
 15000    to    20000          112MB
 20000    and above            more
```

- In addition, for each (concurrent) user after the first, add an additional 32 megabytes of RAM.

Thus, to manage an IP network of 15 000 addresses with five concurrent users, you would need 208 megabytes of RAM.

with large amounts of RAM, paging may occur, so a fast and large disk is an excellent idea. A basic system with NetView, Trouble Ticket and a few applications can probably get away with one gigabyte, but only just, and in most situations—especially considering how inexpensive disk drives are—two, three or more gigabytes would be a good choice. Nonetheless, there are some things that can be done to minimize NetView's machine requirements. These are discussed in Implementation Tip 5.2.

Implementation Tip 5.2

Here are some tips to help reduce NetView's processor and RAM requirements:

- Use the client/server feature to off-load GUIs to other UNIX systems. Each of these will support only one user and can therefore be relatively modest and inexpensive.
- Off-load as much work as possible to intermediate managers. In the case of IP, this can be done very effectively using Systems Monitor. With other protocols, the approaches are not as well developed. In any case, off-loading IP management alone will significantly reduce the load on NetView.
- Tune NetView. One important thing to do is ensure that the object cache used by the *ovwdb* daemon has a slightly larger size, i.e. 5 to 10 per cent, than the number of objects in the Object Database. The cache size is set in the SMIT panel for the *ovwdb* daemon. You can determine the number of objects using the command:

```
ovobjprint | head -1
```

- Another important factor is to make sure that NetView has fast access to an IP name server. NetView accesses this frequently to determine the mapping between IP names and addresses, and it is therefore best to have it close to NetView, e.g. on the same LAN.

Systems Monitor If your network has a large amount of IP, then you will very likely also want to use the Systems Monitor MLM in your management system. As we have seen, this allows you to off-load several kinds of management activities from NetView.

The MLM can be a very cost-effective solution. The software itself is relatively inexpensive and, because it has no GUI on the agent system, the hardware required to run it is very modest. One option is to put it onto a system already in place, which should be fine as long as that system stays up most of the time. Another is to get a low-end AIX or other supported system.

Other management applications You may also want to have Trouble Ticket running at the central site in order to co-ordinate the handling of problems in the network. Like NetView, Trouble Ticket has a client/server structure in which the server can run centrally on NetView's system, collecting problems and maintaining the database, while the clients access it remotely. There is a good choice of platforms you can run the client on, including AIX, Windows, HP-UX and SunOS.

One thing to bear in mind is that the client operating system must be able to support all the software required, which would probably include at least NetView and Trouble Ticket. While the Trouble Ticket client supports several operating systems, at the time of writing NetView's client supports only AIX.

In addition to NetView, Systems Monitor and Trouble Ticket, there are several NetView applications you will probably want to use for management of non-IP protocols. These will be discussed in the next chapter.

5.2.2 Management protocols

It is obvious that the whole show is going to be SNMP-based since that's NetView's bread-and-butter management protocol. There are also a few other protocols and tools used by NetView:

- ICMP, used mainly for PINGing systems.
- *telnet*, which is extremely useful for logging into remote systems to configure, control, diagnose and so forth.
- *rexec*, the one-shot remote command execution tool, is useful for the same kinds of things, but has the advantage that it is easy to incorporate into programs and shell scripts.
- FTP and TFTP are used by many communications devices, e.g. concentrators, routers, bridges, for remote download of software and definition files. They're also useful for retrieving dumps and traces.
- Some NetView applications also use UDP or TCP to communicate with their agents, particularly when SNMP's slow bulk data transport will not suffice.

The use of these tools and protocols raises two important issues:

- The network components must support them. While most new communications equipment does, many networks have older equipment that may not. As we have seen, proxy agents address this requirement.
- The network must support IP. Since all the aforementioned normally run over IP, there must be IP connectivity between NetView and the managed systems. Given that we're looking at multiprotocol networks, this can be a problem, for example, if the backbone network runs SNA but not IP. The solution to this is our next topic.

5.2.3 Transport protocols

Protocol combinations such as SNMP over IPX or TCP over SNA are, of course, possible in theory and even exist in some implementations, but NetView and most agents do not support these. We must always have IP connectivity—or simulated IP connectivity—between NetView and its agents. This is shown in Figure 5.2. Generally, this means that the IP connectivity must exist all the way from NetView to the managed device. If proxy agents are used, IP is required only up to the proxy agent, and then what happens between the proxy and the non-IP network is a private matter.

The same is true for most NetView applications. One notable exception is SNA Manager/6000. All of its communications with NetView/390 must be performed using SNA.

Given all this, it is important we understand how to arrange the IP and SNA connectivity we will require for NetView. In some cases, arranging the required connectivity is trivial, but there are many other cases where it will be tricky. Let's look at these issues in detail.

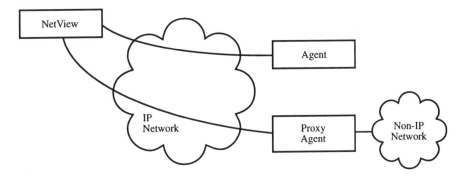

Figure 5.2 IP connectivity required for NetView

Arranging IP connectivity with NetView Let's first consider how to arrange IP connectivity between NetView and its agents. We don't need to worry about LANs since they can easily accommodate IP. We do need to address the common situation that there is an SNA network between NetView and some of its agents.[1] There are several options here.

Easy cases One option is to forget trying to send IP over SNA and just install some IP connectivity. For some organizations this may be easy; for example, there might be a multiplexor network from which a few circuits can be obtained. Or you may have a Frame Relay or X.25-based backbone, in which case you can add NetView's IP traffic to the existing SNA.

SNALINK Another option is to use the SNALINK capability of IBM's NCP (Network Control Program) which runs in IBM 3745 SNA communications controllers. As shown in Figure 5.3, you would connect NetView's system to the 3745 via a LAN—either Ethernet or Token-Ring. At the other end you would have LANs similarly attached to 3745s. With this arrangement, NetView believes it has an IP connection all the way to the managed devices. Actually:

- IP flows between NetView and its nearby 3745.
- The 3745 then encapsulates the IP packets in SNA and sends them through the network to the distant 3745.
- The distant 3745 removes the IP packets from SNA and uses IP to send them to the managed device.

SNALINK requires that IBM's TCP/IP for MVS or VM runs in the hosts owning the 3745s.

AnyNet Another option is to use one of the several versions of IBM's AnyNet. This lets you run an 'application protocol', e.g. TCP or UDP, over a 'transport protocol', e.g. SNA, for which it was not intended. AnyNet supports several protocol combinations, but here we're interested in its 'Sockets over SNA' capability. This allows us to run IP-based protocols such as SNMP over SNA networks.

---

[1] Here SNA could mean either the traditional SNA (i.e. 'subarea SNA') or it could mean IBM's newer Advanced Peer-to-Peer Networking (APPN).

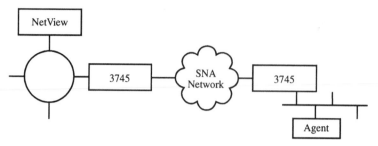

Figure 5.3 Using SNALINK with NetView

AnyNet runs on several platforms, including MVS, OS/2 and AIX. It is also available as a dedicated system, the 2217 Nways Multiprotocol Concentrator. AnyNet comes in two flavours: 'access node' and 'gateway node', as shown in Figure 5.4.

In the case of a gateway node, TCP or UDP runs over IP up to the gateway. There, it is mapped onto SNA for transmission across the SNA network. On the other side, it will be transformed back to IP by another gateway node, or as shown in Figure 5.4, by an access node.[2]

In the case of access nodes, the transformation never really happens. Instead, the AnyNet software runs inside the application's system. Thus the TCP or UDP messages are immediately mapped onto SNA and sent across the SNA network. For example, suppose (as shown in Figure 5.5) NetView runs on an AIX system that is connected to an SNA network and the AnyNet access node software is running in the system. When NetView sends an SNMP (over UDP) message, it is taken by AnyNet instead of the IP subsystem. AnyNet encloses it inside an SNA message and transmits it across the SNA network.

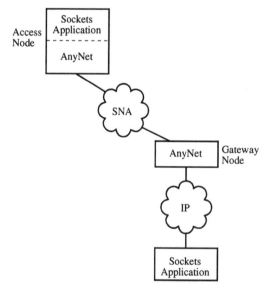

Figure 5.4 AnyNet access and gateway nodes

---

[2] The AnyNets use APPC sessions to carry the TCP and UDP messages.

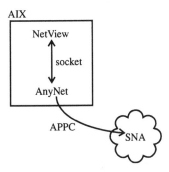

Figure 5.5 AnyNet access node example

One key point about AnyNet is that the communicating applications must use the same application protocol (e.g. UDP). In addition, there must be an AnyNet on each side to transform into and out of SNA.

For NetView and its agents, there are several ways we can use AnyNet to get across the SNA network. On the NetView side we have two choices:

● Run the AnyNet access node software in NetView's AIX and directly connect it to an SNA network. This would be especially suitable for cases where NetView is at a central computing site in an SNA-based network.
● Put NetView onto a LAN or other IP network and then use an AnyNet gateway into the SNA network, as shown in Figure 5.6. This would be suitable if the NetView is not in a location where it is easy to connect directly to the SNA network. It would also be the best choice if there are some IP systems to be managed at NetView's location.

On the agent side, you also need to have AnyNet, in this case, a gateway. Here the AnyNet access node software will generally not make sense—you won't want to have it in every agent.

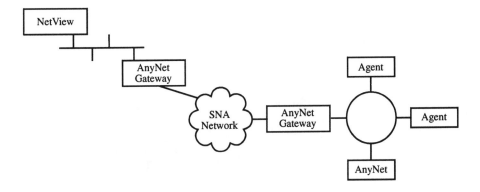

Figure 5.6 NetView with AnyNet

At the time of writing, the AnyNet gateway for Sockets over SNA is available on OS/2 and in the 2217. The access node is available for AIX and other platforms. In addition to SNMP, these also support PING, *telnet*, FTP and the other IP-based tools we require.

Arranging SNA connectivity with NetView/390 Now for the other side of the coin—how to attach NetView to the mainframe, so there can be SNA connectivity for SNA Manager/6000 and any 3270 terminal emulators used to access NetView/390. You will need such an emulator if you are using SNA Manager, and you might need one even if not. For example, you may want to manage the SNA network simply by accessing NetView/390's 3270-based screens.

Thus, the SNA connectivity must support APPC sessions for SNA Manager and LU2 sessions for the emulators.

Easy cases In some cases, it will be easy to arrange SNA connectivity to the mainframe. For example, NetView may reside in the same location and connect to the same LAN. In this case, the mainframe will typically connect to the LAN via an IBM 3745, 3174, 3172 or something similar. These usually allow NetView's system to appear to the mainframe as an SNA PU type 2.1—which is required by SNA Manager.

AnyNet Here, the solution is analogous to running SNMP *et al.* over SNA—there are AnyNet gateways and access nodes available for running SNA over IP. As before, we must use AnyNets in pairs, with a gateway or access node on both the NetView and NetView/390 sides. Some ways this can be accomplished on the NetView/390 side are:

● Run the AnyNet access node in the mainframe.
● Place an AnyNet gateway on a LAN to which the mainframe connects, as shown in Figure 5.7. For example, if there is a Token-Ring or Ethernet local to the mainframe, you could put the OS/2 gateway on the LAN. If there is also an IP router on the LAN, then AnyNet can

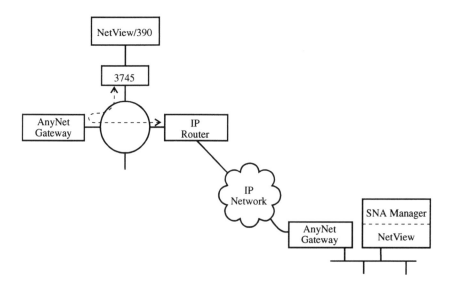

Figure 5.7 NetView/390 with AnyNet gateway

communicate with the IP network through it. Alternatively, the OS/2 could directly connect to the IP network, saving the step of going through the router.

On the NetView side the possibilities include:
- Running the AnyNet access node software in NetView's AIX. In this case, the AIX would directly connect to the IP network.
- Put an AnyNet gateway on the LAN and run the SNA protocol up to the gateway. This is also shown in Figure 5.7.

Multiprotocol routers Most routers support some form of transporting SNA across IP networks. IBM, Bay Networks and Cisco routers, for example, use the Data Link Switching (DLSw) protocol. There are several others. As shown in Figure 5.8, you would usually connect NetView's system to the router via a LAN and, on the other side, another router would connect to the mainframe via another LAN.

5.2.4 Distributed management

Let's now move on to the next topic, performing network management in a distributed manner.

There are several reasons to distribute management responsibility across several locations. These include the need to reflect geographic and organizational divisions of the network, to improve management reliability, and to bring management closer to the users. Broadly speaking, this distribution can be done in one of three ways:

- So that each location can manage only a portion of the network, a style I'll call 'regional'.
- So that all locations can manage all the network, but for different management tasks, a style I'll call 'functional'.
- So that all locations can manage all the network, but one at a time, a style I'll call 'rotating'.

The three styles are shown in Figure 5.9. These are archetypes and there are of course many mixtures possible. Still, they highlight the issues in distributed management. It is important to

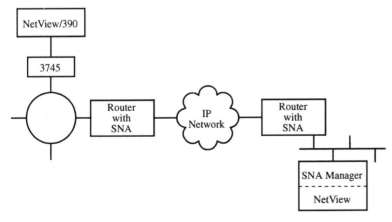

Figure 5.8 SNA over IP routers

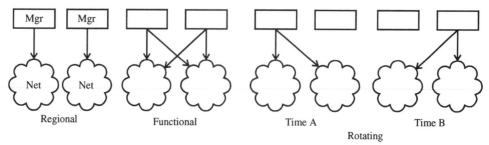

Figure 5.9 Distributed management styles

bear in mind that here we're discussing the distribution of management locations and not distributed management tools such as the Systems Monitor MLM.

In the first chapter, we discussed the general characteristics and issues of distributed management. Here, we'll first look at the requirements each of these styles places on the management system and then how these can be realized with NetView.

Regional style In this style, each site manages a fixed region or 'domain' of the network. This style is used when management is divided by geographic region of the network. For example, New York manages the USA and Amsterdam manages Europe. Or there is a central management centre overseeing most of the network, but local sites managing their own LANs.

The requirements of the regional style are:

- The submaps at each management site must show a subset of the network. Usually they show only the site's domain, though it's also possible they give a broader view of the network.
- The traps coming to each management site will be only those pertaining its domain.
- There may be a need to prevent sites from controlling resources outside their domains.
- The sites will collect information from agents' MIBs and other sources in only their domain.
- It may be necessary to allow some sites to transcend their domains. For example, the users of a LAN may sometimes ask the central management site to perform particular tasks, for example configuring their access router or monitoring their servers off-shift.

Functional style In the functional style, there are not fixed domains, but all sites can manage all parts of the network. The main use for this style is when the management sites perform different kinds of activities. For example, New York might be responsible for software distribution and Amsterdam for operations.

In the functional style, the requirements are:

- The submaps at each site show the entire network. Thus, each site would need to perform topology discovery and status monitoring for the entire network.
- Traps will be sent to the manager responsible for the kind of problem involved. For example, all traps involving software distribution go to New York. That is the goal anyway. In reality, this is fairly difficult to arrange, so alternatively all traps go to all managers.
- There may be a need to prevent sites from performing activities for which they are not responsible. Again this may be difficult to arrange and thus all sites may be able to perform all activities.

- The sites will collect information from agents' MIBs throughout the network, according to their functional requirements.

Rotating style This style is used, for example, in worldwide organizations to change the central management site as the day moves across the earth. Thus, New York is the central manager during the day in the USA, Amsterdam during the European day and so on.

In this style, the requirements are:

- The submaps at the active site must show the entire network. This site performs discovery and status monitoring for the entire network while it is in control.
- Traps will be sent to the site in control. Since this is difficult to arrange, traps may be sent to all managers at all times.
- The active site will be able to control the entire network. Alternatively, all sites may be capable of controlling the entire network at all times, but only the active site will actually do so.
- The site in control will collect data for immediate use, e.g. to check if it indicates urgent problems or to support diagnosis. Data collection for long-term purposes, e.g. generating reports, will usually be performed from fixed locations. Thus, managers must be able to collect from any part of the network.

Hybrid implementation There are several difficulties in implementing the functional and rotating styles. In the functional style, the most serious is that having all managers perform discovery for the entire network will consume far too much bandwidth. In both styles, trap routing is difficult since agents are normally not very clever about how they send traps. In a moment, we will look at ways of handling these problems, but it's worth considering a hybrid implementation that solves the worst problems of the functional and rotating styles.

Here (as shown in Figure 5.10) you first implement a regional structure so that there is one NetView managing each portion of the network. Each NetView receives traps, performs discovery and monitors status for only its portion of the network. Then, you take advantage of NetView's client/server structure, so that any site requiring a global view of the network logs into the NetViews in the other sites to access their data and management functions. Thus, any site has access to management functions for the entire network and yet the management structure is the regional style, the easiest to implement. Unfortunately, this approach is not seamless, since the NetView users must run multiple instances of the GUI and switch among them to manage different domains of the network. Still, the simplicity and efficiency of this approach make it very attractive.

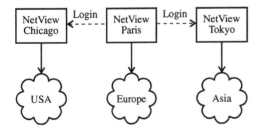

Figure 5.10 Implementation using client/server

Using NetView for distributed management Let's now look at the features of NetView that support distributed management, in the three non-hybrid styles we have considered above. We will do this for each of our four key management tasks.

Problem reporting The most difficult issue in problem management is getting traps to the right NetView. Once there, the rest of the job is not significantly affected by having a distributed management system. Unfortunately, the flow of traps is not something NetView has much control over, since traps' destinations are determined by the agents themselves. Many agents allow you to specify multiple trap destinations, but usually these are fixed and not easy to change from the manager.

In the regional style, this is not a problem since we want the trap destinations to be fixed. In the other styles, it's acceptable as long as you're happy to have all traps go to all managers. On the other hand, you may not want to waste network bandwidth doing this and instead want traps to go to only the relevant manager. This cannot be practically arranged in the agents themselves, but there are two other approaches:

1. Have all traps sent to an intermediary of some sort which then forwards them to the appropriate NetView. In particular, this intermediary could be our old friend the MLM.

   The MLM has a function called the Trap Destination Table which can route traps. As fortune would have it, this table can route traps based on the time of day or the traps' contents.

   Thus, within a given portion of the network you would instruct all agents to send their traps to a particular MLM. This MLM would then forward them to the appropriate NetView based on time (rotating style) or trap content (functional style).
2. Alternatively, you could implement trap routing in the NetViews themselves. Agents would send their traps to the closest NetView, which would forward them to other NetViews as appropriate. In SNMPv1 there is not a manager-to-manager protocol defined to do this, but it would be quite easy to write code in NetView that routes traps based on any criteria you choose.[3]

Network views Another issue is getting the right view of the network shown by the NetViews at the various locations. In this section we'll look mainly at the case of IP, and this approach will generalize to most other protocols, though the details of how will depend on the application producing the submaps.

The issues involved here are:

● The overhead of discovery and status monitoring. This is especially serious in the functional style where several management sites may require a view of the entire internetwork. Even in the rotating and regional styles this overhead can be a problem.
● Restricting views of the network. This is important mainly in the regional style where we may want each site to see only its own domain.

---

[3] The program in Appendix II is an example of how to use NetView's SNMP programming interface, and could be extended to perform this trap routing function.

- Changing the management site that has the global view and is performing the associated discovery and status monitoring. This is relevant in only the rotating style and can be done quite simply by stopping all NetViews except the one that is in control.

The first two issues are more complex and warrant further discussion.

OVERHEAD The frequency with which NetView performs discovery and status monitoring can be decreased, but doing so reduces accuracy. A better solution is to off-load these processes to the MLM, especially status monitoring. If this is arranged cleverly, e.g. with the MLMs placed close to large concentrations of systems, the overhead of having network-wide maps may become acceptable. Note that the MLM is able to perform both discovery and status monitoring on behalf of multiple NetViews, and thus can greatly reduce the overhead involved in having global views at multiple management sites.

RESTRICTING NETWORK VIEWS We can restrict views as required in the regional style by exploiting the concepts of managed and unmanaged networks in NetView. A managed network is one for which NetView performs discovery and status monitoring, and whose details it displays in submaps. A unmanaged network is one in which it does neither.[4] Thus, in the regional style we would arrange for each NetView to 'manage' only the networks in its domain.

There are several ways to control which networks a particular NetView manages. In the present context, the most useful are:

- The Manage and Unmanage functions available in NetView GUI. Here you point at networks and choose whether NetView will manage them. You would do this at each site's NetView according to its requirements.
- The NetView backup manager function. This is intended primarily for allowing one NetView to take over from another when it fails. However, we can exploit its facility for explicitly defining which networks each NetView will manage. Doing things this way has the advantage that we can create all required definitions on one NetView and distribute them to the others.

Controlling the networks that each NetView manages will accomplish most of what we need. It may be necessary to do some fine tuning, however. For example, networks may not correspond exactly to the management domains and it may be necessary to remove some of the resources from particular submaps. The Hide map editing function can be used to do this, as discussed in Implementation Tip 5.3.

Thus, we have much control over what each NetView will show. The only problem now is that if we aren't careful, users will be able to undo all our hard work and see whatever they like anyway. To prevent this, we can take advantage of NetView's maps and their permissions.

We will discuss maps in more detail later, but for now think of a map as determining the set of submaps and symbols a user may see. There can be many such maps in a given NetView, but each user has only one map open at a given time and sees only the submaps and symbols it contains.

---

[4] In this context, the term manage refers only to discovery and status checking, and does not involve traps, for example. Also note that here I'm using the term network in the strict sense, i.e. as opposed to internetwork.

Implementation Tip 5.3

When editing submaps, the best way to remove symbols, e.g. hosts, networks, is to use the Hide function. It's also possible to use the Delete function, which not only removes the symbol, but also NetView's knowledge of the resource. However, with Delete, NetView may once again discover the resource, at which time the symbol will pop back into the submap. Hide, on the other hand, removes only the symbol and prevents this from happening.

    If you Hide a symbol from all submaps, it's also a good idea to Unmanage its resource, so NetView doesn't waste time monitoring it.

The user may have the map open in read-write or read-only mode. In the former case, he can change what is shown at will. In the latter, he can see only what the map contains and cannot change this. In particular, he cannot change which networks are managed and cannot un-hide symbols. Also, any new resources NetView discovers will not be added to maps open in read-only mode. Thus, the user of a read-only map sees only what you allow.

To restrict particular users to read-only maps, you take advantage of maps' permissions. These determine which users can open particular maps and whether they can do so in read-write or read-only mode. These permissions work much as UNIX file permissions do and are controlled using the NetView *ovwperms* command.

Thus, if security is a concern, you can enforce your view restrictions using maps and permissions. You would create special maps for each management site and limit the users there to read-only access. You would also, of course, want to prevent them from creating new maps. You can do this with the *ovwchmod* command.[5]

Note that when a user has a map open in read-only mode they can still use the management functions of NetView. Changes in resource status are also reflected. The user simply cannot edit the map's contents and cannot perform a few key functions such as changing which networks are managed. Thus, restricting users to read-only maps does not prevent them from managing the network.

As noted above, NetView will not add new resources it discovers to maps that are open in read-only mode. The map must be opened read-write to receive these updates. This fact has the advantage that it prevents uncontrolled changes to your restricted maps. It has the disadvantage that users will not see new discoveries in their domains. A solution to this dilemma is to open the restricted maps periodically and let everything new pour in. Afterwards you can tidy them using the Hide function.

Network operations The main issue for operations in a distributed management environment is restricting control functions when security matters. This is especially important in the regional style.

The main technique available here is to use community names and passwords in the network's components to restrict access. For example, all agents in each domain could use a community name known only at its management site. Access to equipment, using other tools such as *telnet*, can be controlled with an analogous password scheme.

---

[5] To do this you issue 'ovwchmod -G go-w' from the *root* user ID.

Network monitoring and reporting Collection is initiated and controlled by managers and thus in each of the three styles the managers simply collect what they need. Where security is an issue, community names can be used to restrict access.

5.3 SUMMARY

Designing the architecture of a network management system can be a complex task. As we have seen in this chapter, you must consider many issues including:

- The hardware and software required for the management system.
- Which management protocols and tools to use, and how to arrange connectivity between managers and agents to support these.
- How many locations will manage the network and how they will co-operate with each other.
- Whether to distribute the management system itself using tools such as the Systems Monitor Mid-Level Manager.

Many people feel that it shouldn't be this difficult and perhaps one day you will be able to buy a network management system that you just plug into your network and start using immediately. Until then, it is important to remember that a well managed network is an extremely valuable asset for any organization and is well worth the time and expense.

## SIX

MANAGING NON-IP ENVIRONMENTS

As we have seen, NetView is a good solution for managing IP networks, especially when used with Trouble Ticket and Systems Monitor. For other protocols and environments, it is necessary to find a NetView application and proxy agent. In this chapter, we will review the key applications and proxy agents available for managing non-IP environments, starting with higher-layer networking protocols and moving toward the lower layers. An explanation of the many protocols is, of course, beyond the scope of this book, so I've assumed that if you are interested in managing a particular protocol then you probably know something about it.

6.1 SNA NETWORKS

Earlier we discussed the use of SNA Manager/6000 for traditional SNA networks. What remains is to discuss the management of SNA's successor, APPN.

NetView can manage APPN networks if they include IBM 6611 routers or other APPN nodes supporting SNMP. The 6611 is capable of functioning as an APPN Network Node and in that role it provides a private MIB extension with data about the APPN network. The 6611 can also generate traps when it detects problems in the APPN network.

The 6611's MIB extension has a great deal of information, as described in the box.[1] Among the more interesting is the topology of the APPN network. APPN Network Nodes such as the 6611 maintain topology databases in which they keep information about all other Network Nodes in the network, and about the links connecting them. The main purpose of this database is to support routing. It does not include information about End Nodes or the links connecting them to Network Nodes, since routing through these is not possible.

---

[1] The MIB module can be found in the file /usr/OV/snmp_mibs/ibm-6611-v1r3.0.mib on a NetView system.

6611 APPN MIB

The MIB contains APPN information divided into groups as follows:

- **Node Group**   information about the 6611 itself:
  - *General*   name, network ID, node type and capabilities
  - *Port*   configuration and status of each APPN port
  - *Link Station*   configuration and status of each link station
  - *SNMP*   counters of SNMP requests and errors
  - *Memory Use*   by the APPN control point in the 6611
  - *XID*   counters of XIDs exchanged with adjacent nodes.
- **APPN Topology Group**   Network Node topology as held in the 6611's topology database.
- **Local Topology Group**   6611's End Node topology.
- **Directory Group**   contents of the 6611's APPN directory. This directory holds information about where applications (LUs) reside in the APPN network.
- **Class of Service Group**   information about 6611's Class of Service tables. These are used for making routing decisions.
- **Intermediate Session Group**   describes sessions being routed through this 6611 and includes accounting information for them.

Thus, even if there is just one 6611, it will know the complete Network Node topology and will make it available in its MIB.[2] It will also provide information about its own End Nodes and their links. It will not, however, know about other End Nodes. Thus, a manager will be able to collect End Node topology only for 6611s (and any other Network Nodes supporting SNMP).

A 6611's MIB information can be accessed with NetView's MIB tools including the MIB Browser, MIB Application Builder and MIB Data Collector. In addition, Router and Bridge Manager for AIX (RaBM), a NetView application from IBM, has support for this MIB. First, RaBM is able to display several counters that describe utilization and traffic for the APPN protocol in the 6611. Second, it can collect information from the topology groups and present it in NetView submaps.

Router and Bridge Manager adds a symbol to NetView's Root Submap which represents the APPN networks for which it has topology. Beneath this symbol is a hierarchically structured set of submaps showing APPN topology information in increasing detail. The symbols in the submaps are coloured to reflect the statuses of the APPN network components.

Another way to view the information in the 6611 MIB is with a set of applications you can obtain from an IBM server on the Internet. This package uses NetView's MIB Application Builder to create formatted views of 6611 MIB groups, including those for APPN.[3]

---

[2] If an APPN network is divided into subnetworks, then a Network Node knows only the topology of its own subnetwork.

[3] The package of applications is called 6611APPS and you can get it via anonymous FTP to 6611ftp.cary.ibm.com.

6.2 DECNET NETWORKS

DECnet currently exists in two forms—the proprietary Phase IV which is in widest use and the newer OSI-based Phase V. At the time of writing, there are two NetView applications for managing DECnet Phase IV:

- DNM from ki Networks. DNM is implemented on the AIX version of NetView.
- Digital's POLYCENTER DECnet Manager. This is implemented on the NetView version for Digital UNIX.

Both products are able to display DECnet Phase IV topology in NetView submaps and also to show devices using DECnet's Local Area Transport (LAT) protocol. Let's look in more detail at one of these applications, ki's DNM.

In addition to its DECnet management capabilities, DNM has many others for general-purpose network management. Here we will focus on its role in DECnet management. DNM works with the DNA product, also from ki, which provides a DECnet Phase IV protocol stack on the AIX system. This allows DNM to communicate with systems in the DECnet network.

DNM places three symbols in NetView's Root submap—one representing the topology of DECnet networks, a second representing that of LAT services and nodes and a third representing nodes whose consoles can be accessed from DNM.

DNM displays DECnet topology as follows:

- Under the DECnet icon, there is a submap showing all DECnet areas known to DNM.
- For each area, there is a submap showing the topology of the routers and hosts within.
- For each router and host, there is a submap showing its DECnet interfaces.

Colour is used in all these submaps to depict resources' statuses.

There are also several DNM functions you can invoke from these DECnet submaps. You can display and change the characteristics of DECnet nodes, lines, links, circuits and areas. You can also execute the Network Control Program (NCP) on a host selected in a submap. This gives you console access to network management functions on the host itself as well as other hosts to which it can connect using the NICE protocol (Network Information and Control Exchange).

Under the LAT symbol in the Root submap, there is a set of submaps showing LAT terminal servers, hosts and services. In these, you can select a terminal server and display or change its global characteristics or the characteristics of specific ports. You can also open a console session to a terminal server.

Under the Console Manager symbol in the Root submap, there is a submap showing nodes whose consoles can be accessed from DNM, using for example Digital's Maintenance Operations Protocol (MOP). From here you open the console and interact directly with the node, or view its console log.

DNM also creates SNMP traps and sends these to NetView for problems it detects in the DECnet and LAT protocols. It is also possible to use the Console Manager function to create traps from messages written to devices' consoles.

6.3 NETWARE NETWORKS

There are two possibilities for managing NetWare environments from NetView. Each works with a proxy agent to translate between the NetWare IPX world and SNMP, as shown in Figure 6.1:

- IBM's LAN Management Utilities for AIX (LMU for AIX), a NetView application that works in conjunction with an LMU/2 proxy agent running on an OS/2 system. This approach supports other LAN workgroup environments as well.
- NetView's OpenMon facility, which works in conjunction with Novell's NetWare Management System (NMS) acting as a proxy agent.

Let's look at both of these approaches.

6.3.1 LMU for AIX

LMU for AIX manages several LAN workgroup environments, in particular, those with:

- IBM OS/2 LAN Servers.
- NetWare Servers.
- OS/2, DOS and Windows workstations. These must be running the IBM LAN Requester or the NetWare Requester.
- Apple Macintosh systems running System 7.

LMU for AIX requires one or more LMU/2 systems serving as proxy agents. In addition to being a proxy agent for NetView, LMU/2 can be a standalone manager for workgroup environments. In the standalone case, LMU/2 is placed on the same LAN (or group of bridged LANs)

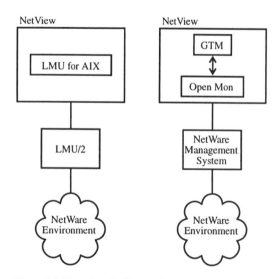

Figure 6.1 Managing NetWare environments

as the workstations. It uses IPX and NetBIOS to communicate with agent software running on the workstations. (This agent software is supplied with LMU/2.)

LMU for AIX brings the functions offered by LMU/2 to the NetView platform, thus serving as a way to concentrate in one place the management carried out by several LMU/2s, as well as integrating these into the NetView GUI. Thus, to understand LMU for AIX it is important to understand LMU/2.

LMU/2's functions include:

- Topology display of the workgroups. There are submaps showing the workstations being managed, and colour is used to represent their statuses. LMU/2 uses a 'heartbeat' mechanism in which the managed workstations periodically send it a message indicating they are alive and well.
- An alert mechanism for detecting exceptional conditions in managed workstations. These alerts can be displayed on the LMU/2 station. LMU/2 can also automatically react to them or forward them to other management systems including NetView/390 and IBM's LAN Network Manager.
- A set of utilities for collecting many kinds of data about the workstations, including machine configuration, installed software, performance statistics and system activity statistics, e.g. processes running. LMU/2 can save this information in a DB2/2 database which may be queried and displayed by LMU/2 or with standard SQL.
- A facility for issuing commands from LMU/2 to the managed workstations. In the case of OS/2, DOS and Windows, the command results can also be returned for display by LMU/2. The commands can be issued to a single workstation or they can be broadcast to several. They can also be issued automatically according to a schedule.
- Other goodies thrown in for good measure and completeness, including a shutdown/reboot utility for OS/2 and NetWare, and a utility for dialling a pager in response to an alert. There are several others.

Now let's consider how LMU for AIX brings these functions to the NetView platform. It consists of two major components:

- The LMU Application, which runs under NetView's *OVw* process, providing the LMU GUI.
- The *lmuTopod* daemon, which interacts with the LMU/2 proxy agents to collect topology and status information. *lmuTopod* stores this information in the GTM Database and *xxMap* uses it to produce NetView submaps showing the managed workstations.

The majority of the functions available from LMU/2 are also available from LMU for AIX, specifically:

- Submaps showing the managed workgroups (details are in the box). Throughout these submaps, colour is used to indicate the statuses of the managed systems.
- The LMU/2 proxy agents can send traps to NetView. These are displayed in the NetView Events window and processed by the rest of NetView's trap-handling machinery. These traps can be sent for any exceptional condition that causes an alert in LMU/2. LMU/2 configuration options determine which are actually sent.

LMU for AIX Submaps

- LMU for AIX places a symbol in the NetView Root Submap. This represents all LMU-managed resources.
- Selecting this symbol opens a submap known as the 'LAN Network Submap' in which each symbol represents the 'domain' or group of workstations managed by a particular LMU/2.
- Selecting a domain opens a 'LAN Submap' which shows one symbol for each of its workstations.
- Selecting a workstation opens a Node Submap which shows its network interfaces.

- LMU for AIX makes it possible to access the data LMU/2 collects and stores in its database. The proxy agent makes this available through a MIB extension.[4] This MIB extension can be browsed and otherwise processed with the usual NetView utilities. In addition, LMU for AIX provides windows for viewing it.
- LMU for AIX provides a facility for remote execution of commands on managed workstations. This sends the command to the appropriate LMU/2 proxy agent, which then forwards it to the target workstation. The command response is returned to AIX (if the target workstation is OS/2, DOS or Windows).

6.3.2 OpenMon and NMS

The other approach for managing NetWare environments is to use Novell's NMS as a proxy agent. Here, NMS communicates topology information to NetView's OpenMon facility. OpenMon is an interface IBM provides for vendors to use in building topology agents. In this case, the Export Service of NMS sends the topology information.[5] OpenMon passes it on to GTM which stores it in its database so that *xxMap* can build submaps.

A new symbol is added to NetView's Root Submap, representing the topology reported by NMS. Beneath this symbol is a hierarchy of submaps showing:

- NMS stations
- IPX networks
- IPX routers
- IPX segments
- NetWare servers
- NetWare requesters
- Hubs

---

[4] The LMU/2 proxy agent MIB extension is defined in the file /usr/lpp/lmu6000/install/snmp_mibs/lmu2.mib. It is also included in the softcopy materials available on the Internet at www.mcgraw-hill.co.uk (check on editorial information for professional computing).

[5] At the time of writing, the Export Service software can be obtained free of charge from Novell's FTP server on the Internet (ftp.novell.com).

At present this solution provides topology information only and not status. Thus, all the resources are coloured green in the submaps. IBM and Novell are however working on several improvements to this solution. In addition to this topology information, NetWare servers and clients can also send traps to NetView.

The OpenMon solution would be attractive in cases where all that's needed is topology, status (eventually) and traps at the NetView station. This may be the case, for example, if NetView is being used as the overall multiprotocol manager and needs only a general view of the NetWare environment, while detailed management is performed at the NMS station. The LMU for AIX solution is best in cases where there are also a significant number of OS/2 LAN Servers and Requesters and where LMU's additional facilities for the NetWare environment are required.

6.4 RMON PROBES

An extremely important aspect of network management is monitoring and controlling LANs—Ethernets, Token-Rings and others. One very interesting topic in this area is the use of special SNMP agents known as Remote Network Monitoring (RMON) probes. These probes are placed on Ethernet and Token-Ring LANs where they observe activity and derive useful information which they make available in their MIBs. Managers such as NetView can then access this information and use it to understand LAN performance, configuration and faults. Generally, an application in the management system will digest and interpret the data from the RMON probes' MIBs. The MIBs themselves have been standardized by two RFCs, collectively referred to as 'the RMON MIB'.

The RMON MIB was originally defined in RFC 1271 for Ethernets only. RFC 1513 extended coverage to Token-Rings. Between the two, an amazing amount of information is defined making it possible to:

- Measure traffic flowing on LAN segments. It is possible to monitor overall traffic as well as traffic flowing from individual systems or between pairs of systems.
- Collect many other measurements of LAN performance and faults.
- Track measurements over time.
- Trace packets flowing in LANs.[6]
- Collect complete topology and status information for monitored segments. Managers can use this to produce graphical views of the LAN.

There are several RMON probes available, typically packaged as dedicated devices, but sometimes sold as software for Windows, OS/2 or UNIX. Examples of dedicated probes are:

- Axon Networks' Ethernet LANservant
- Wandel and Goltermann Technologies' IDMS 3113 Remote Segment Monitor

Examples sold as software are:

---

[6] To be consistent with RMON parlance, I'm using the term 'packet' to refer to what we called 'frames' in the earlier discussion of the IP protocol. Also, in this section the term 'segment' will be used to refer to an individual LAN (and not a group of LANs bridged together).

- Network General's Cornerstone Agent (which runs on Windows)
- IBM's RMONitor Agent for OS/2

It is also possible for communications devices such as concentrators, bridges and routers to incorporate RMON probes. Given the trend to jam as many different functions as possible into single boxes, it is likely this will be common in the future. Regardless of their packaging, RMON probes are directly connected to the LANs to be monitored and then communicate with a manager using SNMP, potentially across a WAN.

It is possible to use standard MIB tools such as those supplied in NetView to collect, analyse and present data from RMON probes These are especially useful if you want to create custom applications. It would also of course be quite handy to have a ready-built application to interpret the information and there are several of these. Some are stand-alone applications, running on operating systems such as Windows. Others are integrated into enterprise management systems, for example, IBM's RMONitor for AIX which runs on NetView.

Let's look at the RMON MIB itself, and then at the RMONitor for AIX application.

6.4.1 RMON MIB

An RMON probe monitors one or more LAN segments and to do this will have an interface that connects it to each of them. Because information flowing in an Ethernet or Token-Ring passes through all attached systems, the probe can watch the traffic and get a good picture of the LAN's performance, faults and configuration. It can also make copies to provide a tracing function.

In Ethernet LANs, this is especially easy to arrange, since Ethernet adapters make all data passing through them available to software. Thus, in an Ethernet, the probe can use a standard adapter in most cases. In Token-Ring, it's more complicated, since although Token-Ring adapters will see all data on the LAN, most pass along to software only the data destined for the particular system. Thus, in Token-Ring LANs, the probe must use special 'promiscuous' adapters which make all data visible to software.

However the probe derives its information about the LAN, it places it into the MIB extension defined by the RMON standards. This MIB is divided into 13 groups as shown in Figure 6.2. Implementation of each group is optional, though some groups depend on others. The probe will normally have a large amount of information in its MIB since it has information for each segment, and for each system attached to the segment. Tables are used extensively to hold this information.

```
Statistics
History
Host
Matrix
Host Top N
Alarm
Event
Filter
Packet Capture
Token-Ring Station
Token-Ring Station Order
Token-Ring Station Configuration
Token-Ring Source Routing
```

Figure 6.2 RMON MIB groups

Let's now review the groups of the RMON MIB. Here I will discuss the purpose of each group and some of the more interesting details. Those wishing for more detail should consult the RFCs.

Statistics Group This group provides performance and fault statistics for each of the monitored segments. These can be used to understand the amount of traffic flowing on a segment and how frequently various types of errors occur. The statistics are maintained as counters that start at zero when the probe initializes and increase thereafter. The manager can sample these periodically to understand the current characteristics of each segment.

The Statistics Group is divided into three subgroups, one for Ethernet and two for Token-Ring. In each, the counters are held in tables to allow for probes that monitor more than one segment. Each row of the table holds the counters for a particular segment.

The subgroups are:

- **Ethernet** This has the traffic and error counters for Ethernet LANs. These are derived from the packets received by the probe and the events it detects on the LAN. Because the probe sees all traffic, the counters describe the overall behaviour of the segment. The counters include:
  - Total octets and packets received.
  - Multicast and broadcast packets received.
  - Error of various kinds, for example collisions and jabbers.
  - Packets of particular sizes received. These are divided into six categories: packets that are 64 octets in length, packets of 65 to 127 octets, packets of 128 to 255, and so forth.
- **Token-Ring Promiscuous** This subgroup has statistics for Token-Rings. The probe derives them from adapters it has that operate in promiscuous mode. The statistics here describe the data traffic flowing on the ring. They exclude control traffic (which is measured by the other Token-Ring subgroup). The counters here are very similar to those in the Ethernet subgroup. The main differences are:
  - There are no error counters, since these maintained in the other Token-Ring group.
  - Instead of six categories for packet sizes, there are ten, since packets in Token-Ring can be much larger than in Ethernet.
- **Token-Ring Mac-Layer** This subgroup has statistics the probe derives from medium access control (MAC) packets it receives.[7] The statistics here can be used to detect several types of errors in the Token-Ring. The counters include:
  - Total MAC packets received and the total octets in these.
  - Beacon packets and beacon events (the latter being the number of times the ring has entered the beacon state).
  - Ring purge packets and events.
  - Claim token packets and events.
  - Counters of several other packet types and corresponding events.

History Group This group holds historical statistics about the segment. The statistics are the same as those in the Statistics Group, but here they are maintained over time. Thus, while the Statistics Group allows you to understand average behaviour of the LAN, this group lets you see

---

[7] MAC packets are used to carry out control functions in Token-Rings.

in detail how the LAN behaves at different times. For example, you could determine the time of day at which LAN utilization is highest and how busy it is during that period. Or you could determine the time that a particular type of error started occurring.

This group is implemented as a control table and three data tables. The control table is used to determine the way historical measurements are kept; the data tables contain the actual historical data. The data tables correspond to the three tables in the Statistics Group.

To start historical collection, the manager sets some objects in the control table. These determine the frequency at which the probe will collect statistics and how many 'samples' it will maintain. For example, the manager might instruct the probe to collect one sample from a particular Ethernet once every 15 minutes. Then, at the end of each such period, the probe would calculate the most recent statistics and save these as one sample in the Ethernet data table. The counters in the sample will be the same as those in the Statistics Group except that they will measure the change over the measurement period.

The probe can be collecting many sets of historical statistics at one time. Thus, it could monitor one Ethernet every 15 minutes and another every hour. In each set, the probe maintains samples up to the limit specified by the manager. When this is reached, the probe discards the oldest samples.

Host Group This group lists all hosts the probe has discovered.[8] It indicates the segment in which each host resides and thus can be used by a manager to understand the LANs' topology. The group also includes traffic and error counters for each host. These are a subset of those maintained in the Statistics and History Groups, and can be used to understand how different hosts affect the performance of the LAN. The counters maintained for each host are:

● Packets sent and received
● Octets sent and received
● Erroneous packets sent
● Broadcast and multicast packets sent

Matrix Group This group contains information about conversations, i.e. data exchanges, between hosts. The information can be used to understand the amounts of information exchanged between pairs of hosts. This is stored in the form of two-dimensional matrices, as you might expect. For each pair of conversing hosts, the Matrix Group contains the following counters:

● Total packets
● Erroneous packets
● Octets

These are maintained in two sets of counters, one for each direction between the two hosts.

---

[8] In RMON parlance, a host is any station in a LAN segment, that is, anything with an adapter connecting it to the LAN. Thus, a host could be an IP host, a router, a bridge, a workstation and so on.

Host Top _N_ Group This group can be used to find the _N_ hosts that have the largest values for some measurement. For example, this could be used to find the 10 hosts in a segment that have the highest number of outgoing packets. The measurement may be any of:

- Packets sent or received
- Octets sent or received
- Erroneous packets sent
- Broadcast packets sent
- Multicast packets sent

The manager instructs the probe to perform the measurement by setting some objects in a control table. The results are then placed in a data table.

Alarm Group This group lets you perform thresholding on probe measurements and generate traps and create log entries when thresholds are crossed. The mechanism used here is similar to those NetView and Systems Monitor use to threshold MIB variables. The Alarm Group could be used, for example, to send a trap when the collision counter for an Ethernet exceeds a particular value.

Event Group This group consists of two tables:

- The Event Table, which controls how the probe handles the events it detects. It is used, for example, to determine whether a crossed threshold in the Alarm Group will cause a trap or merely a message to the log.
- The Log Table, which defines a log for events detected by the probe. Each entry of the table contains a log message text string and a time stamp.

Filter Group This group, along with the Packet Capture Group, allows tracing and analysis of packets flowing on a LAN. Here you define filters that select a subset from all the packets flowing on the segment. These are counted and you may also indicate that each packet passing the filters should cause an event. As with the Alarm Table, such an event may cause a trap to be sent or a message logged. You can also have the packets saved in the Packet Capture Group.

　　The filtering mechanism here is quite powerful and flexible. Filtering can be performed by any data in the packet, and by packet attributes (e.g. whether it has a particular kind of error).

　　For a full explanation of the Filter Group see Stallings (1993). Alternatively, if you have a good supply of aspirin on hand, see the relevant sections of RFC 1271.

Packet Capture Group This group implements the buffer for packet capture. Using the Filter and Packet Capture Groups, the probe can perform the detailed line tracing required for diagnosing LAN problems.

　　There are two tables here:

- The Control Table determines the number of packets to save and several details of how this will be done. You can control, for example, which part of each packet will be saved.
- The Capture Buffer Table is the actual buffer in which packets are saved. Each entry contains a captured packet, its capture time and several details about it.

Token-Ring Station Group This group contains information describing the Token-Rings monitored by the probe. It contains two tables:

- A control table in which there is one entry describing each ring. This contains global information for the ring, including the number of stations and the ring state, e.g. normal, ring purge, beaconing.
- A data table describing the stations in the monitored rings.[9] For each station, it gives the address, NAUN (Nearest Active Upstream Neighbor), status, ring enter and exit times, and several error counters.

Token-Ring Station Order Group This group has a single table that gives the NAUN order for each of the monitored rings. The manager can use this to understand the rings' topology.

Token-Ring Station Configuration Group This group provides a means to get configuration information about stations and also to remove them from the ring. There are two tables:

- The first is a control table containing one entry for each station known to probe. There are two interesting objects here. One can be set by the manager to remove a station from the ring. The other can be set to initiate a query of configuration information for the station. This includes the station's location, microcode level, group address and functional addresses.
- The second table is where results of queries are placed.

Token-Ring Source Routing Group This group contains statistics about the source-route bridging carried out in monitored rings.

6.4.2 RMONitor for AIX

RMONitor for AIX is a NetView application that works with RMON probes to collect and present information about LAN segments. It will work, for example, with IBM's RMONitor Agent for OS/2. It makes use of all groups defined in the two RMON RFCs except the Packet Capture and Filter Groups.

RMONitor is accessed from the NetView GUI. Its most basic display is called the Network Monitor (shown in Figure 6.3). There is a symbol for each monitored segment, and colour indicates its status. The status is determined by comparing probe measurements to thresholds you define. For example, you could define a threshold that causes a segment to be considered marginal if its packet rate exceeds a certain level. Or you could define a segment to be critical if the number of collisions per second exceeds a particular value. You can arrange to have this window display all segments or only those with particular statuses. This gives you a way to see which segments are in trouble.

If you want to see details for a segment, you can use the Segment Monitor window. This will create tables and graphs of probe measurements for the segment as a whole. For example, you can see a graph showing the Ethernet errors for a segment. This would show a graph in

---

[9] A station is essentially the same thing as a host, but is the term used in the RFC for Token-Rings.

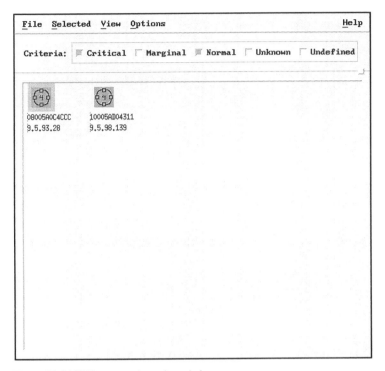

Figure 6.3 RMONitor network monitor window

which each line represents a particular kind of Ethernet error. You select the kinds of information you want to see using 'attribute groups', which are sets of related probe measurements. The tables and graphs may be for historical or current measurements.

There is also the Host Monitor window, which you can use to create tables and graphs of information from the Host, Host Top N and Matrix Groups. For example, you can see a graph showing the traffic exchanged between two hosts. Or you can see a graph showing traffic sent by a particular host or a group of hosts.

One nice feature of RMONitor is that, when it is used with the RMONitor Agent for OS/2, it can collect measurements of traffic for particular protocols, e.g. SNA or IPX. This information can be extremely useful for understanding the impact of a protocol on the LAN. This function is based on non-standard counters in the IBM probe's MIB.

RMONitor also has a data collection function that can upload data from RMON probes and store it in local files. This is provided in addition to the NetView collection function to meet the special requirements of RMON probes. For example, the RMONitor collection function is capable of performing a batch upload of data from the History Group at a particular time, like the middle of the night, to avoid bringing the network to its knees just to make sure it's running well.

6.5 TOKEN-RING LANS

In addition to RMON probes, there are several other options for detailed management of Token-Rings from NetView. Let's look at some of these.

6.5.1 LNM for AIX

Probably the best option here is to use IBM's LAN Network Manager for AIX. LNM for AIX is a NetView application that manages Token-Ring and FDDI LANs. It can also manage LAN bridges that conform to the bridge MIB standard defined in RFC 1286. It presents configuration, topology and status information for these, and also supports operation and configuration. It maintains its topology and status information in the NetView GTM Database.

To perform these tasks, LNM for AIX relies on several kinds of agents, as shown in Figure 6.4. These can be divided into four types:

- The LNM for OS/2 proxy agent for Token-Ring management
- SNMP agents that provide Token-Ring topology and status information
- SNMP agents for LAN bridge management
- SNMP agents for FDDI management

Let's consider the first three of these agents. (Discussion of the FDDI agent is deferred to Section 6.7.)

LNM for OS/2 proxy agent LNM for OS/2 is a standalone management tool for Token-Rings which can also serve as a proxy agent to LNM for AIX. It displays the topology of rings, stations, bridges and concentrators in graphical views. It also collects alarms and statistics, and allows commands to be issued to control the LAN.

LNM for OS/2 can also manage a large number of Token-Rings, but all of these must be connected together with bridges. Thus, it is suitable for managing a single location, but not sev-

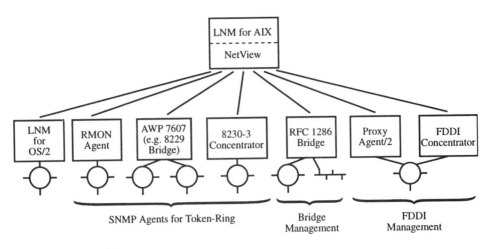

Figure 6.4 LNM for AIX agents

eral (unless the several locations are connected with remote bridges). A higher-level manager is required to manage several locations. One possibility is NetView/390. Another is LNM for AIX.

When serving as a proxy agent to LNM for AIX, each LNM for OS/2 communicates with it using SNMP and TCP. Thus, many locations can be managed as long as it is possible to communicate with them using IP.

Each LNM for OS/2 sends Token-Ring topology and other information to LNM for AIX. Topology information is stored in the GTM Database and NetView's *xxMap* uses it to create submaps. LNM for OS/2 also sends traps to NetView when there are problems in the LANs and these are displayed in NetView's Events window. In addition, LNM for AIX provides functions to control Token-Ring LANs and to display performance and fault information for them.

SNMP agents LNM for AIX can manage Token-Rings via SNMP agents with particular MIB extensions. In this approach, as with the LNM for OS/2 proxy, LNM for AIX displays submaps showing the topology of Token-Rings and their resources. It also provides performance and fault information for them. The operational capabilities available here however are more restricted. For example, in the SNMP agent approach you cannot remove a station from a ring, as you can with the OS/2 proxy.

LNM for AIX can manage Token-Rings through SNMP agents that support one of the following MIB extensions:

- An IBM private MIB extension known as 'AWP 7607'.[10] This is implemented at present in IBM's 8229 Token-Ring/Ethernet bridge.
- An IBM private MIB extension implemented in the IBM 8230 model 3 Token-Ring concentrator.
- The RMON MIB (RFCs 1271 and 1513). As we have seen, these MIB extensions contain topology and status information for Token-Rings.

LNM for AIX bridge management In addition to its Token-Ring management capabilities, LNM for AIX can also manage LAN bridges that conform to the bridge MIB defined in RFC 1286. This MIB provides information about source routing and transparent bridges and thus can be used with Token-Ring, Ethernet and FDDI bridges. The MIB also provides for bridges that use WAN facilities such as digital lines, Frame Relay and even X.25 networks to perform remote bridging. From this MIB, LNM obtains information about the bridges themselves—as opposed to the LAN and stations. This makes it possible to present submaps showing the configuration of bridges and their ports and also to present windows with configuration, performance and fault details.

6.5.2 Intelligent Hub Management Program for AIX

IHMP is an IBM application for NetView designed to manage the IBM 8250 and 8260 intelligent LAN hubs. The 8250 and 8260 are each built as a chassis hosting a set of modules. These

---

[10] AWP is an acronym for Architecture Working Paper. These are internal IBM papers that document architectural issues in networking.

modules perform LAN concentration, bridging, routing and other networking functions. They do so for Token-Ring, Ethernet, FDDI, ATM and other environments.

IHMP adds a symbol to the NetView Root Submap representing the hubs it is managing. Below this, there is a hierarchy of submaps (as described in the box). In all these submaps, colour is used to depict the statuses of the represented resources.

IHMP Submaps

IHMP provides a hierarchical set of submaps showing the hubs it is managing, as follows:

- The top of the hierarchy is the Network Level Submap. This has one symbol for each hub being managed.
- Selecting a hub symbol opens a Hub Level Submap. This shows a diagram of the hub which includes the chassis, each installed module and its status. There are also symbols indicating temperature, power supply and fan status.
- Selecting a module symbol opens a Module Level Submap. This has a picture of the module with symbols representing its ports and trunks. There are also symbols representing stations, routers and bridges connected to the module.

A nice feature of IHMP is its integration with LNM for AIX. When both are installed, you can navigate from the submaps of one to the other. Thus, from an LNM submap showing an 8250 in the context of a LAN, you can open an IHMP Hub Level Submap. Similarly, in IHMP submaps showing stations, LAN segments or bridges you can open submaps showing these in the context of LNM's view of the LAN.

In addition to navigating through pretty pictures of 8250s and 8260s, you can open various windows from within the submaps, including those allowing you to:

- Display and modify the configuration of hubs, modules, ports and trunks.
- Display information about hubs' fans, power supplies and temperature.
- Download microcode to a module.
- Reset modules or the hub itself.
- Display, in an interpreted way, the values of MIB variables measuring the performance of the hub. You can also set up thresholds for generating traps when these go outside defined limits.
- Open a NetView Events window showing traps for a particular hub.

In Token-Ring environments with 8250s or 8260s, IHMP provides an important tool for managing hubs. It is also possible to understand the topology and status of each Token-Ring by looking at the ports and stations shown in the Module Level Submaps.

6.5.3 Native NetView support

Another option for managing Token-Rings—if you are unable to use any of the other approaches—is to take advantage of NetView's IP management capabilities. These alone provide a certain amount of Token-Ring management when the systems on the LAN support IP.

They will appear in NetView's IP submaps and will be correctly shown as residing on a Token-Ring, i.e. they will be laid out in a circle as opposed to the segment layout used for Ethernet. The statuses of the Token-Ring adapters can be inferred from the IP statuses displayed.

The Interfaces Group of MIB-II can be viewed (using for example the MIB Browser) to get information about Token-Ring interfaces on the LAN. The objects in this group have information that is independent of the protocols running on the interfaces. Thus, you can determine an interface's status, type, speed and LAN address. You can also access several traffic and error counters. This much gives you a good picture of what is happening in a particular station, as well as of the overall LAN.

In addition, any traps sent by the stations can be received by NetView. It is very likely that the LAN will have a hub or bridge that supports SNMP and can also generate traps when problems occur.

There are however some limitations to this approach:

- Only those adapters running IP will be noticed by NetView.
- You can browse the MIB-II interface information for only those systems supporting SNMP. Only these can send traps.
- NetView is not aware of the difference between a single LAN and a group of bridged LANs. NetView displays LANs from an IP point of view and here such a group is treated as a single LAN.
- If you don't have a bridge or hub that generates traps, it is very likely you will miss many problems.

6.6 ETHERNETS

The options for managing Ethernets from NetView are fewer than for Token-Rings, mainly because there is no Ethernet equivalent of LNM for OS/2. Still, there are several ways to manage Ethernets from NetView.

6.6.1 LNM for AIX

LNM for AIX can manage Ethernet bridges, as we have seen. This is of course limited to information about the bridges themselves, e.g. you don't get submaps showing Ethernet topology.

6.6.2 Intelligent Hub Management Program for AIX

As we have just seen, IHMP manages IBM 8250 and 8260 LAN hubs. These support Ethernet and thus IHMP can be an important aspect of Ethernet management from NetView. Also, if you're using 10BaseT Ethernet (where each station directly connects to the hub) IHMP's Module Level Submaps will show the topology and status of the Ethernet.

6.6.3 Other bridge and concentrator management applications

Just as IHMP manages the IBM 8250 and 8260 hubs, there are NetView applications from other vendors to support their bridges and hubs, including the Ethernet capabilities of these. For example:

● Bay Networks' Optivity can display and configure their hubs, switches and bridges.
● Chipcom's ONdemand Network Control System (NCS) can manage their Oncore Switching System and ONline System concentrators.
● LANNET's MultiMan/6000 manages their Multinet hubs.

There are several others.

6.6.4 Native NetView support

The situation here is directly analogous to the native support for Token-Ring. You will get views of the Ethernet segments from an IP viewpoint and can collect data from the MIBs in hubs, bridges and stations. NetView can also receive traps from the various components of the Ethernet.

6.7 FDDI

For managing FDDI LANs from NetView, the options are similar to those for Token-Rings. LNM for AIX has specific functions for managing them. In addition, it is possible to manage FDDI LANs from an IP viewpoint, using NetView's native IP management functions, with the same capabilities and limitations as for Token-Ring and Ethernet. Here, let's focus on LNM for AIX.

LNM for AIX has a sub-application designed to manage FDDI LANs. It does this in conjunction with an OS/2 application known as the Proxy Agent/2 (see Figure 6.5). This is an SNMP proxy agent that attaches to FDDI rings and monitors them using the Station Management Protocol (SMT) for FDDI, either version 6.2 or 7.3.[11] The proxy then interacts with NetView by placing information about the LANs into a MIB extension defined by either RFC 1285 (for SMT version 6.2) or RFC 1512 (for version 7.3). In either case, there are also some IBM-defined extensions to the MIB that improve the effectiveness of LNM for AIX's management.

From the information in the proxy agent's MIB, LNM is able to create submaps showing the stations on each FDDI ring, their statuses and information about their ports. From LNM you can also control the operation of the stations, adding or removing them from the ring and enabling and disabling the ports and several functions of the stations. The Proxy Agent/2 also monitors the SMT protocol on the ring for status reporting frames (SRFs) indicating problems and translates these into SNMP traps.

LNM for AIX can also manage FDDI concentrators (as opposed to rings and stations) using SNMP. It is best at managing IBM 8240 and 8244 FDDI concentrators, but can also manage

---

[11] SMT is a protocol defined by the American National Standards Institute (ANSI).

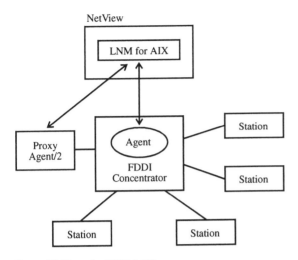

Figure 6.5 Managing FDDI LANs

non-IBM concentrators. LNM for AIX creates submaps of the concentrators, showing their ports, operating parameter and connections to FDDI rings. It also allows you to configure and control the concentrators.

6.8 X.25 NETWORKS

X.25 is not really a network protocol, of course, but rather an interface standard. It defines the interface between a DTE (data terminal equipment, e.g. a workstation) and DCE (data circuit-terminating equipment, e.g. a switch in a packet switching network). Still, when we speak of X.25, we often mean networks that provide an X.25 interface, while using some other protocol within. Thus, we have two cases to consider: managing the X.25 interface and managing the network providing the X.25 service.

The second case is not really an X.25 management question at all, since any protocol may be used within this network as long as it provides X.25 interfaces at its edges. This network will often be owned and managed by a PTT or other service provider. It may also be owned privately, and use a proprietary protocol devised by the vendor of the network's equipment. If you are lucky, this will have SNMP management capabilities.

NetView will be able to manage X.25 DTEs and DCEs if their hosting systems have SNMP agents, and if there is IP connectivity to them. At the time of writing, there do not appear to be any NetView applications available for X.25 environments, so NetView's general SNMP management tools will have to suffice.

A limited but useful amount of management information will be available if the agent implements only MIB-II. Additional information will be available if the agent implements one or more of the MIB extensions for X.25 defined in RFCs 1381 and 1382.

RFCs 1381 and 1382 go together, so that a system implementing X.25 would normally support both:

- The RFC 1381 MIB contains objects for the LAPB layer (link layer) of the X.25 protocol. It consists of four tables that allow the manager to read and change LAPB interfaces' configurations, and also to understand their performance and faults.
- The RFC 1382 MIB contains objects for the packet layer of X.25. These allow the manager to read and change the system's packet-layer configuration, to see which virtual circuits exist and to get performance and fault information about the packet-layer protocol in the system.

In addition to these two MIBs, some X.25 products support private MIB extensions containing data specific to their design. If the agent in a DTE or DCE implements a standard or private MIB extension, the normal NetView tools, e.g. MIB Browser, MIB Data Collector, can be used to manage them.

6.9 FRAME RELAY NETWORKS

The situation with Frame Relay networks is analogous to X.25. We have two issues. One is managing the Frame Relay protocol proper, that is, the interface between the DTE and the DCE. The other is managing the network providing the Frame Relay service. Since that network's protocol is not part of Frame Relay proper, we will skip the question of managing it, and focus instead on the interface and the service.

In general, the DTE will be a Frame Relay Access Device (FRAD), router, bridge or other networking device on the customer premises. The DCE will generally be a switch owned by the Frame Relay service provider which is located remotely and connected to the DTE via an access line, e.g. T1 or E1.[12] The DTE's system will usually contain an SNMP agent. On the DCE side, the service provider will often have a proxy agent accessible by the customer. Through this, the customer can view and manage his use of the Frame Relay service.

There are two RFCs defining MIB extensions for each of these cases—RFC 1315 for managing Frame Relay DTEs and RFC 1604 for the proxy agents.

The RFC 1315 MIB consists of three tables that describe the DTE's Frame Relay interfaces and allow them to be configured. The tables also contain fault and performance information.

The RFC 1604 MIB is intended to be implemented in an SNMP proxy agent owned by the service provider. The customer accesses the agent from his management station via SNMP/UDP, which would usually run over a Frame Relay virtual circuit. The MIB provides information about the performance, faults and configuration of the Frame Relay service. If the agent allows appropriate variables to be set, it can be the vehicle for configuring the service, e.g. create or delete a permanent virtual circuit. The MIB allows management of the Frame Relay service, but does not provide anything for managing the network itself.

If an agent implements either of these MIB extensions, or a private MIB extension for Frame Relay, then the normal NetView tools, e.g. MIB Browser, MIB Data Collector, can be used to manage the DTE or the Frame Relay service.

An example of an RFC 1604 implementation is the SNMP proxy agent provided by WilTel as part of their Frame Relay service. The agent implements a subset of RFC 1604, focusing on performance and utilization information. It also implements traps from the RFC. In addition to

---

[12] It is also possible that the DCE is owned by the 'customer', when the frame relay network is private.

this proxy agent, WilTel provides a Frame Relay management system called WilView/X which allows the customer to configure and administer the Frame Relay service. This is not based on SNMP. Instead, the customer accesses WilView/X using the X protocol across the Frame Relay network.

Many communications devices support the RFC 1315 MIB, for example IBM's Route-Xpander/2, IBM's 6611 and 2210 routers, and Cisco and Bay Networks routers.

6.10 ATM NETWORKS

At the time of writing, both the standards for ATM and its management are under development. However, there are already ATM products shipping from many vendors and thus management products are already available. These conform to whatever standards are available and fill in the gaps with private MIB extensions and protocols, with an eye to likely future developments. Further confusing the matter is that there are two camps on the question of which management protocol to use for ATM—one made up largely of telecommunications providers, who see CMIP as the best protocol, and another, whose members are mainly from the data communications world and see SNMP as the best choice.

ATM is seen as ultimately becoming the all-pervasive medium over which every kind of electronic information is transmitted—voice, data, video, virtual reality karaoke competitions and the rest. Thus, the phone companies are quite interested and play a leading role in its standardization. It therefore seems that CMIP will have a significant part in ATM management. Indeed, there are already products on the market, e.g. IBM's Broadband Switch Manager, that support ATM management using CMIP. On the other hand, SNMP is well accepted in the data world, and I strongly suspect that in the end most of the ATM management performed there will use SNMP. I will therefore focus on the SNMP side of things in this section.

There are two sets of ATM standards relevant to the SNMP world. The first are the specifications produced by the ATM Forum, a group of vendors, users, phone companies and others that has been formed to promote and expedite ATM standardization. The other set consists of the RFCs produced under the auspices of the Internet Engineering Task Force, the group responsible for Internet standards. The two sets of ATM standards have not been produced in isolation. The people involved work together by sitting on each other's committees and sharing information.

The ATM Forum's standards documents are being developed in the context of a network management model shown in Figure 6.6. There are six management interfaces defined. In all, the concepts of private and public networks are important. A public network is one owned by a telephone company or other provider, which is used by many different organizations and users. A private network would generally be owned and used by only one organization.

The six ATM Forum management interfaces are:

- **M1** The interface between a private management system and a private ATM device (e.g. a router, bridge or workstation in the private network).
- **M2** The interface between a private management system and a private ATM network.
- **M3** The interface a private management system uses to manage a portion of a public ATM network, doing so by interacting with a proxy agent in the public network. This would typically be used by subscribers to manage their service.

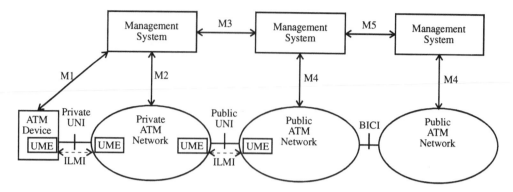

Figure 6.6 ATM Forum network management model

- **M4** The interface a public, i.e. service provider's, management system uses to manage a public ATM network.
- **M5** The management interface used between two public networks.
- **The Interim Local Management Interface (ILMI)** This is used on the ATM User to Network Interface (UNI) to exchange configuration and fault information between private ATM devices and private networks, and between private ATM networks and public ATM networks.[13]

At the time of writing, there are ATM Forum specifications for the M3 and M4 interfaces. In addition, the ILMI is documented in the UNI Version 3.1 specification (The ATM Forum, 1994).

In the ILMI, there are UNI Management Entities (UMEs) defined on each side of the UNI. Each implements a MIB defined in the UNI specification. The UMEs exchange information from their MIBs using SNMP. These MIBs include information about:

- The physical and cell-layer configuration of the ATM interface
- Cell-layer faults
- The configuration of virtual connections and virtual links

In M3, the private manager uses SNMP to access a proxy agent in the provider's network. The proxy agent implements a MIB based on the MIB-II System Group, the RFC 1573 Interfaces Group (an update to the MIB-II interfaces group), several groups from the RFC 1695 ATM MIB (discussed below) and groups from several other RFCs covering transmission media over which ATM will run.

The M4 specification is currently based on the use of CMIP, though there may be an SNMP-based specification in the future.

---

[13] The UNI is the interface between the ATM user and an ATM switch. There is a public UNI which (The ATM Forum, 1994) 'will typically be used to interconnect an ATM user with an ATM switch deployed in a public service provider's network'. There is also a private UNI which 'will typically be used to interconnect an ATM user with an ATM switch that is managed as part of the same corporate network'.

6.10.1 RFC 1695 ATM MIB Extension

The ATM MIB extension defined in RFC 1695 is especially important to ATM network management because it defines portions of the MIBs used in ATM Forum specifications, and also because it can be the basis for private SNMP-based ATM management, i.e. the M2 interface. It would normally be implemented on a device with one or more ATM interfaces.

Details of the MIB extension are given in the box.

ATM MIB

The ATM MIB defined in RFC 1695 consists of the following groups of managed objects:

- **ATM Interface Configuration Group** This group describes the ATM configuration of each interface. This includes its ATM-layer address, the maximum and current number of virtual paths and virtual connections, and some information describing the interface's role in the ILMI and SNMP protocols.
- **ATM Interface DS3 PLCP Group** This group contains performance statistics for the DS-3 Physical Layer Convergence Protocol used for carrying ATM cells over DS-3, i.e. T3, lines.
- **ATM Interface TC Sublayer Group** This group contains configuration and state information for interfaces that use the Transmission Convergence sublayer for carrying ATM cells over SONET (Synchronous Optical Network) lines.
- **ATM Virtual Link Groups** This consists of two groups. One allows the manager to understand and manipulate virtual path links. The other group allows the manager to do the same for virtual channel links.
- **ATM Cross-Connect Groups** This consists of two groups used to understand and control cross-connections between virtual path links and virtual channel links in an ATM switch or network.
- **AAL5 Connection Performance Statistics Group** This group contains performance statistics for virtual channel connections using the AAL-5 protocol. AAL-5 is the ATM service used by higher-layer protocols, e.g. IP, for sending data traffic.

6.10.2 ATM Campus Manager

Moving on from the rarefied world of network management standards, let's consider NetView applications for managing ATM, of which there are two at this writing, both from IBM. The first is the Nways Broadband Switch Manager for AIX, designed to manage the IBM line of 2220 switches which support ATM and other protocols. Broadband Switch Manager uses the CMIP support in NetView to manage these switches, which makes sense when you consider that much of the market for this kind of equipment is in the telecommunications world. The second application is the ATM Campus Manager for AIX, which uses SNMP to manage IBM's 8260 LAN hubs. These hubs—which we have already briefly considered when we looked at the Intelligent Hub Management Program for AIX—are used in building LANs and campus networks based on Ethernet, Token-Ring, FDDI, ATM and other protocols.

ATM Campus Manager (known to the initiated as 'ATMC Manager') manages the ATM aspects of 8260s. As we have seen, the ATM management standards are still being developed and therefore ATMC Manager currently handles only IBM 8260s and ATM networks constructed from them.

ATMC Manager adds a symbol to the NetView Root Submap representing the set of submaps it provides for ATM networks. These submaps are built by GTM and *xxMap*, and use colour to indicate the statuses of managed components. The submaps show:

- The network of 8260s and the ATM links that connect them.
- The ATM details of each 8260, including its ATM interfaces.

From the submaps, you can access several windows and functions for detailed ATM management. You can display performance information, such as call statistics, traffic counts and bandwidth-in-use statistics. There are also many windows available that display configuration information for 8260s and their ATM interfaces. You can see a list of the ATM interfaces in an 8260, and for each interface you can:

- Display interface speeds and media types.
- Display an interface's switched and permanent virtual circuits.
- Track a virtual circuit, displaying the nodes and links along it. For each node, this displays the circuit's virtual path and virtual connection identifiers.
- Create and delete permanent virtual circuits.
- Display an interface's virtual path connections and virtual channel connections.
- Display an interface's virtual path links and virtual channel links.
- Track a virtual link. This is analogous to the virtual-circuit tracking function.

ATMC manager also provides functions for downloading code to 8260 ATM modules and for uploading dumps, traces and logs.

Because there are two applications for managing 8260s, ATMC Manager has facilities that integrate it with IHMP, allowing you to jump between IHMP and ATMC Manager views of the 8260. For example, if you are looking at an 8260 in an ATMC Manager submap, you can jump into the IHMP submap for the 8260 to see information about its power supply and temperature.

6.11 SUMMARY

In this chapter, we have seen some of the more significant NetView applications and proxy agents available for managing environments other than IP. There are of course other environments you may wish to manage, and applications and proxy agents are available for many of these today. IBM and several other companies continue to develop new ones as well. The best source for the latest information is the most recent version of the *NetView Association Catalog* (IBM, 1995a).

SEVEN

KNOWING WHEN IT'S BROKEN—PROBLEM REPORTING

In this chapter we will look at how to perform problem notification in a NetView-based management system, that is, for any problem that may occur in the network, how to notify the right people. Doing just this much with any management system is not trivial and in many installations has not yet been achieved in a comprehensive manner. This area will be the main concern of the chapter, although at the end we will also look at how to manage and track problems once notification has been done.

The basic building blocks of our system will be NetView, the Systems Monitor Mid-Level Manager and Trouble Ticket.

7.1 REQUIREMENTS

Let's review what a good problem notification system should do:

- Report problems from any part of the overall network, regardless of the location, protocol, equipment or media involved.
- Accept traps as well as reports from people, e.g. phone calls, e-mail messages, screams of agony.
- Provide a basic set of information about each problem:
  - Unique identification of the problem resource and its type
  - Time and date at which the problem occurred
  - The nature of the problem
- It would be nice to have some supplemental information as well:
  - Seriousness
  - Probable causes
  - Recommended actions to solve the problem
  - Diagnostic information—some diagnostic codes or even a dump of relevant memory contents
  - Location of the problem resource

- Filter problem notifications using any of several criteria, including the resource's identity, its type, the kind of problem that occurred and the time it occurred. The filters must be able to determine whether the problem notification is simply logged or if a person is actually notified.
- Perform at least a basic level of correlation. If multiple notifications arrive that all describe the same problem, it would be useful for the manager to correlate these and tell the management staff only once about the problem.
- Route notifications to one or more people based on any of several characteristics of the problem, including:
  - Problem type
  - Resource identity
  - Resource type
  - Resource location
  - Resource's owning organization
  - Time of occurrence
- Keep a log or database of notifications.
- Automatically react to problems by issuing commands or taking other actions.

Let's now look at these requirements in more detail.

7.1.1 Agents and traps

The basic medium of our problem management system will be the humble SNMPv1 trap. As we have seen, its information is quite limited—agent address, codes identifying the problem, enterprise ID and time stamp. This much gives the basic problem information outlined above. For the supplemental information, we must rely on the agent putting this into the trap as variable bindings. The fact that variable bindings have no semantic structure makes them somewhat awkward for the manager to process.

For the traps to reach NetView, we of course require that there be an SNMP agent in each networking component—or a proxy agent supporting it—and that there be IP connectivity from the agent to NetView.

7.1.2 Other problem sources

Many problems are reported by people and a comprehensive management system needs to provide an easy way for them to do so. These people may be members of the management staff responding to phone calls or may be the users themselves. It would also be useful for the system to accept problems sent as e-mail messages, especially if they are structured in a way that software can process. There are other more exotic possibilities as well, for example problem submission via voice mail. NetView isn't designed to handle problem reports other than traps,[1] but as we'll see there are problem management systems that can, including Trouble Ticket.

---

[1] Here, as elsewhere, we are not considering NetView's CMIP capabilities.

7.1.3 Filtering

There are two major reasons to perform trap filtering:

1. To minimize the number of traps flowing through the network and using its bandwidth. For this purpose, it will be desirable to filter as close to the source as possible. Ideally, filtering would be done in the agent itself, but more realistically it can be done in an intermediate manager, such as the Systems Monitor MLM.
2. To avoid presenting extraneous traps to the management staff. Here it doesn't matter where filtering is performed as long it is reasonably flexible and effective.

Below we will look in detail at filtering in NetView, Systems Monitor and Trouble Ticket.

7.1.4 Notifying people

There are many ways to notify the management staff of problems. In the best case, this will be done in the context of an overall problem management system so that its other capabilities can also be used.

Let's consider some possibilities for notifying people:

● Simply add a line of text to a list along with all other open problems. This approach has the advantage of simplicity and in small installation could be enough. This approach might also be useful if all problems go through a central dispatcher. Usually, more will be needed.
● Transform the notification into an e-mail message and send it to a member of the management staff. If the e-mail system is good, this could be better than just having a list in a window. Relevant mail functions include sorting by priority, forwarding and attaching comments. If the e-mail system is integrated with a workflow system, this approach could be quite attractive.
● Present the notification using a full-blown problem management system. For example, Trouble Ticket has windows in which the problems assigned to a particular person are displayed. This can be an excellent approach since Trouble Ticket's supporting functions will also be available.

7.1.5 Routing

Regardless of the method used for notifying people, the system will be more useful if it provides for routing notifications to the right people. The most basic way is to have people perform the routing, but it is realistic to expect software to do much of this.

There are several possible criteria software can use to route notifications:

● **Resource type, e.g. IP router versus NetWare server**   For notifications based on traps, the enterprise ID can be used. When people report problems, they can obviously supply the resource type.
● **Resource location**   This is useful in cases where management responsibility is divided by geography. Reports from people can include location information. With traps, it is more dif-

ficult since these normally do not indicate location. Traps do however indicate resource address, and this can be mapped into location using a little database, or with addressing conventions that directly indicate location. It is also possible to get the resource location by issuing an SNMP Get, though this would add complexity into the notification process and would also require that all agents' *sysLocation* variables are reliably maintained.

- **Owning organization** This is useful in cases where management responsibility is divided by ownership of the equipment. If people enter the reports, they can sometimes supply this information. If not, it will be necessary for the management system to derive it, perhaps by looking the resource up in a database. Traps do not include this information and for them it will be necessary to derive it based on addressing conventions or from a database.
- **Time and date** This is useful for routing to people according to work shifts. Traps and reports from people can both include this information.
- **Seriousness** This is usually determined from the resource identity, its type, or the nature of the problem. The nature of the problem can be determined from the trap's generic and specific codes, or—if people are reporting the problems—by requiring them to supply it in a form the routing software can understand, e.g. problem codes.
- **Resource identity** Some resources may be so special that we want to have unique routing for them.

Given that the information required for routing is usually available, or at least can be derived, it should be possible for a system based on NetView, Systems Monitor and Trouble Ticket to implement effective routing. As we'll see below, it is.

7.1.6 Correlation

Networks often generate many traps when just a single problem has occurred. For example, a link's failure may cause the routers on both ends of it to send traps. In addition, logical connections relying on the link may fail, for example SNA sessions or TCP connections, and more traps will come into the network management system. Traffic that was flowing on the link may be diverted to other links which consequently become congested and more traps arrive describing these problems.

Of course, what you really want is just a single notification describing the link failure. Correlation aims to solve this problem. For relatively simple cases such as two routers sending the same kind of trap, correlation is feasible. More complex cases involving secondary symptoms such as congested links require extremely sophisticated correlation logic and, although this is a popular topic in research literature and sales pitches, it is not something that can be practically implemented in real networks yet.

As we will see, NetView has tools to support the feasible kinds of correlation.

7.2 SYSTEM DESIGN

Let's now look at the overall system design of a problem notification system based on NetView, Trouble Ticket and Systems Monitor. As shown in Figure 7.1:

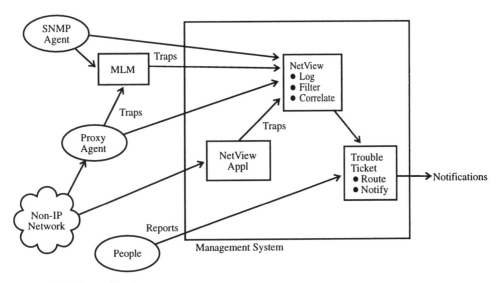

Figure 7.1 Problem notification system

- Notifications come into the system, manifesting themselves in one of several ways:
  - Most simply, the problem occurs in an IP network and an agent sends an SNMP trap which flows directly to NetView.
  - Alternatively, the agent sends a trap to an intermediate manager such as the Systems Monitor MLM. Here, as much filtering as possible will be done. Traps passing the filters will be sent on to NetView.
  - The problem occurs in a non-IP network managed by an SNMP proxy agent. The proxy agent learns about the problem using the non-IP network's protocols and creates an SNMP trap. It sends it to NetView, possibly via an intermediate manager such as the MLM.
  - A NetView application learns of a problem in a non-IP network and sends a trap to NetView (within the system). Applications that do this include ki Networks' DNM (for DECnet networks) and IBM's SNA Manager.
  - NetView itself generates an internal trap in response to something it has learned. These generally pertain to IP networks, for example the Interface Down traps which the NetView *netmon* daemon generates when it cannot successfully PING an interface.

    Alternatively, NetView's *trapgend* daemon creates traps in response to error messages written to the AIX error log. The *trapgend* may be in NetView's system or another.
  - The problem is reported by a person, and entered directly into Trouble Ticket.
- Next, we need filtering, correlation and then routing.

    The best approach will be to perform filtering and correlation in NetView and then routing and notification in Trouble Ticket. NetView has good mechanisms for filtering and correlation and has programming interfaces to extend these if necessary. NetView can also perform routing and notification, but Trouble Ticket is better at these. We also want to incorporate problem reports from people and these come directly into Trouble Ticket. Also, using Trouble Ticket, we can take advantage of its tracking and co-ordination capabilities.

For these reasons, the approach we will investigate in this chapter is to use NetView for filtering and correlation and Trouble Ticket for routing and notification. Of course, you may choose not to use Trouble Ticket, so in this chapter we will also consider the use of NetView for routing and notification.

7.3 IMPLEMENTATION

Let's now consider the implementation of each key aspect of the problem notification system.

7.3.1 Creating traps

In most cases, the creation of traps is not something you need to worry about, since SNMP agents, proxy agents and NetView applications do this quite well. With agents, the most important issue is configuring them to send their traps to the correct NetView or intermediate manager.

There are some other methods of creating traps that are more complicated and deserve some discussion. One of these is transforming SNA alerts from NetView/390 into traps. We discussed this in Chapter 4. Let's look at some others.

snmptrap **command** A simple way of getting traps into NetView is to use either the *snmptrap* or *event* command. *snmptrap* is the more general of the two as it can generate any trap you like. Some examples are shown in Implementation Tip 7.1.

snmptrap is useful when you want to generate a trap quickly from the command line. It can also be called from shell scripts or even C programs. For example, an application program could use it to send traps when it encountered errors.

One thing to note about *snmptrap* is that it works only on systems running NetView. There is also a version of *snmptrap* provided with the Systems Monitor MLM and SIA. Outside NetView and Systems Monitor, you will need to rely on other tools.

AIX error log and *trapgend* AIX has a central log into which it writes error information, and applications can write information there as well. This log is interesting to us here because NetView can monitor it and create traps when certain errors are logged, in particular those which have been marked as 'alertable'. These traps, like all others, are shown in the Events application and processed in the other usual ways.

When a program writes to the log, it does not simply write some error text, but instead logs an error code. This code in turn points to a message defined in a template. This indirection has the advantage of making the error messages independent of application code and easy to update.

By default, AIX marks certain important errors as alertable. It is possible to change which ones are so marked and to have your own applications write alertable information to the log.

The NetView process that monitors the error log and creates traps is *trapgend*. One nice thing about *trapgend* is that it doesn't have to run on a NetView system. Thus, you can distribute *trapgend* to all your AIX systems and monitor them with the trap mechanism. At the time of writing, one NetView licence allows you to distribute *trapgend* to as many AIXs as you like.[2]

---

[2] The SMIT screens for NetView include a tool for distributing *trapgend* to remote systems.

Implementation Tip 7.1

The NetView *snmptrap* command is an easy way to create and send traps. A simple example is:

```
snmptrap erasmus .1.3.6.1.4.1.2 fred 6 123 971
```

This sends a trap to the manager named 'erasmus'. The trap's agent address will be that of host 'fred', and it will have a time stamp of 971. The trap will be enterprise-specific, with enterprise ID of 1.3.6.1.4.1.2, and will have a specific trap code of 123.

It is also possible to include variable binding in the trap. For example:*

```
snmptrap erasmus .1.3.6.1.4.1.2 fred 6 123 971 \
.1.3.6.1.4.1.2.5.3.4.1.1.1 integer 3 \
.1.3.6.1.4.1.2.5.3.4.1.1.5 octetstring "zombie wolf"
```

will include two variable bindings, one with the INTEGER value 3 and the other with the OCTET STRING value "zombie wolf". The leading dots in the variable's object IDs prevent NetView from adding the MIB-II identifier (1.3.6.1.2.1) to them.

There is also a Systems Monitor version of the *snmptrap* command, with a slightly different syntax. To generate the same trap as in the second example, you would use:

```
snmptrap erasmus public 1.3.6.1.4.1.2 fred 6 123 971 \
1.3.6.1.4.1.2.5.3.4.1.1.1 integer 3 \
1.3.6.1.4.1.2.5.3.4.1.1.5 octetstring "zombie wolf"
```

Here you need to specify the community name for the trap. In the NetView *snmptrap*, a default name is used based on its SNMP configuration information for the agent. Another difference is that in the Systems Monitor version you don't put a dot in front of object IDs, since it does not add default prefixes to them.

* In UNIX commands, the character '\' is line continuation.

Thus, *trapgend* and the error log are wonderful things. There is just one problem—the error logging process is complicated and somewhat difficult to understand. The designers have put in so many levels of indirection that it gets to be like a house of mirrors.

If you don't want to know any more about these mechanisms, you might save yourself a headache by skipping the rest of this section. In any case, what follows is an improvement, I hope, over available descriptions. Please refer to Figure 7.2 throughout.

AIX error log The error log is managed by the AIX daemon *errdemon*. Programs add entries to the log by calling one of two system routines—kernel processes use the routine *errsave* and others use *errlog*. The key piece of information a program passes when it logs an error is the 'error ID'. This uniquely identifies the error and also points to an 'error template'. The template describes the error in detail, not using text, but instead using a set of 'codepoints'.

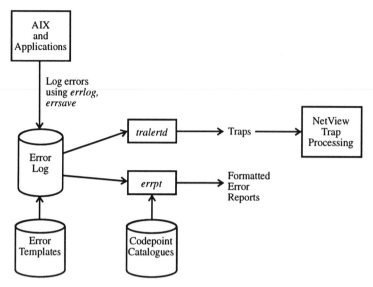

Figure 7.2 The AIX error log and *trapgend*

The program logging an error also passes the name of the resource involved in the problem, and may additionally pass 'detail data' to be logged. This is supplemental information describing the problem and could be some diagnostic codes or even a little memory dump.[3]

The error templates live in the directory /var/adm, but they are not displayable. If you want to see them, you can use the *errpt* command, e.g. 'errpt -at'. To create or otherwise manipulate the templates, you use the command *errupdate*.

The error templates contain the following information:

- The error ID. This is assigned by AIX when the template is created.
- A short label for the error, e.g. DMA_ERR.
- The class of the error—hardware or software.
- Indicators of whether the error is:
  - 'alertable'—should be picked up by *tralertd*.
  - 'loggable'—should be written to the log (and not discarded).
  - 'reportable'—when formatting the log, the user can filter out those which are not reportable.
- A series of codepoints describing the error. These are one or two bytes in length and indicate the nature of the problem, its probable causes and recommended actions for resolving it. If you're familiar with IBM's SNA Management Services, these are based on the Generic Alert architecture.
- Formatting instructions for any detail data.

---

[3] The information that programs pass to *errlog* and *errsave* is defined by a C language structure contained in the file err_rec.h. This file is in the directory /usr/include/sys.

When someone wants to see what is actually in the error log, they use the *errpt* command. This takes the encoded information and formats it into something a person can read. Since most people do not like to read one- and two-byte codepoints, *errpt* translates these into text strings. It does so by consulting a 'codepoint catalogue' that contains the mappings from codepoints to text strings.

There is a default codepoint catalogue provided with AIX which contains mappings for the codepoints used by AIX itself and other installed software. To see it, you can use the *errmsg* command, e.g. 'errmsg -w all'. You can also use *errmsg* to update the catalogue.

Figure 7.3 is an example of an error template—for loss of power—and shows the codepoints used for the error description and probable causes, among others. Figure 7.4 is the formatted version of the log entry created when I pulled the plug on my RS/6000. (It has the codepoints interpreted.)

```
ERROR ID 74533D1A

Label: EPOW_SUS
Error Class:   H
Error Type:    UNKN
Loggable: YES    Reportable: YES    Alertable: NO

Error Description
1400

Probable Causes
0200
0201

Failure Causes
0200

        Recommended Actions
        0200
        3302
        0000

Detail Data
Power status register
```

Figure 7.3 Example AIX error template

There is an additional interface into the error log worth mentioning and that is the *errlogger* command. This gives AIX users a way to write a text message into the log, e.g. 'errlogger We have got problems'. Of course, all the usual codepoints and the rest of the machinery are involved, but they essentially just indicate there is a message. The actual message text is included as detail data.[4]

trapgend The NetView daemon *trapgend* registers to *errdemon* its interest in the error log, and thus receives copies of everything that's marked as alertable. *trapgend* transforms these log entries into traps and sends them to NetView—which may be running locally or remotely.

---

[4] The *errlogger* mechanism uses the template for error ID AA8AB241.

```
ERROR LABEL:        EPOW_SUS
ERROR ID:           74533D1A

Date/Time:          Mon May 8 07:55:55
Sequence Number:    385
Machine Id:         000020053100
Node Id:            aix4
Error Class:        H
Error Type:         UNKN
Resource Name:      SYSIOS
Resource Class:     NONE
Resource Type:      NONE
Location:           NONE

Error Description
LOSS OF ELECTRICAL POWER

Probable Causes
POWER SUBSYSTEM
INTERNAL POWER UNIT

Failure Causes
POWER SUBSYSTEM

        Recommended Actions
        CHECK POWER
        IF PROBLEM CONTINUES TO OCCUR REPEATEDLY THEN DO
        THE FOLLOWING
        PERFORM PROBLEM DETERMINATION PROCEDURES

Detail Data
Power status register
8000 0000
```

Figure 7.4 Formatted error log entry

The traps built by *trapgend* are enterprise-specific[5] and have specific codes equal to the error IDs of the corresponding log entries. They include several variable bindings. These are explained in Appendix I. The bindings contain much of the same information one finds in SNA Management Services alerts and this allows the traps to be easily translated by *tralertd*.

If you decide to use this mechanism for your own applications, you will want to create your own templates using *errupdate* (as described in Implementation Tip 7.2). You will probably also want to use NetView Event Configuration so that when the traps are logged and displayed by NetView they will be nicely formatted. To understand exactly how *trapgend* sets up the variable bindings for a particular error, the best thing to do is cause the error to occur and then look at the results in trapd.log.[6]

Systems Monitor SIA as a trap source There are two major ways that Systems Monitor can alert you to problems in the network:

● The first is when using the MLM as an intermediate manager. Here you can use its Threshold Table to generate traps based on data the MLM collects from SNMP agents. This is discussed in Section 10.3.5.

---

[5] Their enterprise ID is 1.3.6.1.4.1.2.6.4.1.2.1.

[6] This log file is kept in the directory /usr/OV/log. To see the variable bindings for a trap, you need either to ensure there is no event configuration for it or to use the $* symbol in its configuration string.

Implementation Tip 7.2

If you want your applications to use the AIX error log, here's an example of how to do it. First, you would define an error template, using the *errupdate* command with input similar to:

```
+ LARRY_ERR:
  Class= S
  Log= True
  Report= True
  Alert= True
  Err_Type= TEMP
  Err_Desc=EB01
  Prob_Causes= 5004
  Fail_Causes= E800, 6312
  Fail_Actions=1601, 0000
  Detail_Data = 4, 58, DEC
  Detail_Data = 4, 59, DEC
```

AIX would assign this error an ID of A4D4D187. Then the following C program can refer to the template using these IDs. (This program needs to be compiled with the '-l rts' option.)

```
#include <stdio.h>
#include <stdlib.h>
#include <string.h>
#include <sys/select.h>
#include <sys/errno.h>
#include <sys/err_rec.h>

int main(int argc, char **argv) {
    struct eb {
        int errorid;
        char resname[16];
        int detail1;
        int detail2;
    } errbuf;
    errbuf.errorid = 0xa4d4d187;
    strcpy(errbuf.resname,"fred");
    errbuf.detail1 = 37;
    errbuf.detail2 = 38;
    printf("%d\n",errlog(&errbuf,28));
}
```

You might also want to make additions to the codepoint catalogues for your error template. You can use the *errmsg* command to do this.

- The other is when using the SIA's File Monitor Table. This we will cover here.

The File Monitor Table (FMT) is intended to be used on systems throughout the network to alert you to various kinds of changes in their files. When the SIA detects these changes, it sends traps to an SNMP manager such as NetView. The kinds of changes the SIA can detect are:

- The presence of a particular character string in a file. The SIA would typically monitor a log file for one or more strings indicating a particular error condition. When the SIA detects the string, it generates a trap containing the relevant line of the file and other information needed to figure out exactly what happened. This is probably the most interesting capability of the FMT for our purposes since it allows you to integrate error logs into the SNMP trap mechanism.
- The presence or absence of a particular file. With this capability you can check whether the system has certain software installed, for example, programs known to have viruses or software that isn't licensed.
- A change in the size, content, permissions, owner or group of a file. When combined with the monitoring for presence and absence, this capability can be used to ensure that crucial files are present and not altered. For example, you can ensure that configuration files or software package files are intact.

The FMT offers endless Orwellian possibilities.

To start an instance of file monitoring, you must create an entry in the FMT. The FMT, like all SIA tables, resides in the SIA's MIB extension. You can add an FMT entry in one of the ways discussed in Section 3.5.4.

Regardless of the method used to create the FMT entry, you will set up several objects in it which specify the file monitoring details. A complete description of these can found in IBM (1995f) and also in somewhat more detail in the SIA MIB module.

Going through the FMT objects here would constitute an act of mental terrorism, so instead I'll just give a few examples. Note that the MIB objects involved in the FMT all have rather forbidding names like *smSiaFileMonitorState* in which the *smFileMonitor* prefix is common and the last part unique to the particular object. For brevity I'll simply use this last part.

To monitor a particular file for changes in its content, you could set up an entry in the FMT as follows:

- **Name** MonitorFred
- **Description** Watch /tmp/fred for data change
- **State** enabled
- **Type** dataChange
- **PollTime** 10m
- **FullPathName** /tmp/fred

This will cause the SIA to monitor the file /tmp/fred every ten minutes for a change in its data content. If the SIA detects a change, it will send a trap to NetView or another manager. The trap will have the following information:

- Enterprise ID = 1.3.6.1.4.1.2.6.12 (the Systems Monitor Enterprise ID)

- Specific code = 22
- Variable bindings with the following values:
  - The *Name* of the entry
  - The *Description* of the entry
  - The *FullPathName* of the file
  - A formatted time-stamp—e.g. "Sat Jun 17 18:58:41 GMT 1995"
  - The new size of the file
  - The original size of the file

For another example, suppose you set up an instance to monitor a file for a line containing the string 'error:'. This might be done when you want to watch an application's log for error messages. An FMT entry to do this is:

- **Name**   MonLog
- **Description**   Watch /tmp/log for the error message
- **State**   enabled
- **Type**   string
- **PollTime**   30s
- **FullPathName**   /tmp/log
- **ForString**   error:

This would check the file every 30 seconds to see if an error message had been written and if so would send a trap to NetView. The trap would be similar to the one in the first example, with the important difference that the entire line containing the error string would be included in the variable bindings. This makes it possible for the manager to understand what the error condition is.

One nice feature of the FMT is that the basis of the string search can be a regular expression as used in the UNIX *ed* editor or the *egrep* (extended *grep*) string search command. Thus, you can set up sophisticated searching patterns.

There are a few other interesting capabilities of the FMT that are not illustrated in these examples. One is that you can set objects in the FMT entry to specify when it is to be active. For example, the entry can be active only during particular times of day or particular days of the week. Thus, you might monitor an application's log only during the business day when its operation is critical.

Another capability of the FMT is that you can cause it to run commands on the SIA's system immediately before or after the file monitoring occurs. This could be useful, for example, to run a command that reacts automatically to an error or one that recreates a file that was found to be missing. If your command was particularly sophisticated and was able to solve the problem on its own, you might decide to take advantage of another object in the FMT (*TrapState*) which prevents traps being sent to the manager.

Alternatively, you could have a command run immediately before file monitoring occurs to check some conditions on the local system and then write its findings to a file. The FMT could then test the contents of the file to determine if they indicate an error condition. For example, you could run the UNIX *ps* command to write a list of all processes running on the system to a file. The FMT could then check whether a particular process name is in the file and, if not, send a trap to the manager.

7.3.2 Systems Monitor MLM as an intermediate manager

Let's now move on from discussion of trap sources to look at the use of the Systems Monitor Mid-Level Manager as an intermediate manager for handling traps. The goal here is to place MLMs strategically, i.e. close to clusters of SNMP agents, and then configure the MLMs to carry out two important functions:

- **Trap filtering** Perform as much as possible in the MLM to avoid wasting network bandwidth and NetView cycles.
- **Trap routing** In many cases, the manager that should receive traps will change over time, or may depend on attributes of the traps, e.g. fault traps go to one manager and performance traps to another. Most SNMP agents are not able to send traps to different managers depending on time and trap attributes and therefore it is necessary to insert an intermediary such as the MLM.

In both these cases, all agents in an MLM's 'domain' would be configured to send their traps to it. The MLM would then determine which traps to filter and which managers should receive the rest.

Two tables are involved in trap routing and filtering:

- **The Trap Destination Table** This globally determines the NetView or NetViews to which the MLM will route traps.
- **The Filter Table** This controls whether traps are discarded or sent to a manager. It also allows you to route certain kinds of traps to particular managers, overriding the Trap Destination Table.

Let's look at these two tables.

Trap Destination Table Each entry in this table defines a single manager to which traps will be sent. All traps not explicitly routed (by the Filter Table) will be sent to each of the managers defined in these entries.

You set up entries in this table using any of the techniques discussed in Section 3.5.4. Each entry would as usual have a *Name*, *State* and *Description*. In addition, for each entry you would define:

- The host to which traps will be routed. You can list several if you like, and you can also use an alias (referring to the Systems Monitor Alias Table).
- Optionally, a mask. This provides a crude global filtering mechanism for traps going to the destination in this entry. It allows you to determine which of the seven generic categories of traps (based on the generic code) are to be sent. In general, you probably won't bother with this since better and more granular filtering is available in the Filter Table.
- As with other Systems Monitor tables, you can specify that an entry should be active only during certain times of day or days of the week, and do this with much flexibility. This is clearly an important capability for our purposes, since it allows routing to different managers at different times (as required in the Rotating Style of distributed management we discussed earlier).

An interesting feature of the Trap Destination Table is that it can be used to control the proto-col—TCP or UDP—over which traps are sent to managers. It can also change the ports to which they are sent. In normal SNMP, agents send traps to managers using UDP. To be precise, they send the traps to port 162 on the manager. By default, the MLM does also. There are at least two reasons you may want to change this:

- You want to have traps sent using TCP instead of UDP. We discussed the reasons for doing this (and not doing it) under 'Mapping onto transport protocols' in Section 2.2.5. Assuming you wanted to send traps to host helen's port 162 using TCP, you would set the destination host to 'helen+tcp/162'. You would also need to configure NetView to listen on TCP port 162.[7]
- The MLM may be running on NetView's system. You might do this to take advantage of the MLM's filtering, since it has some capabilities NetView's does not. In this case, the MLM would receive all traps first, filter out insignificant ones and pass the rest to NetView. While doing this can be useful, it introduces some problems involving port numbers. The solution involves the Trap Destination Table, and is described in Implementation Tip 7.3.

Implementation Tip 7.3

It's possible to run both NetView and the MLM on the same system. In this case, the MLM would serve as a 'pre-processor' for NetView. This allows you, for example, to use the MLM's trap filtering capabilities instead of NetView's. However, doing this introduces a conflict involving the port to which traps are sent.

By default, both NetView and the MLM listen for traps on UDP port 162. When the two run together, it is not possible for both to listen there. Instead, you can arrange to have NetView listen on a different port. The MLM would then receive incoming traps on port 162, filter out uninteresting ones, and send the rest to NetView's port. This is shown in Figure 7.5.

To arrange this, you do the following:

- Change the port on which NetView listens. You can do this in the SMIT screen for the NetView *trapd* daemon. The port number should be greater than 1023. For example, I've used UDP port 1099.
- Cause the MLM to send its traps to NetView on UDP port 1099 (for example). To do this, you set the destination host in the Trap Destination Table to a special value. For

---

Filter Table This table lets you filter traps coming into the MLM with considerable flexibility. For each trap, the MLM can:

- Forward it to a manager.
- Drive a command to handle it locally.
- Simply log it.

---

[7] This can be done using the SMIT screens for the *trapd* daemon's options.

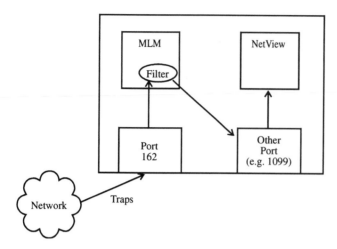

Figure 7.5 MLM and NetView on the same system

The Filter Table also supports the MLM trap throttling function, which allows you to handle traps in ways that depend on how frequently they are received.

When forwarding traps to another manager, the Filter Table lets you control the protocol used (UDP or TCP) and the port number to which they are sent. Normally, traps handled by the Filter Table will be sent according to the specifications in the Trap Destination Table and thus will use the protocol and port number specified there. However, you can override this in the Filter Table. You might do this if you wanted order-sensitive traps to use TCP (e.g. traps indicating that systems have come up or gone done), while others use UDP.

Let's consider the mechanics of this table. There is a set of scalar objects that control some global aspects of filtering and trap reception. Then there is the table itself, in which each entry defines a particular filter the MLM will use.

As with all other Systems Monitor tables, this can be configured using one of the techniques described in Section 3.5.4.

Controlling MLM Trap Reception

It's possible to change the port and protocol the MLM uses to receive traps. (This is the other side of the coin from what was just discussed in Implementation Tip 7.3.) In most cases, you would not change these, and instead would simply take the default of UDP port 162. That is where agents normally send traps. You might change the protocol if this MLM will receive traps from another MLM using TCP instead of UDP.

The MLM's trap reception is controlled by four scalar objects associated with the Filter Table:

- **UdpTrapReception** Determines whether the MLM receives its traps from agents using UDP.
- **UdpTrapReceptionPort** Determines the UDP port number.
- **TcpTrapReception and TcpTrapReceptionPort** These are for receiving traps with TCP.

First, you would configure the global objects as needed. For our purposes here, only one is interesting. *DefaultAction* controls whether the default action for traps is to block or pass them.[8] This determines how traps not matching a filter are handled, and gives you the option of filtering in a positive or negative way.

Next, you would set up some entries in the Filter Table proper to define the actual filters. We can think of these as being in four groups:

1. **General objects**   These take care of the usual naming of the entry, giving it a description, and specifying the times during which it should be active.
2. **Matching objects**   These determine if a given incoming trap matches the filter entry. Each object specifies a particular kind of test to apply to the trap. If it passes all the tests, then it matches the overall filter. The matching objects are:
   - *EnterpriseExpression*, *AgentAddrExpression*, *GenericExpression* and *Specific-Expression*   These test the enterprise ID, agent address, generic and specific code. Several kinds of wildcard matching can be used.
   - *VariableExpression*   This lets you do nearly anything you like to test the trap contents. You can give an expression using special variables to access information from the trap. The expression can use the normal C-like logical operators such as ==, !=, <, >, !, ||, && and so forth. You can also use parentheses to change evaluation precedence. One of the best things about this facility is that it gives you a way to look at the variable bindings in the trap. For example, the expression shown in Figure 7.6 would match a trap with specific code 1234, enterprise ID 4.5.6.7 and whose only variable binding has object ID 2.4.6.8 bound to the INTEGER value 37.
3. **Action objects**   These determine what the MLM does when a trap matches the filter:
   - *Action*   Whether to pass the trap to a manager, block it, or perform throttling.
   - *TrapDestinations*   Here you specify the host or hosts to which the trap is to be sent, overriding the settings in the Trap Destination Table. Thus, you could route traps indicating problems with bridges to one manager and those indicating problems with workstations to another. This object works just like the destination object in the Trap Destination Table. It allows you to specify multiple destinations, to use aliases and to specify the protocol and port number for trap delivery.
   - *MatchedCommand*   A command to be executed when the filter is matched. This gives you a local facility for automatically reacting to traps. The command is executed in the Korn shell and you can pass it information from the trap by including special variables in the command string. These are similar to the variables discussed above for *VariableExpression*.
4. **Throttling Objects**   These let you set up throttles, as we'll now see.

Throttling   Throttling is a technique which is useful when an agent sends a particular trap repeatedly. For example, if an agent sends 100 traps in 30 seconds indicating it has a buffer shortage, you can filter all but the first trap and save yourself the trouble of wading through the rest. Or if you don't want to know about the occasional link error, but do want to know when many occur in a short period of time, you can set up a throttle so that the first link error trap received in a 15 minute period is discarded, but any additional ones are sent to the manager.

---

[8] The objects in the filter table have the common prefix *smMlmFilter*.

```
$SM6K_TRAP_GENERIC_NUM==6 &&
$SM6K_TRAP_SPECIFIC_NUM==1234 &&
$SM6K_TRAP_ENTERPRISE==4.5.6.7 &&
$SM6K_NUM_TRAP_VARS>=1 &&
$SM6K_TRAP_VAR_OBJ_ID1==2.4.6.8 &&
$SM6K_TRAP_VAR_TYPE1==INTEGER &&
$SM6K_TRAP_VAR_VALUE==37
```

Figure 7.6 Example *VariableExpression*

When a trap matches a Filter Table entry whose *Action* is to throttle, then throttling objects are applied. They are as follows:

- *ThrottleType*   This may be *sendFirstN* or *sendAfterN*. *sendFirstN* throttles start blocking after a given number of traps have been received. *sendAfterN* blocks until a given number of traps have been received. Thus, *sendFirstN* traps are useful for situations where an agent will send a burst of traps for a single problem, while *sendAfterN* traps are useful when you only want to know about traps that occur repeatedly.
- *ThrottleArmTrapCount*   This is the *N* in *sendFirstN* and *sendAfterN*. It indicates the number of traps required for the throttle to take effect or to be 'armed'. When a *sendFirstN* throttle is armed, it blocks. When a *sendAfterN* throttle is armed, it passes.
- *ThrottleDisarmTrapCount* and *ThrottleDisarmTrapTime*   You specify one or both of these to control when a throttle is disarmed. *ThrottleDisarmTrapCount* specifies the number of traps that will disarm the throttle. The count starts with the first trap received after the throttle is armed. *ThrottleDisarmTrapTimer* specifies the maximum length of time from receipt of the first trap (the one that armed the throttle) until the throttle is disarmed.
- *ThrottleArmedCommand* and *ThrottleDisarmedCommand* may optionally be used to execute commands when the throttle is armed or disarmed.

There are several ways to use throttles. The most straightforward is to limit bursts of a particular type of trap. Suppose you want to receive at most three 'out of memory' traps from a given agent in any 15 minute period. You would set:

- *ThrottleType* to *sendFirstN*
- *ArmTrapCount* to 3
- *DisarmTimer* to 15 minutes

Alternatively, you can use throttles to ignore 'noise' level traps and pass them only when they occur frequently. Suppose that you want to receive a 'link error' trap only when there have been more than 10 in any 30 minute period. You would set:

- *ThrottleType* to *sendAfterN*
- *ArmTrapCount* to 10
- *DisarmTimer* to 30 minutes

Still another possibility is to use throttles to decrease a particular trap by a given ratio. Thus, if you wanted the manager to receive only one out of every three occurrences, you would set:

- *ThrottleType* to *sendFirstN*
- *ArmTrapCount* to 1
- *DisArmTrapcount* to 2

7.3.3 NetView trap filtering

Let's look now at the filtering mechanisms in NetView. Although it is wise to do as much filtering in the intermediate manager as possible, it is almost certain that NetView filters will be required as well. One reason may be that not all agents are covered by intermediate managers, for example those agents close to NetView or those in segments too small to justify an MLM. Another reason is that you may have NetView applications that generate traps locally, for example IBM's SNA Manager or ki Networks' DNM. Also, NetView itself generates traps and you may wish to filter these too.

There are two ways to perform filtering in NetView. First, there are filters proper, which we will consider in this section. Second, there are rulesets. Rulesets are a more powerful way to perform filtering in most cases and also to incorporate other features such as trap correlation and automatic reaction to them. The process of defining rulesets is also much easier to grasp since you can use the very intuitive Ruleset Editor.

In most cases, you would want to use rulesets instead of filters because of their many advantages. As we will see in a moment, however, there are cases where filters can be used but rulesets cannot. Thus, we will look at both.

Filtering model There are several ways filters and rulesets are used in NetView:

- The Events and Event History applications both use filters to ensure that only significant traps are shown. Events applies filters to traps as they come into NetView. Both Events and Event History use filters to determine which historical traps they will display.

    Events can also use a ruleset to filter its display, while Event History cannot. When Events is using both filters and a ruleset, it will display only those traps which pass the ruleset *and* at least one filter. (While Events can have several active filters, it can have only one active ruleset. The reason for this will be apparent from the discussion below.)
- Filters are used to determine which traps the *tralertd* daemon receives and thus which are translated into SNA alerts. Rulesets are not used in this case.
- Filters are used by NetView applications that connect to the SNMP programming interface. In this interface, there are two ways applications can receive traps. Most simply the application connects by calling the *OVsnmpTrapOpen* routine in which case it receives all traps coming into NetView. Alternatively, the application connects with *nvSnmpTrapOpenFilter*, in which case it receives only those traps that pass a specified filter. Rulesets are not used in the SNMP programming interface.

The important thing to notice is that each use of filters and rulesets is independent of the others. Thus, the filters used by applications have no effect on what is shown in Events. Equally, the filters and rulesets used by one operator's Events have no effect on what is shown in another's.

Filter semantics and the Filter Editor A filter is a logical expression that takes as input certain trap fields and other characteristics of the trap, and then determines whether to pass or block it. The inputs to a filter are:

- Enterprise ID
- Generic code
- Specific code
- Sending agent
- Time it was logged in NetView
- How frequently it is being received (for throttling)

These filters, known in NetView parlance as 'filter rules', can be defined in two ways:[9]

- By using the Filter Editor
- By directly coding filter rules and placing them in a file

In either case, the result is one or more filter files, each of which contains one or more filters. As we'll see, the most flexible way to create filters is by coding them directly, but it is easier (at least in the beginning) to use the Filter Editor. Let's look at the editor first.

The Filter Editor window has four main sections, some or all of which you fill in to create a filter:

1. **Event identification** Here you set up filtering based on the meaning of the trap, that is, the type of problem or other occurrence the trap is describing. You do this based on the trap's enterprise ID, generic code and specific code. You can do this in a positive or negative manner, i.e. only those traps matching pass, or all except those matching pass.

2. **Object identification** This is a rather high-falutin way of saying 'agent identification'. In this section, you list one or more agents from which this filter will either block or pass traps. You can also specify that traps from all agents will pass.

3. **Time range** This section allows you to filter out traps based on the time and date they are received in NetView. You do this by specifying a starting and ending time/date. You must always specify time and date together so that while you can have traps pass from (say) 9:00 on 4 July to 17:00 on 5 July, you cannot have traps pass between 9:00 and 17:00 every day.

4. The fourth section allows you to set up throttles. These come in two flavours, and their capabilities are a subset of those available in the MLM and rulesets. In either flavour, you specify a time interval and a 'frequency'. You then choose the flavour:
   - **'Less than or equal to'** This is similar to the MLM's *sendFirstN* throttles. Here the frequency indicates the maximum number of times the trap can pass the filter within the time period. Thus, if you specify a frequency of 3 and an interval of 60 seconds, and the trap occurs 100 times in 60 seconds, only the first three will pass the filter and then all others will be suppressed until the 60 seconds are over. Then the next three will pass.
   - **'Greater than or equal to'** This is similar to the MLM's *sendAfterN* throttles. Here you specify that a particular trap must be received more than a certain number of times within the interval before it passes the filter. For example, if you specify a frequency of

---

[9] Filter rules have nothing to do with rulesets.

10 and interval of 60, and the trap occurs 100 times in 60 seconds, then the first nine will be suppressed but the tenth will pass. The next 90 will be suppressed. After that 60 seconds, another 10 traps would have to occur to cause another to get through the filter.

The criteria specified in these four sections of the Filter Editor window are combined so that any trap matching all four will pass the filter.

Compound filters We have so far considered only 'simple filters'. There are also 'compound filters' which can also be defined with the Filter Editor or directly in files. These are built by ANDing or ORing two or more other filters (compound or simple) together. In the AND case a trap must match all included filters to pass the compound filter, while with OR the trap may match any. Although any single compound filter can use only one of AND and OR, it is possible to combine AND and OR by including other compound filters.

What is the purpose of these compound filters? Much of what they can do is available by having multiple simple filters active at once, as you can do, for example, in the Events window. Doing this has the same effect as using OR, which is to say that if the trap matches any of the active filters it will be shown in Events. Still, it is easier to refer to a collection of simple filters as one compound filter (which, for example in Events, means typing one rather than many lines to define which filters are to be used).

In addition, compound filters are helpful when you want to filter out all traps except certain ones, that is, use a negative filtering approach. This requires AND logic in all non-trivial cases and thus is not possible without compound filters. For example, suppose you want to filter out generic traps 0 and 3 for all systems and also filter out specific trap 123 for enterprise *xyz*. To do this, you would define two simple filters:

1. A filter that matches everything except generic traps 0 or 3.
2. A filter that matches everything except traps with specific code 123 for enterprise *xyz*.

You would then AND these together in a compound filter. The result would be that:

- Generic traps 0 and 3 would not pass the first simple filter. Thus, the AND of the compound filter would be false.
- Specific trap 123 for enterprise *xyz* would not pass the second filter. Thus, the AND would be false.
- All other traps would match both filters, and for them the AND would be true.

Defining filters to NetView Both simple and compound filters reside in files. There is a sample in /usr/OV/filters/filter.samples and you can add your own filters to it. If you want to be tidy about it, you can set up your own files. In Events and other applications that use filter rules, you always specify both a file name and a rule name, so where you put the filter files doesn't really matter. Most applications put theirs in the directory /usr/OV/filters.

While the Filter Editor is an easy way to create and update these files, you get more flexibility if you code them directly. You will also find yourself coding them directly if you write programs that use the *nvSnmpTrapOpenFilter* routine to receive filtered traps. When you invoke this routine, you do not pass filter file and rule names, but instead a raw filter string.

Filter files Each filter file is just a good old ASCII file containing a series of filter rules, each of which begins with a line giving its name:

```
RuleName=Fred
```

Next there will optionally be a description of the rule, for example:

```
RuleDescription=Some text to describe the rule
```

Then you get down to the actual logic. You use one or more conditions, as described in the box, and connect them with the operators AND (&&), OR (||) and NOT (!). You may also use parentheses to override the default operator precedence (e.g. to give OR precedence over AND). For example:

```
RuleContent=CLASS=1.2.3.4 && !(IP_ADDR=9.180.180.207 ||
                              IP_ADDR=9.180.180.208)
```

This filter would pass all traps with an enterprise ID of 1.2.3.4 and with an agent address other than 9.180.180.207 or 9.180.180.208.

You can also make compound filters. As is the case with the Filter Editor, you can use AND, OR and NOT logic. For example, suppose you have two simple filters named 'Billy' and 'Ethel', and you want to combine them using negative AND logic, i.e. block anything that matches both of them. This could be done as follows:

```
RuleName=Billy_AND_Ethel
RuleContent=!((FilterName=Billy &&
              FilterFile=/usr/OV/filters/myfilters) &&
             (FilterName=Ethel &&
              FilterFile=/usr/OV/filters/myfilters))
```

Conditions allowed in filter rules

- CLASS=value
  specifies the enterprise ID.
- IP_ADDR=value
  specifies the IP address or host name.
- LOGGED_TIME <= time/date, LOGGED_TIME >= time/date
  works the same as time/date ranges in the Filter Editor.
- PRESENT = SNMP_TRAP
  used as a way of saying any trap will match. It exists to distinguish between traps and CMIP events. For our purposes, it has very little use except in cases where we want to create a filter that passes all traps.
- SNMP_TRAP=value
  for matching on the generic code.
- SNMP_SPECIFIC=value
  for matching on the specific code.
- THRESHOLD <= frequency && TIME_PERIOD = time_period
  for setting up a 'Less than or equal to' throttle.
- THRESHOLD >= frequency && TIME_PERIOD = time_period
  for setting up a 'Greater than or equal to' throttle.

Filtering events with a program As we have seen, NetView filters stick to the mainline fields of the trap message and allow only basic filtering logic on these. As such, they are much less sophisticated than the MLM's filtering mechanism and NetView's rulesets. In most cases, one of these will provide the functions you need, but there may be cases where you would like to write your own program that can access the incoming traps, do whatever it likes to filter them and then passes the interesting ones along to whatever is the user interface for displaying traps to operators.

If that user interface is the Events application, it will be difficult to do this. Although it is easy to write programs that receive traps on the SNMP programming interface, there is no way to put one in the flow of traps going into Events. In other words, your program can filter all it likes, but, because the filters used by Events will be independent from those used in your program, Events will be unaffected.

There is a slightly hokey way to get around this, as shown in Figure 7.7:

- First you would have Events use a ruleset to discard all traps except those with a special community name you invent. This must be a community name that no real traps will include.
- You would then write a program that receives traps from the SNMP interface and determines which are interesting enough for the operators to see.
- The program transforms all interesting traps so that they use the special community name and re-sends these to NetView.
- They will pass the ruleset and Events will display them.

There are several possible variations on this scheme, but in all of them something in the traps must be changed. Doing this cannot be described as aesthetically pleasing. Nor is running traps through NetView's trap-handling machinery twice, which for example would mean duplicate

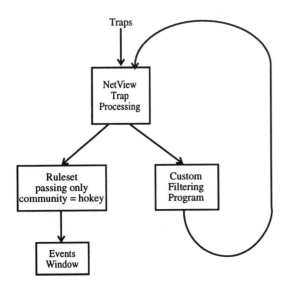

Figure 7.7 Controlling Events display with a filtering program

logging. Below we will see that one good alternative is instead to use Trouble Ticket as the user interface for trap display. In that case, it will be possible to write your own filtering program (without being hokey).

7.3.4 Filtering with rulesets

Rulesets are a powerful and easy-to-understand method of filtering, correlating and automatically reacting to incoming traps. In this section, we will look at their basic features and how they can be used for filtering. Later in this chapter, when we discuss correlation, and also in Chapter 9, we will look at their other capabilities.

We can think of a ruleset as a flow diagram that specifies how NetView will handle incoming traps. The diagram consists of nodes and lines. Each node specifies a particular step in processing incoming traps and the lines indicate the relationships between the nodes.

Suppose, for example, you wanted to create a ruleset to pass only those incoming traps which:

- Have the RMON enterprise ID, specific code 1 and the second variable binding set to the string 'mudshark'.
- Or have the RMON enterprise ID and specific code 2.

Figure 7.8 shows a ruleset that will do this:

- The beginning of the diagram is a node that represents all incoming traps. These 'flow' from the node into the two branches of the ruleset.
- In both branches, the Trap Settings node is first used to determine whether an incoming trap has a given enterprise and specific code. A trap with the RMON enterprise and specific

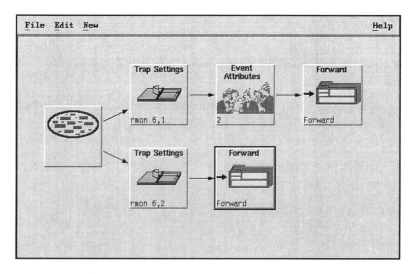

Figure 7.8 Ruleset Editor window (for this window capture, I used a beta version of NetView 4, which is why the leftmost node has its label missin)

code 1 will pass the top Trap Settings node; one with the RMON enterprise and specific code 2 will pass the bottom node.

- In the top branch, a passed trap will continue on to the Event Attributes node which checks its second variable binding, and passes only those traps which have it set to 'mudshark'.
- Finally, in either branch, traps that have made it through to the Forward node will have passed the ruleset. They will be displayed in any Events window that uses the ruleset.

Rulesets have the advantage that they can filter on any part of a trap's information. The Trap Settings node can test the enterprise ID and both generic and specific codes, checking all three in one node. The Event Attributes node can test these as well as anything else in the trap, though one node is required for each attribute tested. Both these nodes can use equal-to or not-equal-to as the test and thus filtering can be done positively—specifying which traps pass—or negatively—specifying which are to be blocked. The Event Attributes node can also use as its test:

- greater-than
- less-than
- greater-than-or-equal
- less-than-or-equal

Thus, filtering can be done with much flexibility.

It is also possible to perform throttling with rulesets. This is similar to MLM throttling. Here you use the Threshold node which performs the actual throttling. You also use Event Attributes and Trap Settings nodes to select the traps you wish to throttle. In the Threshold node, you specify a time period and a count. You also specify the type of the throttle—*First*, *At* or *After*:

- With *First*, the throttle will pass traps up to the count and then block for the rest of the time period.
- With *After*, the throttle will pass only after the count.
- With *At*, the single trap that is received at the count will pass.

These have the same sorts of uses we discussed earlier for MLM throttles.

There are many other nodes that can be used in rulesets, and we will review these later when we look at correlation and operations.

Each ruleset is stored in an individual file, and these are normally contained in the directory /usr/OV/conf/rulesets, though you can put them anywhere you like. The files are not in a form you can edit directly.

7.3.5 Using Trouble Ticket as the user interface

While NetView's Events is a good user interface for displaying traps, a much more powerful one is Trouble Ticket with its substantial machinery for routing, notification, tracking and other aspects of problem management.

If Trouble Ticket will be the user interface, we first need to get traps into it from NetView. As we have seen, Trouble Ticket's model of the world makes a distinction between symptoms and the underlying problem. To support this model, Trouble Ticket uses two kinds of objects—incident reports and trouble tickets. The former represent symptoms and the latter represent actual problems. Thus, incident reports are the first stage in making a problem manifest to Trouble Ticket and our task is to create them from the traps NetView receives.

There are two major ways this can be done:

1. Let Trouble Ticket do it automatically.
2. Write some code to pick up traps from NetView and pass them to Trouble Ticket as incident reports.

Obviously, the first approach is the easier.[10] It also has the advantage that Trouble Ticket will use any Event Configuration defined in NetView and thus will display the configured text descriptions in the incident reports, rather than the raw information from traps. However, in this approach, you will not be able to take advantage of NetView rulesets since these are not applied to the flow of traps into Trouble Ticket.[11]

Trouble Ticket has its own filters for incoming traps. These are very similar to NetView's, and thus are less powerful than rulesets. They allow you to filter based on the enterprise ID, generic and specific codes and the sending agent. They provide throttling, in a way somewhat more elaborate than with NetView. They also provide a basic correlation mechanism that allows you to associate a trap with another that resolves it. They do not allow you to filter or correlate using the variable bindings within the trap.

In many cases, these capabilities will be enough. The most common use of filtering is to eliminate traps that indicate insignificant but frequently reported occurrences. Examples are traps indicating that workstations have come up or gone down. Trouble Ticket can easily perform this kind of filtering.

However, you may want to do something more sophisticated and take advantage of NetView rulesets, or even provide your own filtering and correlation logic. For this, you will need to write code that picks up traps and creates incident reports from them. There is one significant disadvantage to doing this. The Event Configuration information is not available to your program. It will simply receive the trap information in essentially raw form and from this create incident reports. Your program could, of course, read the trapd.conf file itself and use this information to create meaningful text descriptions for the incident reports. Or you could create your own event configuration scheme independent of NetView's. However, either of these will require significant programming effort. Thus, the question is one of power and flexibility versus simplicity.

In the following sections, we will consider two approaches for writing your own code that receives traps from NetView and creates incident reports:

1. Receiving traps from the SNMP programming interface.
2. Writing a command that is driven from NetView rulesets, given each trap's information as parameters.

---

[10] To cause Trouble Ticket to automatically create incident reports from traps, you answer 'yes' to the question 'Collect NetView/6000 events' in its SMIT configuration screen.

[11] Neither are NetView filters, but then this is not a significant issue, as we are about to see.

The second approach has the advantage of allowing your program to see the traps after they have been through ruleset processing and thus take advantage of their correlation capabilities. The first approach is cleaner from a programming point viewpoint since it will receive the trap information from a programming interface rather than having it passed as command parameters.

Incident reports can be created not only from traps, but also by people who fill in Trouble Ticket forms or send specially formatted e-mail messages. While it will usually be desirable to filter and correlate traps, it is less important to do so with reports from people since they generally do not flood in at the rate traps do. Thus, it is not a serious problem that the approaches above apply only to traps.

Let's now look at how we can employ a 'pre-filtering daemon' to receive traps from the SNMP programming interface and pass them to Trouble Ticket as incident reports.

Pre-filtering daemon A pre-filtering daemon is a process that will always be running in the NetView system. It receives traps from NetView, discards uninteresting ones and passes the rest to Trouble Ticket.

As shown in Figure 7.9, a pre-filtering daemon works as follows:

1. It first opens a connection to the NetView SNMP programming interface to receive incoming traps.
2. When a trap arrives, the daemon looks at it and decides whether it is significant or not.
3. If the trap is significant, then the daemon builds the information for an incident report and calls Trouble Ticket's *cmd_in* command to create the incident report.

Let's look at each of these steps in more detail.

Connecting Opening the connection for receiving traps can be done in one of two ways:

● You can use the *OVsnmpTrapOpen* routine to receive all traps and events.
● You can use the *nvSnmpTrapOpenFilter* routine to receive only a filtered subset. You might want to do this to combine the best of NetView filters with your own logic. Notice that *nvSnmpTrapOpenFilter* is really a superset of *OVsnmpTrapOpen* since you can always use the former with a filter that lets everything through (for example 'PRESENT= SNMP_TRAP').

Once the session is open, the daemon waits for traps to arrive. When one does, the program calls an SNMP programming interface routine such as *OVsnmpRecv* to get the trap.

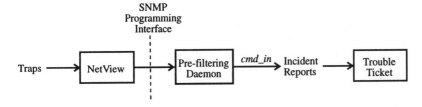

Figure 7.9 Pre-filtering daemon

Filtering The daemon then parses the trap and goes to work deciding whether it is significant enough to be passed onto Trouble Ticket. This part of the routine is potentially the hardest, depending on what your filtering criteria are. In easy cases, you may just need to check an address or test one of the variable bindings. Easier still, you may just rely on the NetView filters you specified with *nvSnmpTrapOpenFilter*. In more difficult cases, you might need to make a query to a database or consult some other external data source.

Sending to Trouble Ticket If the routine decides the trap should pass, then the next step is to issue the *cmd_in* command to send an incident report to Trouble Ticket. *cmd_in* is a tool that can pass many kinds of requests to Trouble Ticket. It expects to be passed one parameter—the name of a little file containing the request and its parameters.

An example request file is shown in Figure 7.10. The file includes a set of fields and their values. These describe, for example, the information to be included in an incident report being created. One interesting field for our purposes is *Organization,* which we can use to determine whom Trouble Ticket will notify when the incident report is created. Here the notification will be routed to the person designated in the Trouble Ticket database as the contact for that organization. (There are other ways to perform notification in Trouble Ticket and we will look at these in Section 7.3.8.)

```
Incident_Report_Submission {
Summary          =  "LAN Adapter Failed"
StartDate        =  "01/01/95 9:45 a"
Count            =  "1"
Impact           =  "2"
Location         =  "Building 7"
Detail           =  "Ethernet card failed on PC in Office 732"
Client           =  "Smith, Ed"
Organization     =  TechSpt
Resource         =  "ed.acme.com"
Reporter         =  "Bennett, Larry"}
```

Figure 7.10 Input file for *cmd_in*

Let's consider a few of the other fields in the file:

- *Count* is the number of incident occurrences covered by this report. In other words, if the failure happened three times and you are reporting all of these, then you would use 3 for *Count.*
- *Impact* is your perception of the extent to which this event affects the network or system. It can be either 'None' or a number 1 through 5 in which 5 is the most serious.
- *Client* indicates the affected contact for the resource, in other words the person who has just lost three hours' editing because his PC went down.

The pre-filtering daemon must prepare such a file for *cmd_in*. The most obvious way to do this is to write the file to a working directory. Once this has been done, you can use the UNIX *system* routine to invoke *cmd_in* with the file name as its parameter. If you find using files to pass parameters a bit distasteful, you could take advantage of the fact that *cmd_in* can read this same information from standard input.

An example pre-filtering daemon can be found in Appendix II. With this approach, you can build a bridge from NetView to Trouble Ticket. As we've seen, it's possible to do this without writing your own code. However, a pre-filtering daemon allows you to combine NetView's filtering logic with your own and thus create much more powerful filtering than you could if you relied only on Trouble Ticket's filters.

7.3.6 Reducing duplicate notifications

Closely related to the question of filtering is that of correlating the several traps or incident reports that are related to a single problem. There are two major ways this can be approached:

- Wait until traps and reports from people have manifested themselves as incident reports in Trouble Ticket and there perform manual correlation.
- Use the correlation capabilities of NetView rulesets. One consideration is that there is no programming interface for receiving traps after ruleset processing, as there is for filtered traps. Thus, the pre-filtering daemon cannot take advantage of any correlation performed by rulesets.

    It would be possible however to modify the approach slightly and (as shown in Figure 7.11) use the action capabilities of rulesets to drive a pre-filtering program. Aside from this difference in how it receives traps, the program would be essentially the same as the pre-filtering daemon. We will look at these action capabilities of rulesets in Section 9.3.4 under 'Using rulesets'.

Let's now look at the two approaches for correlation.

Manual trap correlation Once incident reports have been created, they are collected together in a big conceptual bucket known as 'unattached incidents'. This consists of the incident reports that have not yet been associated with a trouble ticket.

You can open a window (known, appropriately enough, as the Incident Report List) listing all incidents known to Trouble Ticket. Here you'll see incidents that are attached to particular trouble tickets as well as unattached incidents. You can filter this window (using its Search Tool) so that it shows only unattached incident reports. You can then attach these to trouble tickets. If this is done so that all related incident reports are attached to the same trouble ticket, then this window can serve as the basis for a manual correlation system.

There is a feature of Trouble Ticket that can help with gathering together related incident reports into a trouble ticket—in particular for the case when you have many related incidents for a single resource and want to attach them to a single ticket quickly. The feature allows you to select a resource from a NetView submap and then request Trouble Ticket to show you a list of all unattached incidents for it. You can then select and attach from this list (see Implementation Tip 7.4).

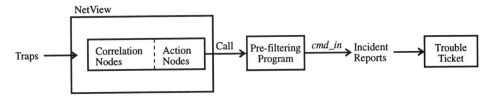

Figure 7.11 Pre-filtering program called by rulesets

Implementation Tip 7.4

To create a new trouble ticket with some or all of the unattached incidents for a particular resource, use the following procedure:

1. Point at the resource in a submap and press the right mouse button to bring up the context menu.
2. From this, select 'Review Incident Reports'. This opens the list of unattached incidents for the resource.
3. Select the ones you want and press the 'New Ticket' button.

This assumes, of course, that the incident reports for a given problem will all refer to the same resource. This will not always be true and thus, in many cases, you will still have to rely on grouping them from the list of unattached incidents.

Using rulesets Another approach is to use the correlation functions of NetView rulesets. These, of course, apply only to traps and not to incident reports. The crucial feature rulesets offer is memory of the traps that have recently been received. This is necessary to determine whether a trap that has been received at a given time is related to one received slightly earlier.

Rulesets are a tool and you must determine the details of how they actually carry out correlation. There are samples provided with NetView, but you will need to determine for your network precisely which traps will be correlated and under which circumstances.

Rulesets are intended mainly for relatively straightforward kinds of correlation. For example, they can easily handle cases where one trap indicates a failure and another its resolution. This much is quite useful, since if a network resource has a problem that lasts only briefly, correlation will prevent an unnecessary trap from wasting your operators' time.

Another case rulesets can handle is where two or more particular traps indicate a single problem. Here, if you know which set of traps indicates the problem, then the ruleset can combine them into a single one. For example, suppose that when a router has a memory error, it sends two traps—one with specific code 38 and another with 39. It may be that receiving just the trap with code 39 indicates this problem, in which case you don't need correlation at all but could simply use filtering to eliminate the redundant trap. However, if both traps are needed to indicate the single failure, then correlation would be useful since it could combine the two.

It is also possible in theory that rulesets could be used to perform the really difficult kinds of correlation that require analysis of the relationships among network components. For example, suppose an important link in the network fails and traffic is diverted onto other links, which consequently become congested and cause more traps. Here you may wish to know only about the primary problem of the link failure. Or suppose a link that connects NetView to a portion of the network fails and NetView generates several traps because it believes that the resources there have gone down. In complex cases such as these, you could create rulesets to correlate the traps, but the analysis and definition work would quickly become too complex for practical use.

Still, rulesets should give you a very good start to performing correlation in your network. The correlation tools provided are quite flexible and the Ruleset Editor makes it easy to use them. Let's look at how correlation works.

Correlation depends on several ruleset nodes. You can combine these with the nodes we discussed earlier for filtering or with any other ruleset nodes.

The most fundamental nodes are Correlate Attributes and Resolve. With these two, you can perform the simple kinds of correlation. For example, suppose you want to correlate the generic SNMP *linkDown* trap with *linkUp*, so that if a link goes down but comes back up within a few minutes, then the two traps will be correlated and cancel each other. Let's further suppose you would like the *linkDown* trap to be displayed in Events until the *linkUp* is received. The ruleset shown in Figure 7.12 will do this.

The two Event Attributes nodes select *linkUp* and *linkDown* traps from the incoming stream. *linkDown* traps then pass on to two other nodes—the Forward node which causes them to be displayed in Events, and the Correlate Events node. *linkUp* traps also go into the Correlate Events node.

This correlation node includes a matching criterion—that the first variable bindings of the *linkUp* and *linkDown* traps must be equal (in the *linkUp* and *linkDown* generic traps the first variable binding is set to the name of the link involved). It also specifies the amount of time the *linkDown* trap will be held waiting for a *linkUp*. If the matching criterion is met within this time, then correlation occurs, and the *linkDown* trap is passed to the next node, Resolve, which will retract it from Events.

You could extend this kind of ruleset into one that correlated more than two traps by using multiple Correlate Events nodes.

There are several other nodes you can use for correlation:

- **Set Database Field**   This will set the value of an object's field in the NetView Object Database. This would usually be an object representing a network resource. The Set Database Field node can be used to remember information about a trap or to change an attribute of the object in response to a trap.

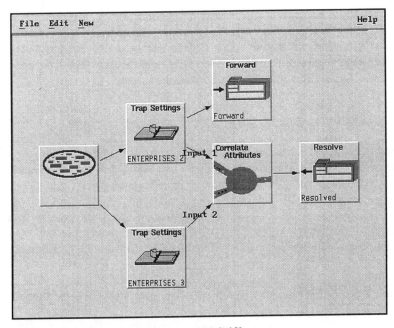

Figure 7.12 Ruleset to cancel *linkDown* trap with *linkUp*

- **Query Database Field**   This tests the value of a field on a particular object and, when the test is successful, passes processing onto the next node in the ruleset.
- **Set Global Variable and Query Global Variable**   These are similar to the Set and Query Database Field nodes, but allow you to store and test information independently of particular objects.

With these ruleset nodes, it is possible to get quite elaborate in the trap correlation you design. The main limitation will be the amount of knowledge you can obtain about the trap patterns in your network, and the amount of complexity you are willing to have in your rulesets.

7.3.7 Creating incident reports manually

Up to now we have focused mainly on problem notifications that originate as traps. They can also, of course, come from people. Often, this will be a member of the management staff who's responding to a phone call, though there are other possibilities. In any case, Trouble Ticket supports manual creation of incident reports with its Incident Report window.

In this window, you provide:

- Two items of text description—'incident summary' and 'incident detail'
- The name of the resource involved in the problem
- Other details of the problem, including its 'impact'

Once this has been done, the incident report is submitted and goes into the pool of unattached incidents.

There is also an e-mail interface for incident report creation, so that an e-mail message containing the information for a new incident report can be sent to Trouble Ticket.[12] These are sent to a special user ID on Trouble Ticket's system, which you define for this purpose. This facility has several uses. One is that you have remote operators who cannot access Trouble Ticket. Another is that you could write an application with which users report their own problems and have the application e-mail the information to Trouble Ticket.

7.3.8 Routing and notification

Once traps have passed filtering and made it into Trouble Ticket as unattached incidents, you can put Trouble Ticket's machinery to work managing them. The first step is to route them to the appropriate people, and in this section we will look in detail at how to do this.

Here I'm assuming you want to notify based on incident reports rather than on trouble tickets. On the other hand, you may want to notify people when trouble tickets are created. You might do this, for example, if manual trap correlation is used to group incident reports into trouble tickets before passing them to individual operators. In either case, the solution is essentially the same.

Trouble Ticket's notification scheme depends on two logical entities you must define— 'Notification Rules' and 'Notification Methods'. The former determine who will be notified for

---

[12] The format of these e-mail messages is very similar to the input files for *cmd_in*.

particular events, while the latter determine how. The overall notification process is depicted in Figure 7.13.

Records involved in notification To support notification, you must create some 'inventory records' in the Trouble Ticket database, using either Trouble Ticket forms or its import facility. The latter method is best for when you have a large number of records to define or already have the information in another database.

Specifically, you must define records for:

- **Contacts** These represent people Trouble Ticket will notify and for other reasons you must know about. The records include information such as name, user ID, e-mail address and organization. In addition, these records include the names of Notification Methods to use.
- **Organizations** These records create a level of indirection so that you can refer to an organization rather than directly to a person. Thus, if the person representing the organization changes, you don't have to update all the places that refer to him. In an organization record, you can define information such as its name, a short description, the name of a contact and a contact telephone number. For the notification process, the only things that matter are the organization and contact names.
- **Resource Classes** These records define the classes to which resources belong. Much of the information here can be pulled in when creating a record for a particular resource. The information in resource class records includes, among other things:
  - The type of the resources in this class, e.g. workstation, router, terminal.
  - The family to which the class belongs (by default there are Hardware, Software and Service).
  - The number of problems a resource in this class must have before it is considered 'chronic', and a time period to which this number applies, e.g. five failures in six months is chronic.

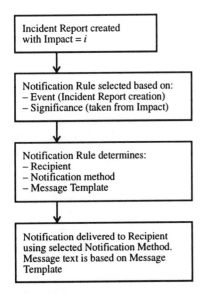

Figure 7.13 Trouble Ticket notification process

- A reference to the service level agreement that applies to resources of this class.
- Most importantly, the name of the responsible organization for this resource class, which is pulled into resource records and can determine where to send notifications.
- **Network resources** These describe the resources themselves. Each record includes:
  - The resource name.
  - Its class.
  - Lots of identifying information such as model number, manufacturer, release, serial number and so on.
  - Information useful for problem management such as the MAC address, location and the names of relevant vendors.
  - A little log in which remarks about the resource can be placed.
  - Contact information. The name and phone number of the person who uses or is otherwise affected by the resource.
  - The responsible organization. This can determine where to send notifications.

Trouble Ticket can automatically create records for resources known to NetView. In addition, Trouble Ticket has predefined resource class records that should cover most other kinds of resources you require.

Notification Rules Once the necessary records have been defined, the next step is to create Notification Rules. Each such rule tells Trouble Ticket to notify someone when a 'notification event' occurs with a particular 'significance'.

Notification events are occurrences within Trouble Ticket relating to incident reports, trouble tickets and others. Here are some examples of notification events:

- Incident Report created
- Incident Report modified
- Trouble Ticket opened
- Trouble Ticket fixed
- Incident Report attached to Trouble Ticket

Any such event will have a 'significance' associated with it. Significance is a value between 1 and 5 (the highest significance is 1), and is determined in different ways depending on the notification event. For example, in the case of Incident Report Created, significance is taken (confusingly) from the value given as the 'impact' when the incident report is created.

A different Notification Rule may be specified for each permutation of notification event and significance. For example, you could have one rule for Incident Report Created when the incident has a significance of 3, and another for Incident Report Created with significance of 1. You could have still other Notification Rules for the Trouble Ticket Opened event.

Each Notification Rule indicates the person to be notified, the 'urgency' of doing so, and a 'Message Template' to determine what the person is told.

In the Notification Rule, the person to be notified is defined either directly by name or indirectly by specifying their 'role' (see Figure 7.14). For example, in the case of Incident Report Created, one of the following roles may be specified:

- **Reporter** The person who created the incident report.

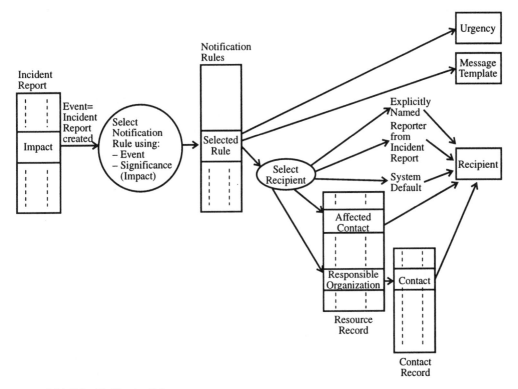

Figure 7.14 Using Notification Rules

- **System Default Contact**   This you define to Trouble Ticket.
- **Affected Contact**   The person defined as being affected by problems with the resource (e.g. the owner of a malfunctioning workstation).
- **Referring Organization**   Trouble Ticket will find the responsible organization from the problem resource's record. It will then look in that organization's record to find their contact. This is the person Trouble Ticket will then notify.

If you wish to notify more than one person, you create a separate Notification Rule for each of them.

Alternatively, when setting up a notification rule, you can give the name of a script to be driven rather than a person to be notified. This can be handy if you simply want to bypass the rest of Trouble Ticket's machinery for notification and do it yourself. It also provides a way to create trouble tickets directly from incident reports, without the manual step of using windows to create the ticket and attach the incident.[13]

At the beginning of this chapter, there is a list of several criteria the system should be able to use for routing problem notifications. Now we can see that Trouble Ticket provides four of

---

[13] In directory /usr/lpp/tt6000/samples/ntf_meth there's a sample script that will create a trouble ticket using this technique.

these: resource identity, resource type, owning organization, and seriousness of the problem. It doesn't handle the other two: time of occurrence and resource location.

Should you require either of the latter, you can employ a little trick that involves a slight misuse of the Affected Contact field in incident reports. This field is intended primarily to contain the name of the person who uses the broken resource or who is otherwise affected by its status. However, there is nothing in Trouble Ticket requiring you to use it this way and thus you could instead interpret Affected Contact as the person to be notified. Because Affected Contact is a field you can set when you create an incident report with *cmd_in*, you could have your NetView pre-filtering daemon make the routing decision in any way you choose and then fill in Affected Contact accordingly.

Notification Methods Once the recipients have been determined, Trouble Ticket carries out notification according to a Notification Method it selects. This may be one of the two pre-defined methods:

● *Notification*, which uses Trouble Ticket's Notifications window
● *Email*, which as you might guess uses e-mail

Alternatively, you can create your own custom methods to do more exotic things like sound an alarm to wake an operator from his afternoon nap.

Trouble Ticket selects the Notification Method according to the urgency indicated in the Notification Rule. This urgency may have one of the four values *Emergency*, *High Priority*, *Normal* and *Low Priority*. It selects the particular Notification Method to use by looking in the recipient's Contact record, where you will have defined a method for each of the four urgencies (this urgency is called 'priority' in the Contact record).

The result is that for each person you determine an appropriate way to notify them depending on how urgent the situation is. For example, you could use e-mail for *Normal* and *Low Priority*, a pager-based method for *High Priority* and door-to-door search for *Emergency*.

Let's now look at the two pre-defined Notification Methods, as well as custom methods.

Notifications window One option is to use Trouble Ticket's Notifications window, shown in Figure 7.15. For each notification, a one-line note will be added to a list in the window. The idea is that people will open this window and watch for new notifications. The window can also beep when new notifications arrive.

A useful feature of this window is that it allows you to require acknowledgement and will keep an eye on those who are tardy, prompting them with pop-up windows and even reporting them to others in the organization. Also, the window shows each notification's urgency and status, and the notifications may be sorted by urgency, status and event type. They can also be removed from the window.

For each notification, there will be a message header (the one-liner for each list item) and some message text (shown when more detail is requested). Both these bits of text are obtained from the Message Template.

The message header and text may embed environment variables which resolve to details about the particular situation. For example, the message for Incident Report Created can embed the following information from environment variables:

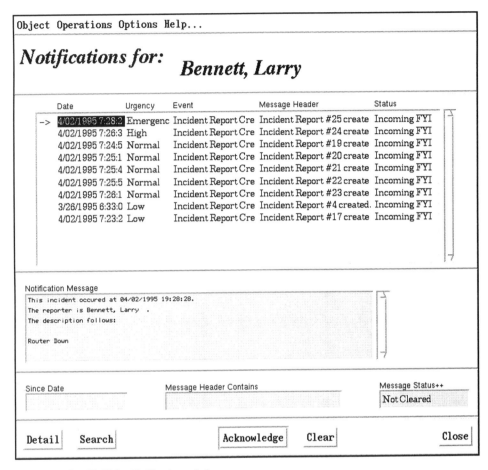

```
Object Operations Options Help...
```

Notifications for: *Bennett, Larry*

Date	Urgency	Event	Message Header	Status
-> 4/02/1995 7:26:2	Emergenc	Incident Report Cre	Incident Report #25 create	Incoming FYI
4/02/1995 7:26:3	High	Incident Report Cre	Incident Report #24 create	Incoming FYI
4/02/1995 7:24:5	Normal	Incident Report Cre	Incident Report #19 create	Incoming FYI
4/02/1995 7:25:1	Normal	Incident Report Cre	Incident Report #20 create	Incoming FYI
4/02/1995 7:25:4	Normal	Incident Report Cre	Incident Report #21 create	Incoming FYI
4/02/1995 7:25:5	Normal	Incident Report Cre	Incident Report #22 create	Incoming FYI
4/02/1995 7:26:1	Normal	Incident Report Cre	Incident Report #23 create	Incoming FYI
3/26/1995 6:33:0	Low	Incident Report Cre	Incident Report #4 created.	Incoming FYI
4/02/1995 7:23:2	Low	Incident Report Cre	Incident Report #17 create	Incoming FYI

Notification Message
```
This incident occured at 04/02/1995 19:28:28.
The reporter is Bennett, Larry  .
The description follows:

Router Down
```

Since Date	Message Header Contains	Message Status++
		Not Cleared

| Detail | Search | | Acknowledge | Clear | | Close |

Figure 7.15 Trouble Ticket Notifications window

- Incident impact
- Incident report number
- Problem description
- Incident reporter
- Affected contact
- Responsible organization

For example, in a Message Template you could place the following header:

```
Incident Report #$REF_ID$ created.
```

And then this text:

```
This incident occurred at $WHEN$.
The reporter is $NAME1$.
The description follows:

$DESC$
```

An example of the text produced by the latter is:

```
This incident occurred at 02/09/1995 22:50:10.
The reporter is Bennett, Larry.
The description follows:
The Ethernet wiring on the fourth floor is faulty.
```

E-mail Notifications can also be sent as e-mail. In the Contact records, you can specify people's e-mail addresses, and then when a notification event occurs, Trouble Ticket sends them a
note. Its content will be determined by the Message Templates. (The header determines the subject line and the text the body of the note.) This method is useful if you don't want to install
Trouble Ticket clients for everyone on the management staff. One disadvantage, though, is that
you don't have the capability for acknowledgement, prompting stragglers and reporting them.

Here's an example of a note generated by Trouble Ticket for Incident Report Created, based
on the example templates above:

```
To: root@erasmus.isc.uk.ibm.com
From: TT6000.Notification
Subject: Incident Report #240 created.

This incident occurred at 02/09/1995 22:50:10.
The reporter is Bennett, Larry.
The description follows:

The Ethernet wiring on the fourth floor is faulty.
```

Roll your own Alternatively, you can create you own custom Notification Method. To do this,
you provide Trouble Ticket with its name, a short description and the name of a shell script that
implements it. You can define this information in the Notification Methods window.

The shell script will have access to several environment variables giving information about
the notification event, including:

- Message Template text with variables expanded
- Message Template header with variables expanded
- User ID from the Contact record for this recipient
- Contact's work telephone number
- Contact's fax number
- Contact's voice mail number
- Contact's beeper number
- Contact's e-mail address

Your shell script can then do all sorts of exotic things, for example making phone calls, sending
faxes and dialling pagers.

Example The flows through Trouble Ticket are somewhat complicated, so let's consider an
example:

- A technician spills a cup of coffee into a bridge, which short-circuits, isolating several users from the network.
- One such user calls the help desk and an operator there opens an incident report. In the report, he enters the name of the bridge (BRIDGE13), an impact of 2 and the text description 'Bridge drowned'.
- This causes an Incident Report Created event, and Trouble Ticket searches for a Notification Rule to handle this event with a significance of 2.
- The Notification Rule it finds indicates that the Responsible Organization should be notified, and that the urgency of doing so is *Normal*. It also specifies a Message Template similar to the example given above.
- Trouble Ticket looks in the Resource record for BRIDGE13 and finds that the Responsible Organization is 'LAN Support'. It then looks in the Organization record for LAN Support and finds that the Contact is Fred Smith.
- Trouble Ticket next looks in Fred's Contact record to determine how to notify him. In this record, it finds that for an urgency of *Normal*, the Notification Method to use is *Email*. Fred's e-mail address is also obtained from this record.
- Trouble Ticket then constructs a note from the Message Template and sends it to Fred's e-mail address. The note will contain, among other things, the name of the bridge and the text 'Bridge drowned'.

7.3.9 Doing without Trouble Ticket

Trouble Ticket is a good approach for problem notification and routing, and also supports many other aspects of problem management. Still, you may not want to splash out for Trouble Ticket, in which case you can still do a reasonable if more limited amount of problem management with just NetView. In this section, we will look at what can be done.

Events NetView's Events window can serve as a basic problem notification system. You would have each operator log into NetView and watch their own copy of Events. Each trap that's not filtered will appear as a card or a line of text.

The filtering here will be performed by NetView's filters or rulesets. In general, you will want to use rulesets instead of filters.

There is no explicit support in Events for routing traps to particular operators. However, since each operator can use different rulesets, they can be used to build a routing mechanism. A routing scheme based on resource identify, resource type, problem seriousness or time of occurrence could work well since NetView rulesets can access this information from traps. Routing based on location would work if the resource addresses used a convention to indicate location. Creating the rulesets could be tedious, though. The same is true for routing by owning organization.

The actual presentation of traps in Events is good and there is provision for co-ordinating several operators who are working with the same set of traps. An operator can delete a trap so that it will be removed from all operators' Events windows. Also, operators can add notes to traps and these can be seen by all other operators. While these provisions are not as powerful as the tracking and co-ordination mechanisms in Trouble Ticket, they can be used as a way to monitor which operators are handling which problems, and which have been resolved.

Thus, Events can be useful where sophisticated routing, tracking and co-ordination are not required, e.g. with a small number of operators. Let's review some of its presentation capabilities as well as those of its close relative, the Event History application.

Trap presentation in Events One nice feature of Events is its ability to create multiple Events 'workspaces'. These come in two flavours, dynamic and static. You can move cards from the main Events workspace into static workspaces. The idea is that you can pull out one or more related traps and keep them together for convenience. This capability can be useful for holding all traps related to a particular problem while it is being resolved.

Workspaces created in this manner are called static because new traps are not added to them. This is in contrast to dynamic workspaces, which are updated. The Events window normally shown in the NetView GUI is an example of a dynamic workspace.

You can create additional dynamic workspaces, which are useful if you want to have different workspaces monitor different kinds of traps. For example, you might want to have one window that shows only critical traps, while another shows everything else. Or you might want to have one for critical router traps and another for critical server traps.

Each dynamic workspace can have its own criteria for determining which traps it displays. Example criteria you can use are:

- Event category, e.g. All, Topology, Status, Error
- Event severity, e.g. Cleared, Minor, Major, Critical
- Event source, e.g. agent, *netmon*-related, *tralertd*
- Filters
- Rulesets

Event History You also have the Event History application at your disposal. This allows you to look at older traps in NetView. Event History is extremely similar to Events. The main differences between the two are:

- Event History is not dynamically updated for new traps.
- Event History does not support rulesets.
- Both display historical traps when they initialize, but they do not necessarily display the same ones, i.e. Event History might go farther back in time than Events, depending on how you have things arranged.

Both Events and Event History get the initial set of traps they display from the files ovevent.log and ovevent.log.BAK.[14] The primary history file is ovevent.log, and NetView writes each new trap there. When ovevent.log exceeds its maximum allowable size, it is moved into ovevent.log.BAK (overwriting anything already there) and then cleared.

The point here is that ovevent.log and ovevent.log.BAK together hold a set of historical traps which both Events and Event History read when they initialize. Each however will read a potentially different number from these, depending on some customizable controls. These are explained in Implementation Tip 7.5.

---

[14] These reside in the /usr/OV/log directory.

Implementation Tip 7.5

The number of historical traps that Events and Event History display is controlled by two files in the /usr/OV/app-defaults directory.
   The file Nvevents has two settings that control the Events window:

- *nvevents.maxLoadEvents*   The maximum number of historical traps Events will display.
- *nvevents.maxNumEvents*   The overall maximum number of traps Events will display at any time. When this is exceeded, Events will roll the oldest ones out of the display.

The file Nvela contains one setting to control Event History:

- *nvela.maxLoadEvents*   The maximum number of traps Event History will display in its window. At start-up, it will load the most recent traps from ovevent.log and ovevent.log.BAK up to this maximum.
- By playing with these three settings, you can arrange things up so that Events shows only recent traps, while Event History shows these as well as older ones. By default, all three of the settings are set to 500, which means that initially Events and Event History will show the same thing, although after a time Events will show newer traps and will usually roll some of the older ones out of its window.

7.4 MANAGING AND TRACKING PROBLEMS

So far we have focused on the question of how to notify members of the management staff when problems occur. For some organizations this much will be enough. If your organization is relatively large, however, and several people and organizations are involved in fixing problems, you would probably benefit from having a software system assist in keeping track of all open problems, their statuses and who is responsible for fixing them. In addition, you would probably benefit from reporting tools to let you know how long it is taking to fix problems, how long particular vendors and departments take to complete their part of the job and which equipment is having the most problems.
   Trouble Ticket has been designed to work with NetView in the problem management process and as such is a likely candidate for the job. It has many pre-built functions to support problem management, while at the same time having hooks and customization features to let you adapt it to your own procedures. In this section, we will focus on how you can use Trouble Ticket to do the tracking, co-ordination and reporting aspects of problem management.

7.4.1 Trouble tickets

The basic currency of Trouble Ticket is the trouble ticket—all the other functions revolve around these. As we have seen, a trouble ticket represents a problem and can have several incident reports associated with it, each representing a symptom.

Trouble tickets can be created in several ways:

- People can create them using Trouble Ticket windows. They can attach related incident reports.
- As we saw in Section 7.3.8, Trouble Ticket can be configured to create tickets automatically for each new incident report.
- Programs can create tickets using *cmd_in*.
- People and programs can create tickets by sending e-mail messages.

Once created, a trouble ticket serves as the basis for the several tracking and managing facilities. The most basic of these is simply the existence of the ticket in the database. The ticket can be accessed and updated to track the status and progress of each problem. A trouble ticket contains information such as whether the problem is open or closed, the names of the people and organizations responsible for resolving it and textual details. As the problem's resolution progresses, this information can be updated and used to organize the people working on it.

You can also search the database and list tickets meeting various criteria. For example, you can list all high priority open tickets, all tickets for a given resource or all tickets that have been open long enough to require escalation.

This much gets you a good distance down the road to keeping things organized. There are also other useful facilities built around trouble tickets, including:

- Notification
- Escalation
- Action plans
- Service level agreements
- Reporting

Let's look at these facilities.

7.4.2 Notification

We have already looked at Notification Rules in the case of incident reports, but they can also be used to notify people of key moments in the life of a trouble ticket, for example its creation, the assignment of the ticket to an organization and changes in its trouble code, e.g. Open, Pending, Closed. These events can cause entries to appear in a person's Notifications window, generate e-mail messages and invoke scripts to perform custom notification. Thus, Notification Methods are useful for keeping people informed of each ticket's status and also for alerting them to actions they may need to take.

7.4.3 Escalation

Escalation is a process that notifies people when a trouble ticket has been open too long. There are 10 escalation levels defined and the idea is that you designate the amount of time trouble tickets will spend at each level before moving to the next. Each time a ticket moves to a new escalation level, a notification event occurs, and thus, by using Notification Rules, you can inform the appropriate people that the ticket may require special attention.

Some problems are of course more important than others and require faster escalation. For example, if a core router is down for more than an hour, you may want to let the head of the networking department know, while if the Token-Ring card in someone's PC is down, you may want to wait a couple of days before escalating.

To accommodate this, each 'trouble ticket' is given a priority (1–5) to represent its seriousness. You then define the length of time tickets of each priority will spend at each escalation level. Thus, for low-priority problems you might let them stay at each level for a day, while for high priority you might move them each hour. Also, for really critical problems you can give zero as the time they spend at low escalation levels so that they are immediately escalated to high levels.

The movement of a trouble ticket to each of the 10 different escalation levels causes a different notification event and therefore you can configure different notification recipients and methods for each. For example, you can have tickets escalated to level 1 cause a message to be sent to the help desk manager, level 2 cause him to be paged and level 3 send a note to his boss.

7.4.4 Action plans

An 'action plan' can be associated with a ticket, listing the actions that are to be carried out in resolving a problem. For each action, you give a description, the internal organization or vendor responsible for performing it, a scheduled start and stop time and other details.

The action plan can be modified, for example to update the status (started, delayed or completed) or to change the start and completion times. A log of comments on the action can also be maintained.

For example, if a bridge fails you may create an initial action plan in which you schedule a technician to perform remote diagnosis. If he determines that replacement of a card in the bridge is required, then you can update the plan with an action to order the card and another action for a technician to install it.

By maintaining the information in the action plan, you can keep up to date on the actions being taken to solve the problem. In addition, as we will see, the times recorded for the start and stop of each action can be used for reporting and analysing the response time of various organizations and vendors and, by the service level agreement facility, to monitor the progress of each action.

The creation and modification of each action can trigger a notification event. Thus, you can have Trouble Ticket notify the vendor or internal department that they have a new action, or notify a co-ordinator that an action has been completed.

7.4.5 Service level agreements

SLAs give you the capability to track the resolution times for entire problems, i.e. to track at the trouble ticket level, or to track the resolution times for each action within a ticket. Thus, you can measure the network control centre's service to its users (ticket-level tracking) and you can measure the performance of the vendors and internal departments that are called upon by the network control centre (action item tracking).

To use this facility, you first create some SLAs. In each, you specify a vendor or internal organization to which it applies. You also specify a restoration time, i.e. the amount of time a ticket or action must be completed within. You can also give a definition of working hours (e.g. Monday through Friday, 9–5), so that elapsed downtime is measured only during these hours. Once all this has been done, you can assign an SLA to each trouble ticket or action item that's created. Trouble Ticket then tracks the completion of the ticket or action, recording the total elapsed time and elapsed working hours. This information can then be used to generate reports which you can use to see how you and other organizations are performing against your SLAs.

7.4.6 Reports

Trouble Ticket provides you with several pre-built reporting tools, and you can also create your own. In the latter case, you can use the *rgen* utility provided with Trouble Ticket which extracts information from the database using an SQL subset query language. Alternatively, if you run Trouble Ticket with one of the relational database servers it supports, you can use that server's query tools.

The pre-built reporting tools provided with Trouble Ticket come in two sets—one intended for on-line use, i.e. displayed in a window, and another intended for printing or other off-line display.

The on-line reports are:

- **Open Ticket Analysis**   This provides a count of the numbers of open tickets within each priority level.
- **Unattached Incident Analysis**   This provides a count of the number of unattached incident reports, broken down by incident impact.
- **Action Assignment Summary**   This provides a list of the individuals and vendors who have been assigned actions and, for each, gives an estimate of the amount of assigned work and a count of assigned actions.
- **Restoration Summary**   This gives a list of all open trouble tickets with their estimated times of restoration (based on the schedules in the tickets' actions). It also shows the amount of time each ticket has been open, its priority and a summary of its actions.
- **Related Trouble Tickets**   This shows a list of all trouble tickets open for a selected resource.
- **Status History**   This shows a summary of the changes a ticket has gone through, including the status at each step, the reason code for the status change, the person who made the change and the time and date.

The off-line reports are:

- **Escalation Report**   This shows the escalation levels for all escalated trouble tickets.
- **Chronic Elements Report**   This shows the resources in the network that fail frequently. This is determined from the number of problems (trouble tickets) that have occurred for each resource, as compared to the threshold number and time period you define in the resource's class. For example, you could specify that resources of class Bridge will be considered chronic if they have more than three trouble tickets in 30 days.

- **Resource Performance Report** This shows the mean time to failure and mean time to repair for each model of equipment in your network.
- **Vendor Response Time Report** This shows the actions performed by each vendor and the time taken to complete them, as well as average completion time for all the vendor's actions.
- **Tickets Out to Vendors Report** This gives a report of all the tickets with actions currently assigned to vendors.

7.5 SUMMARY

Problem notification is the most basic and important aspect of network management and there are plenty of options for carrying it out in a NetView-based system. Ensuring that all important network components can send traps to NetView is the first step. To do this, it may be necessary to use proxy agents and tools that monitor message logs. Once the traps are in NetView, they should be filtered and correlated to eliminate redundant information. In medium and large networks, it is also a good idea to employ intermediate managers, such as the Systems Monitor MLM, to filter close to agents and thus reduce traps' impact on the network.

The area where you have the most choice is how to present problem notifications to the management staff and how they are tracked and managed while the problems are being resolved. This depends mainly on your organization and the kind of computing infrastructure you already have in place. In all except the smallest installations it will make sense to have some sort of formal process for notification and tracking problems. This may be something simple, perhaps a paper list or a shared file maintained by those involved in problem management. As the NetView Events window becomes increasingly sophisticated, you may choose it as the means of notifying your staff and organizing outstanding problems. If you require a more comprehensive solution, you will likely choose a full-blown problem management system such as Trouble Ticket.

EIGHT

SEEING IT—GRAPHICAL NETWORK DISPLAY

In this chapter we'll look at how to get NetView to draw pictures of the network, giving an understanding of its topology and status, and providing a graphical context for issuing commands and invoking other applications. The goal is to make NetView's graphical depiction of the network as comprehensive as possible, so that all networking protocols, media and equipment types are included. In most networking environments, NetView or one of its applications will provide a ready-made solution. For other environments, we will investigate ways of building custom solutions.

8.1 REQUIREMENTS

A good network presentation system should:

- Present views of all significant resources in all relevant networking environments.

    Ideally, these resources could be logical as well physical, so that in addition to physical resources such as links, routers and workstations, the views could include sessions and other logical connections, protocol entities, e.g. the IP layer in a workstation, and software resources, e.g. the buffer pool in a router.
- Depict resource attributes with symbols and associated windows.

    The most common example of this is using the colour of a symbol to represent whether the corresponding resource is up and running or flat on its back. It would also be nice to represent other resource attributes with colour, e.g. turn a bridge yellow if it is discarding frames. It is also important that the system provides windows to present detailed attributes of the resources, e.g. a window showing the current configuration parameters for a bridge.
- Provide well-organized and flexible views.

    By default, the system should create a set of views that is sensibly organized, and it should also allow these to be changed to reflect business organization, geography and other criteria relevant to the particular network.

- Allow easy and effective view navigation.

    It should be easy to move from one view to another based on relationships relevant to the management staff. For example, it should be possible to go quickly from a view showing the overall IP internetwork to one showing the details of a component network or to move from a detailed view of a router to one showing all the networks it serves.

- Allow functions and applications to be launched from views.

    Generally this would be done by selecting a resource in a view and then typing or selecting a function from a menu.

- Integrate information for different protocols, equipment and environments.

    It is natural to divide our set of views by protocol so that for example we have one group showing the network from IP's point of view and another from DECnet's. However, many resources will participate in multiple protocols. For these, it is important to be able to understand how the different protocols' views of the network are related and to move easily among them.

- Do all this automatically and dynamically.

    The management system should be able to collect all the information it requires without people helping it along, and as the network changes it should update this information accordingly.

- Make its data available to other applications.

    Clearly, such a system will have all sorts of interesting information about the network, and other applications should be able to use it too. For example, an inventory tracking system would need much of the same data. One way to share the data is to maintain it in a sensibly organized relational database.

Systems capable of performing all the above in a completely consistent and flexible way for all networking environments do not exist. Still, NetView when used with the right applications is capable of doing the majority of this for the most significant networking environments.

8.2 SYSTEM DESIGN

The overall design of the NetView-based graphical presentation system is shown in Figure 8.1 for IP networks and Figure 8.2 for others. In the IP case, NetView's *netmon* daemon collects network topology and status information, and places it into the Topology and Object Databases. The *ipMap* process then uses this as well as information it maintains in the Map Database to create a set of submaps depicting the network.

For other networking environments, the presentation system is analogous, but NetView applications, proxy agents or a combination of the two collect the topology and status information. This is put into the GTM and Object Databases and *xxMap* produces the submaps.

8.3 IMPLEMENTATION

We have already seen the details of how NetView presents IP topology and also reviewed several ready-built NetView applications for presenting topology of non-IP environments. Still, there are two areas of NetView's graphical presentation that remain for us to cover:

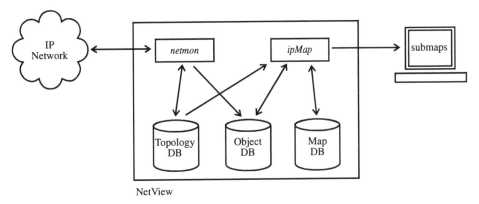

NetView

Figure 8.1 IP network presentation system

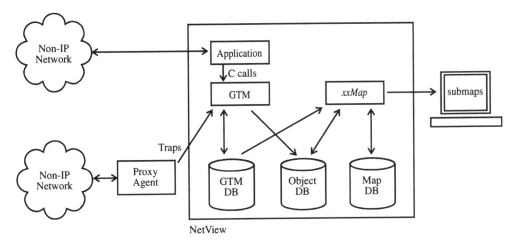

NetView

Figure 8.2 Non-IP network presentation system

- How maps, submaps and other aspect of presentation are handled in all protocols.
- The techniques for handling non-IP topology when there is not a ready-built solution.

In this chapter we will look at these two areas.

8.3.1 Maps and submaps

Two important concepts in the NetView GUI are maps and submaps. Submaps are easy to understand—they're simply the views or diagrams that NetView uses to depict a portion of a network. The concept of maps is more slippery, so let's look at it in a bit more detail.

We can think of a map as the overall environment in which a particular instance of the NetView GUI runs. Anyone using the GUI will have a particular map open, and this determines what they see and what they can do. Specifically, a NetView map consists of:

- A set of submaps
- A set of symbols used in those submaps
- Any customization that has been carried out on the submaps and symbols
- A set of applications available in the map and some configuration parameters for them
- Global parameters controlling behaviour of the map and its submaps, including the status propagation scheme to be used

In a given NetView installation, there will be one or more maps defined. By default there is one—the map named 'default'—but you can create more so that for example system programmers have more extensive maps than operators do.

Many NetView users may have a given map open at once. However, only one may have it in read-write access mode. Any others will have it read-only. If a user has read-write access, then he can change the various parameters of the map and can also customize the submaps within. Users with read-only access cannot make these changes, but they can still carry out all important management functions, including issuing commands and performing SNMP Sets to control the network.

Maps have permissions associated with them to control who is allowed read-write and read-only (or indeed any) access to them. These permissions, which are administered with the NetView *ovwperms* command, work very similarly to UNIX file permissions. In particular, they control the access based on the user's login ID and group ID.

Probably the most important use of maps is to present different views of the network to different NetView users. For example, you might have one map which provides a global view of the network for system programmers, while other maps give operators a view of only the portion of the network they are managing.

A related issue is controlling which management functions particular users can use. For example, you might have a function that resets a router and want only a few people to be able to use it. Controlling access to such management functions is not done with maps, but instead using the NetView security functions we will see in the next chapter.

8.3.2 Objects and symbols

NetView has two related but distinct entities it uses to represent network resources—'objects' and 'symbols':

- Objects represent the resources themselves. For example, objects represent systems, interfaces, links, networks and internetworks.
- Symbols represent the views of these resources in particular submaps. For example, a symbol could represent a host as shown in the submap for a segment.

Thus, there are potentially many symbols for any single resource, but there will be only one object. In most cases, each symbol will derive its status from the 'underlying' object. For example, all the symbols for a router will have their statuses derived from the single router object.

Objects can represent 'real' resources such as the interfaces on IP hosts and routers or they can be 'compound' and represent collections of real resources. Examples of compound objects are those for LAN segments, IP networks and internetworks. The objects representing IP hosts are also compound since a host is considered to be the collection of its network interfaces. Objects can also be used arbitrarily by applications since NetView's programming interfaces make them convenient places for long-term storage of many kinds of information.

Symbols can correspond to any kind of object, so that a symbol can represent a real resource such as an interface or a link, or a compound resource such as a network. There are 'icon symbols' which are used for interfaces, systems, networks and so on, and 'connection symbols' which represent, for example, links in networks.

A symbol can have two kinds of behaviour:

- It can 'explode' into a child submap when it is double-clicked. For example, an IP network symbol explodes into a child submap showing the network's components.
- It can execute a program when it is double-clicked. This provides an easy way of invoking applications from submaps.

Objects are maintained in the Object Database. Each has a set of attached fields in which information about it is stored. Some are attached by NetView, for example the object's 'selection name' which uniquely identifies it. Other attributes may be attached by applications. The fields attached to a particular object can be changed through the 'Field Registration Files', stored in directory /usr/OV/fields/C, or through the NetView *OVw* programming interface.

Some common fields on objects, in addition to selection name, are:

- IP Hostname
- IP Status
- *sysDescr* and other fields for the MIB-II System Group
- *isNode*
- *isRouter*
- *isWorkstation*

To see all the objects in your NetView and their fields, you can use the *ovobjprint* command.

Symbols are maintained in the Map Database and have attributes including:

- **Label** The label displayed in submaps.
- **Status** The status displayed, e.g. normal, marginal, critical.
- **Status Source** The source of status for the symbol. This may be 'object', in which case the status is the same as the underlying object's, 'compound', in which case the status is derived from the symbols in the child submap, or 'symbol', in which case the status is set by an application.
- **Symbol Variety** This may be either 'icon' which means a symbol appropriate for a node, e.g. router, workstation, or 'connection', which means one appropriate for a link between two nodes.
- **Symbol Type** This specifies the 'class' and 'subclass' of the symbol. The class determines the outline shape of the symbol and the subclass determines the bitmap that is placed inside. For example, there is a class called *Network* and all symbols of this class have a cir-

cular outline. One subclass within *Network* is *IP Network* which has a little network-like bitmap drawn inside.[1]

● **Plane location** This indicates whether the symbol is in the 'application plane' of a submap or the 'user plane'. All symbols exist in the application plane except in exceptional circumstances, e.g. when a user creates a symbol and no application can find a resource corresponding to it. This can happen, for example, if you define a workstation and place it into a submap before NetView has discovered it. Symbols that exist in the user plane have a shadow behind them which makes them seem to float above the submap.

● **Behaviour** This controls what happens when you double-click the symbol with the left mouse button. It can be either Explode, in which case the child submap is displayed if it exists, or it can be Execute, in which case a program you have defined for the symbol is executed.

You can see the symbols defined to NetView by dumping the Map Database with the *ovmap-dump* command.

8.3.3 Status

Each symbol shown in a submap is coloured according to its status, which may be one of the following:

● **Normal** Green for nodes and black for links.

● **Acknowledged** Dark green for nodes and black for links. This means the resource is in a status less desirable than normal, e.g. marginal or critical, but the user has issued the Acknowledge command against the resource to indicate that she is working on the problem. Thus, NetView does not poll or otherwise manage the object and its status is treated as Normal in status propagation.

● **Marginal** Yellow for both nodes and links. This may be used for a compound resource when some but not all of its resources are down. It may also be used to indicate a degradation in a non-compound resource, though *ipMap* does not use it this way. It is possible however, using Event Configuration, to have particular traps cause a resource's status to change to marginal. For example, you could configure a trap which indicates that a router's disk has crashed to cause its symbol to be marginal.

● **Critical** Red for both nodes and links. This means the resource is in very bad shape, probably down or unreachable.

● **Unknown** Light blue for nodes and black for links.

● **Unmanaged** Wheat. This means NetView is not attempting to monitor the status of the corresponding object, nor to perform discovery within it if it is compound.

● **User status 1** Pink for nodes and black for links. The meaning of this is user-defined. For example, you can instruct NetView to change resources to have this status upon receipt of specified traps. In status propagation, this is treated the same as normal.

---

[1] The definitions of the symbol types are in several files in the directory /usr/OV/symbols/C. These files point to families of bitmap and bitmap mask files in the directory /usr/OV/bitmaps/C. NetView selects one particular bitmap and mask from the family based on the scale of the submap in which the symbol is being drawn.

- **User status 2**   Violet for nodes and black for links. This is like user status 1 except that it is treated as critical in status propagation.

ipMap determines the statuses of non-compound symbols, i.e. those representing interfaces, by PINGing and sets these to normal or critical depending on whether the interface responds. Other applications use whatever mechanism has been chosen. For example, *xxMap* determines symbol status from information stored in the GTM database.

For a compound symbol, status is derived from the statuses of the symbols in its immediate child submap. NetView provides a choice of three schemes for doing this. Note that only one such scheme may be in operation at any time within a map and this scheme applies to all protocols represented in that map.

The schemes are:

1. **Propagate most critical**   In this scheme, the symbol has the same status as the most critical symbol in its child submap.
2. **Default**   This is essentially a 'propagate most critical' scheme mitigated by some provision for normal statuses to balance critical ones. The most significant difference is that the compound symbol will not be critical if it contains some symbols with normal status. The (mind bending) details of this scheme are in the box.
3. **Propagate at threshold value**   The status of the compound symbol is determined from the percentage of symbols in the child submap that have an undesirable status. Specifically, it is based on the percentage that have a status of marginal, critical or user status 2. Two thresholds are defined:
    - The percentage beyond which the compound symbol will be marginal
    - The percentage beyond which it will be critical

Default Status Propagation Scheme

- The compound symbol is normal if all symbols in the child submap are normal, user status 1, acknowledged, unmanaged or unknown. In addition, at least one symbol must be normal, user status 1 or acknowledged.
- The compound symbol is critical if at least one symbol in the child submap is critical or user status 2 and no symbols are normal, user status 1 or acknowledged.
- The compound symbol is unknown if all symbols in the underlying submap are unknown or unmanaged.
- Otherwise it is marginal.

8.3.4 Submap layout and customization

There are several ways NetView can lay out the symbols in a submap—ring, bus, star, tree, point-to-point and row/column. These are shown in Figure 8.3. The layout is chosen when the submap is created by a user or application. For example, *ipMap* uses:

- Point-to-point for the Internetwork and Network Submaps

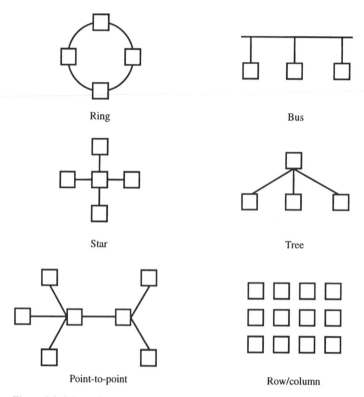

Figure 8.3 Submap layout types

- Ring or bus for the Segment Submap
- Row/column for the Node Submap

Once the layout has been established for a submap, it cannot be changed.

Still, there are several ways you can change NetView submaps to improve their appearance and usability. All of these require that you have the map in read-write mode:

- Move symbols around on a submap.[2] You can arrange the nodes the way you like and the connections follow along. This works only in submaps with point-to-point layout, e.g. the IP Internet submap, or those with no layout algorithm.
- Add a background graphic. You might, for example, add a map of your country and move symbols to show their geographic location. The graphic can be in either GIF (CompuServe Graphics Interchange Format) or XBM (X11 monochrome bitmap format). There are several background graphics provided with NetView, mainly for countries and for the states of America.
- Cut a group of resources from one submap and move them to another. This can be useful if a submap is unreadable because it simply has too many symbols. For example, the Internet

---

[2] To do this you place the cursor over a symbol, hold down the middle mouse button and the Control key, then drag the symbol.

Submap can become quite cluttered and you may need to move some of its resources to other submaps. There are restrictions on how and in which submaps you can do this. For example, you cannot cut a router symbol and place it inside the Node Submap for a host. What exactly is allowed depends on the application owning the symbols involved. In the case of *ipMap*, the rules are complicated, but, put simply, you can cut and paste only in Internet and Segment Submaps, which as fortune would have it are the two places you will likely wish to do so. Details are in Implementation Tip 8.1.

- Delete nodes or links from a submap. Doing this is a little tricky since the underlying object may be represented by symbols in other submaps. You must choose whether to delete the symbol just in this submap or in all submaps. In the latter case NetView will probably redis-cover the object at some point and it will reappear. In the former case things will work the way you want as long as you don't later delete more symbols for the object. A better option (as discussed in Implementation Tip 5.3 in Section 5.2.4) is to first Unmanage the resource and then Hide it in the relevant submaps. This reliably prevents rediscovery.
- Attach comments to network resources.[3] These are saved in the NetView Map Database and are not Set to the agent's MIB or in any other way communicated outside NetView. One advantage of this technique for maintaining notes such as contact and location is that it does not rely on the owner of the resource putting the information into its MIB.

Implementation Tip 8.1

If you have submaps with too many symbols in them, you can create new submaps and move some of the symbols into them. For IP submaps, there are two ways you can do this:

- You can subdivide the Internet Submap. Specifically, in the Internet submap you would first create a new Location or Internet symbol. You would then cut a group of symbols from the Internet Submap and paste them into the child submap of the symbol you cre-ated.
- Similarly, you can divide a Segment Submap. You would first create another segment symbol in the parent Network Submap. You would then cut symbols from the old Seg-ment Submap and paste them into the new one.

In both cases, you should use cut and not copy to ensure this works properly. All of the rele-vant operations are accessed from 'Edit' on the main menu bar or the context menu.

8.3.5 Techniques for non-IP presentation

Let's now look at how NetView can present non-IP network topology. The desired result is to have a set of submaps representing the networking environment in question, and it is generally held that these should look and behave consistently with the NetView IP submaps. There are three methods for doing this:

---

[3] To attach comments, select 'Modify/Describe ... Object' from the context menu for the relevant resource and then fill in the comment field of the window.

- Take advantage of NetView's General Topology Manager. In this case, a program provides GTM with topology, status and general layout information, and then the NetView *xxMap* application takes care of actually building the submaps.
- Use the *OVw* programming interface. Here the program explicitly creates the submaps and symbols, updates them as the network changes, and performs all the other details of presentation.
- Create the graphics without NetView's help, instead using X Windows and other GUI frameworks, with all the hassle that implies.

There are advantages to all these approaches. GTM—although somewhat tricky to get your mind around in the beginning—is the easiest since here the program is simply declaring facts about the environment and leaving *xxMap* to do the dirty work. In addition, GTM has the correlation mechanism we will cover below that allows users to see the relationships between multiple protocols and to navigate from one to another easily. Also, GTM has the advantage of ensuring a certain level of consistency with other applications since the details of presentation and navigation are controlled by *xxMap*.

Many applications, however, use the *OVw* interface. The same interface is supported under Hewlett-Packard's OpenView and thus programs using it can be more easily ported between NetView and OpenView. Also, the GTM approach is much like using a high-level programming language rather than assembler. GTM saves a lot of programming effort, but you may be able to produce faster code if you use the *OVw* interface.

Implementing a topology application without any help from NetView, using X Windows or another GUI framework instead, would make sense only where applications require portability beyond NetView and OpenView.

In general, the approaches other than GTM are suitable only for application vendors and perhaps a few very large and sophisticated organizations wishing to create custom network management applications. On the other hand, GTM is easy enough to use that many organizations can take advantage of it and I'll therefore cover it here.

8.3.6 Topology agent

Your task, should you decide to use the GTM approach, is to build a 'topology agent' that will supply GTM with topology and status information, either by sending it special traps or by making calls to the GTM programming interface.

The topology agent will carry out the following major tasks:

- Collect topology information for the non-IP network. This will usually be the hardest part of the job, though the difficulty will vary considerably, depending on what sort of management system is available for the non-IP network. Ideally, there will already be a management system there which understands the complete topology and which provides convenient programming interfaces for accessing it. If not, you will have to invent a scheme to collect the information.
- Translate the topology information, and send it to GTM using either traps or C calls. This part is relatively easy once you understand the GTM data model and interfaces.

- Monitor the non-IP network for changes, and communicate these to GTM.

There are several ways you might want to structure the agent.

- Implement it all locally on NetView's system. This is the most straightforward if you can get away with it. It will generally require that there is a protocol stack on NetView's system supporting communication with the non-IP network. In this approach, the agent could use either C calls or traps to send information to GTM, though in most cases C calls would be the best approach.
- Implement it remotely. This approach would be suitable if there is no way to communicate directly with the non-IP network from NetView's system, e.g. there is no protocol stack. Here the topology agent would serve as a gateway or proxy agent, as shown in Figure 8.4. The agent would communicate with the non-IP network using its protocol, translate the topology and status information and then send it to NetView across the IP network. Here you would almost always use traps since although the C calls do work remotely, e.g. make the call on one system to communicate with GTM on another, they must be performed on a system that supports NetView, which presumably your gateway wouldn't.
- Split the function, with some running locally and some remotely on a gateway, as shown in Figure 8.5. This is similar to the previous approach except that rather than sending GTM traps to NetView, the gateway would communicate with a NetView application. Thus, it would send the topology and status information using a protocol that runs over IP, e.g. TCP or UDP. The NetView application would then pass this on to GTM using C calls or traps.

    There are several reasons to use this split approach. You might want to have as much function as possible in the NetView system, because you have more horsepower available there or because the programming environment is more congenial. Also, by running in the NetView system, the application will have access to other data stored there and could even interact with other management applications. In addition, if you have several instances of your gateway, each for a different network, you might want to have them all interact with GTM through a central point. This could make debugging and maintenance easier, and the application might even perform some integration of the information sent by different gate-

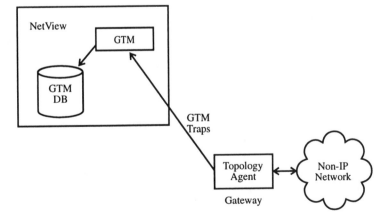

Figure 8.4 Gateway for non-IP topology

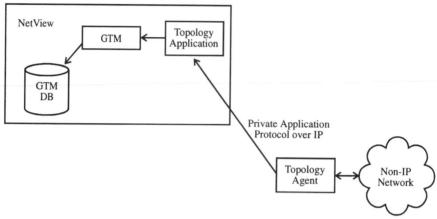

Figure 8.5 Split gateway for non-IP topology

ways. (This is done for example by LNM for AIX, when using multiple gateways to monitor several possibly overlapping Token-Rings.)

Any part of your topology agent that runs on NetView should be packaged as a NetView daemon, and be defined with a Local Registration File so that it may be started, stopped and monitored by NetView.[4] You could also take advantage of the *noniptopod* daemon's capability to start your application automatically when your gateway has been discovered. This is explained in Implementation Tip 8.2.

Implementation Tip 8.2

The *noniptopod* daemon provides a scheme for starting any programs that may be needed to support a topology agent's interaction with GTM. Such a program would be needed, for example, in a split topology agent.

The idea of the scheme is that the remote topology agent must have in it some special MIB objects that no other systems have. *noniptopod* checks for these objects and if it finds them will start the required program. This program could be local to NetView or even remote.

noniptopod works as follows:

- Each time a new SNMP agent is discovered, *netmon* generates a Node Discovered trap.
- *noniptopod* monitors these traps and each time one occurs it polls the agent's MIB for one or more special MIB objects. You must have defined these objects to NetView in a Local Registration File (LRF) in the directory /usr/OV/lrf.
- If *noniptopod* gets a successful response to the poll, then it executes a command you will have defined. This command would start the required program. It could use *rexec* to start a program running on a remote system.

---

[4] Using LRFs for this purpose is discussed in Appendix II.

8.3.7 *xxMap* and protocol switching

Once the agent has provided GTM with topology and status information for your non-IP protocol, *xxMap* will create submaps for it. As shown in Figure 8.6, the submaps *xxMap* will create
are:

- A symbol in the Root Submap representing the non-IP protocol.
- Below this symbol will be the root submap for your protocol. In most cases, this will contain symbols representing compound objects in your topology, e.g. subnetworks.
- Below your root submap, there will be other submaps, organized in a hierarchy, representing progressively more detailed views of your topology.
- At some level, you will reach submaps containing 'box symbols'. These represent systems
  such as workstations, routers, bridges and switches. These box symbols will in turn explode
  into 'box graphs' showing their interfaces. ('Box graph' is a term from the GTM world
  which for our purposes means the same thing as 'Node Submap'.)

It is at the box level that your users will be able to take advantage of NetView's 'protocol correlation' and 'protocol switching'.

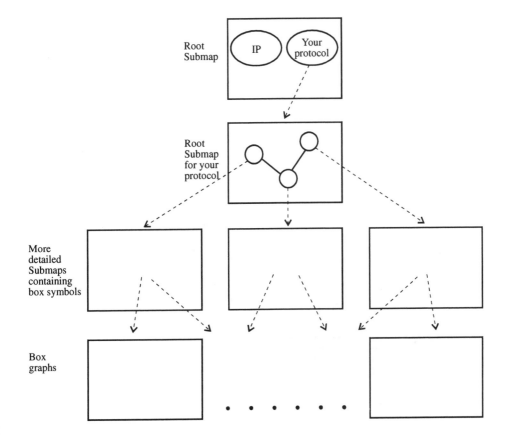

Figure 8.6 *xxMap* submap structure

When there are multiple protocols running in a box, the submaps for each of the protocols will include a different symbol for it. For example, if you have a workstation running both IP and IPX, the box would be shown in the submaps for both of these protocols. Without a correlation scheme, this single box would be treated by NetView as two separate entities. For example, NetView would maintain two objects for the box in its Object Database and there would be no easy way for the user to know that these two objects represent the same workstation.

NetView's protocol correlation and protocol switching address this problem. You can provide GTM with information describing how particular boxes participate in multiple protocols. This information is formulated as 'Service Access Points' (SAPs) which we'll discuss below.

Once this has been done, NetView will merge the multiple objects for a box into a single object. It will also create a single Node Submap for the box, and include this in all the protocols' submap hierarchies.

For example, suppose you have a workstation with an Ethernet interface, and you run the IP and IPX protocols over the interface. As shown in Figure 8.7, the workstation will be treated as

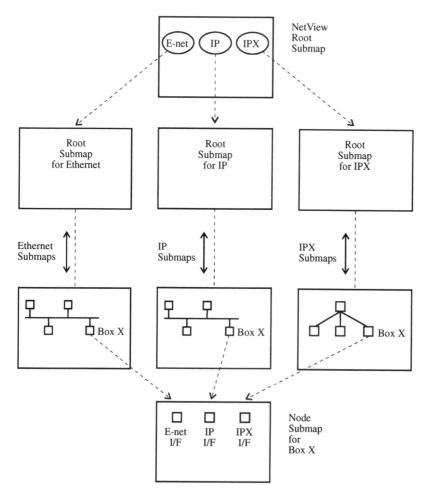

Figure 8.7 Box correlation

a single box and will have a single Node Submap. When you explode a symbol for the workstation—regardless of which protocol's submaps you are in—you will open the same Node Submap for the box.

This submap will have one symbol for each protocol running on the interface, and one for the interface itself. For example, if you have a box with an Ethernet interface which is used for IP and IPX traffic, you would see three symbols, one for the interface in IP, one for the interface in IPX and one for the interface itself.[5] The advantage is that the user can easily see that this single box participates in multiple protocols and can see what these protocols are.

In addition, the user can take advantage of the protocol switching function. In a Node Submap, this allows the user to move to the parent submaps of the box in any of its protocols. For example, you might have arrived at a box's Node Submap by navigating down through the IP submap hierarchy, and once there, want to see how the box fits into the IPX network. To do this, you would use protocol switching to move to the Node Submap's parent in the IPX protocol. You could then navigate within that hierarchy to understand the box's role in IPX.

8.3.8 Topology elements

Probably the hardest part of this business is understanding the topology model used by GTM. The next few sections review it, and if you need more information you can consult IBM (1995d, e).

Your application's traps or C calls indicate to GTM the existence of various network entities and the relationships between these. Because the IBM architects who designed the model are highly educated folk with a taste for the academic, they chose a mathematical sort of terminology for these basic topology elements:

- **Vertices** These represent the lowest-level entities in your topology. In most cases, these would be network interfaces on systems such as workstations and routers. A vertex could also represent the system itself, but in general these are best represented as collections of interfaces.
- **Arcs** These represent connections or other relationships between vertices or graphs. For example, these can represent communications links. They can also represent logical connections.
- **Graphs** These correspond to NetView submaps, and contain vertices, arcs and other elements. Graphs can also contain other graphs. Thus, you might have one graph to represent your entire topology, another for each network within, and still others to represent subnetworks within these.

  Boxes such as workstations and routers are also represented by graphs, since they contain vertices representing interfaces. These have a special name—'box graph'—whereas other graphs are often called 'graph graphs'.

  The symbols for graphs will be explodable so that each opens into a submap showing its contents. The graphs therefore define the submap hierarchy for your topology. The highest graph in the hierarchy is called the 'root graph'. The symbol placed in NetView's Root Submap represents this graph, and when you explode the symbol you will see a submap

---

[5] The details here depend on how the non-IP applications use GTM. It's also possible you would only see two symbols in this example—one for the Ethernet interface in each of the IP and IPX protocols, and no symbol for the interface itself. This would be the case if there were no application providing topology information for the Ethernet protocol.

with the contents of your root graph. From there, you can navigate down into the rest of your submaps.

- **Underlying arcs**   These are used to represent cases where the connections between vertices or graphs are actually made of several arcs. For example, in SNA a 'transmission group' is a logical connection composed of one or more links. Here an arc would represent the transmission group, while underlying arcs would represent the links.
- **Simple connections**   These are similar to arcs in that they represent connections between two vertices, but they represent the connection as seen from a particular endpoint. Thus, they can model situations where the status or other attributes of the connection are different on the two sides. For example, a simple connection can be used to model the case where a link may be down according to one system, but pending connection according to the other.
- **Underlying connections**   As with underlying arcs, these are used to model cases where a connection is actually made of several components.

In most cases, you can skip connections altogether and use arcs instead.

8.3.9 Tables representing topology elements

GTM's service is based on the idea of a 'Topology MIB'. This is a sort of inverted MIB, where the agent sends traps to the manager to update it. The interface used by topology agents to communicate with GTM is based on this MIB, and it is therefore important we understand it.

Think of the Topology MIB as the place where GTM stores its topology information. This is essentially the same thing we have been calling the GTM Database, but in the agent-GTM interface it is useful to think of it as a MIB.

The MIB is divided into several groups, each of which has one or more tables. The tables contain the topology elements. For example, the Vertex Table has one row for each vertex, in which its details are specified.

In general, the tables have indices made of two parts:

- The name of the protocol in question
- The name of a particular element of that topology

For example, in an FDDI LAN, a vertex might represent the interface card in a workstation. FDDI is protocol 15 in the MIB and, if the vertex has the name 'WorkStation7', then its entry in the Vertex Table would have the index 15.WorkStation7. This is not a legal MIB index, but then this is not a conventional MIB.

Throughout GTM, you will see this principle of identifying resources by a combination of protocol and element name. In some cases, additional indices are used. Arcs for example have five indices, four used to identify the two endpoint vertices or graphs and a fifth to provide unique identification when there are multiple arcs between the endpoints.

The groups and tables in the Topology MIB are listed in the box. Appendix III has an example of how they are defined in the MIB. A very useful reference is the Topology MIB itself.[6]

---

[6] The Topology MIB definition is contained in the file /usr/OV/snmp_mibs/drafts/ibm-nv6ktopo.mib on NetView systems. It is also included in the softcopy materials available on the Internet at www.mcgraw-hill.co.uk (check on editorial information for professional computing).

Topology MIB groups and tables

Most of the tables contain topology elements (e.g. each row of the Vertex Table describes a vertex). Other tables describe relationships or hold supplemental information, as noted in each case:

Vertex group

- Vertex Table
- Service Access Point Table—contains SAPs for protocol correlation.

Simple Connection Group

- Simple Connection Table

Underlying Connection Table

Arc group

- Arc Table
- Underlying Arc Table

Graph group

- Graph Table.
- Member Arcs Table—each entry indicates that a particular arc belongs to a particular graph.
- Graph-attached Arcs Table—each entry indicates that a particular arc has only one endpoint in a particular graph.
- Members Table—each entry indicates that a particular vertex or graph is a member of a particular graph.
- Additional Members Information Table—this table is used for graphs that do not have a layout algorithm and instead require fixed coordinates for their members. Each entry in this table gives the coordinates for a particular component.
- Additional Graphs Information Table—each entry provides additional information about a graph such as a label for it or its central vertex as required for certain layout algorithms, e.g. star.

8.3.10 Status model

Status information is stored in the MIB tables along with the topology. It will be stored only for vertices, arcs and simple connections. The status of each graph will be derived from these, using whatever status propagation scheme is in effect for the currently open map.

Rather than represent status in a single variable, GTM uses a model based on OSI network management standards, in which the status of any resource is represented by four variables:

- **Operational State**   This is either *enabled* or *disabled*. *Enabled* covers all the possibilities from fully functional to barely running at all. *Disabled* means absolutely dead.
- **Availability Status**   This modifies the Operational State, and can have values such as *inTest*, *powerOff* and *degraded*. It is 'set-valued' which means it can have several such values, or can be 'empty'.
- **Unknown Status**   This is *true* if the state of the resource is unknown and *false* otherwise.
- **Alarm Status**   This is set-valued and gives information about any recent alarms that have been received for the resource. This would normally be empty, but could also have a value such as *critical*, meaning that a critical alarm has been received for the resource, *major* for a major alarm and so forth.

These four variables are mapped into a NetView status according to the table shown in Figure 8.8.

```
Operational  Unknown  Availability  Alarm          NetView
State        Status   Status        Status         Status
----------------------------------------------------------------
enabled      false    empty         any            normal
any          false    offDuty       any            normal
disabled     false    offLine       any            marginal
enabled      false    degraded      any but crit   marginal
enabled      false    inTest        any            marginal
any          true     any           critical       critical
disabled     false    dependency    any            critical
enabled      false    degraded      critical       critical
disabled     false    failed        any            critical
disabled     false    powerOff      any            critical
disabled     false    notinstalled  any            unmanaged
any          true     any           any but crit   unknown
             -- any other combination --           unknown
----------------------------------------------------------------
```

Figure 8.8 GTM status mapping

8.3.11 Sending topology traps to *gtmd*

Let's now consider how a topology agent provides all this information to GTM using the trap-based approach. The concepts here are the same as those in the GTM programming interface, which we will review below.

The topology agent first sends NetView several traps to create the rows of the MIB tables. These describe the initial topology, status and submap structure to GTM. Later, the topology agent will send more traps to modify this initial configuration, especially to update status.

There are traps defined in the Topology MIB to create, change and delete rows in all the tables we have seen.[7] The traps are described in IBM (1995d). Some examples are:

- *newVertex*   Creates a vertex, adding a row to the Vertex Table
- *newGraph*   Creates a graph
- *vertexStateChange*   Indicates a status change in a vertex
- *deletedArc*   Deletes an arc, removing its row in the Arc Table

---

[7] The traps are enterprise-specific, with enterprise ID of 1.3.6.1.4.1.2 and a specific code from a range beginning with 70000000 (hexadecimal).

A typical topology agent sends traps to GTM as follows:

1. It first sends a *newGraph* trap to define the root graph for the topology.
2. It then sends additional *newGraph* traps to define graphs within the root graph. These subsidiary graphs may represent parts of a network or they may be box graphs representing workstations, routers and other systems.
3. For each of these, the agent also sends a *newMemberTrap* to indicate that the graph is part of the root graph.
4. Next, arcs are created to connect the graphs. For each, the agent sends a *newArc* trap and then a *newMemberArc* trap to indicate that the arc is a member of the graph. The agent should send the arc traps after the graphs they connect have been defined.
5. Additional layers of graphs are created in the same way until eventually the box graphs depicting actual systems are defined. Within these, vertices would typically be defined for the network interfaces. To create a vertex, the agent sends a *newVertex* trap and then a *newMemberTrap* to define the vertex as being part of the appropriate box graph.
6. Finally Service Access Points might be defined to correlate multiple protocols.

Once all this has been done, the GTM database will contain the initial topology for the protocol. Later, the agent will send traps to reflect changes:

● The most common thing to change will be status. For this, the agent sends the *vertexStateChange* and *arcStateChange* traps.
● Resources may disappear from the protocol or may be added. For deletions, there is a set of traps including *deletedGraph*, *deletedArc* and *deletedVertex*. The agent must delete both the entity and any member table entry for it. For additions, the agent uses the same process it did to define the initial topology.

Each topology trap includes a set of variable bindings that contain the actual topology information. This information is of two kinds:

1. Unique identification of the row of the table that is to be created, modified or deleted.
2. The values to which the row's variables are to be set.

For example, consider Figure 8.9, which shows the definition of the *newGraph* trap. The variables *graphProtocol* and *graphName* identify the particular graph and will be the indices for its row in the Graph Table. Other variables then specify the values to be used in the row. The variables of interest are:

● *graphType*   Graph or box
● *layoutAlgorithm*   Star, bus, point-to-point, row-column, etc.
● *userdefinedLayout*   Name of a user-defined layout algorithm
● *graphLocation*   Location the graph represents
● *backgroundMap*   Name of a background map for the graph
● *graphIcon*   Name of the symbol to be used for the graph (this is discussed below)
● *isRoot*   Whether this is a root graph
● *graphLabel*   A label for the graph

```
newGraph TRAP-TYPE
     ENTERPRISE ibm
     VARIABLES { graphType,
                 graphProtocol,
                 graphName,
                 layoutAlgorithm,
                 userdefinedLayout,
                 graphLocation,
                 backgroundMap,
                 graphManagementExtension,
                 graphManagementAddr,
                 graphIcon,
                 isRoot,
                 graphLabel
               }
     DESCRIPTION
      'This trap is issued each time an agent becomes
      aware of a new graph. It is issued each time
      a new graph is added to the graph table.'
      ::= '70000015'h
```

Figure 8.9 Definition of *newGraph* trap

Each of these variables bindings must be given an object ID. These are derived from the naming tree shown in Figure 8.10.

For an example of a topology trap, Consider Figure 8.11. This shows the contents of a trap that would create a root graph named 'Hoosier_Network'. This trap by itself will create an empty graph. Since it is a root graph, a symbol for it will be added to the NetView Root Submap.

One thing to bear in mind is that traps may get lost in the network, or indeed within NetView's system. In the latter case, this can occur if the application sends them too quickly.[8] It is therefore a good idea to put a little delay into your program. Another thing to consider is sending each trap more than once, since duplicates don't do any harm.

8.3.12 Service Access Points

As we've seen, *xxMap* provides protocol switching and correlation when there are multiple protocols running on the same system. GTM supports this process through Service Access Points (SAPs). A SAP is an abstraction that represents the relationship between an entity such as an interface and the higher-layer protocols using it. In the example shown in Figure 8.7, the workstation would have two SAPs, one to indicate that IPX is running on the Ethernet adapter and the other that IP is.[9]

The topology agent would send two *newSapTraps* to create these SAPs. These SAPs would cause:

- The three vertices (Ethernet interface, IPX logical interface and IP logical interface) to be merged into a single object.
- The three box graphs representing the workstation in the three protocols to be merged into a single box graph.

---

[8] I have never noticed traps getting lost, but then normally the AIX system I use is not under stress.

[9] To be picky, SAPs are not required for the IP protocol since NetView includes these in protocol correlation automatically. Here I'm using the example of IP to be consistent with earlier examples, and to keep things simple.

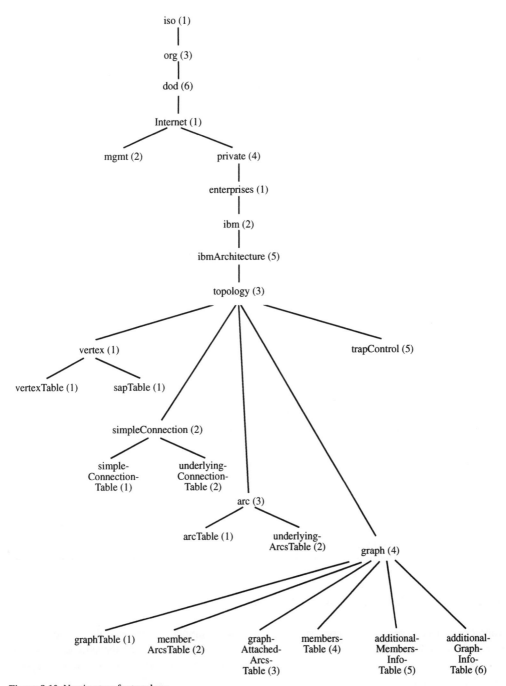

Figure 8.10 Naming tree for topology

```
enterprise ID = 1.3.6.1.4.1.2 (IBM's enterprise)
generic code   = 6
specific code  = 70000015 (newGraph)

Variable bindings:
 graphType         = 3 (graph graph)
 graphProtocol     = .1.3.6.1.2.1.2.2.1.3.6 (Ethernet)
 graphName         = Hoosier_Network (selection name)
 layoutAlgorithm   = 4 (bus)
 userdefinedLayout = not_used (placeholder value)
 graphLocation     = Muncie (a famous town in Indiana)
 backgroundMap     = /usr/OV/backgrounds/indiana.gif
 graphIcon         = .1.3.6.1.2.1.2.2.1.3.11.11 (location)
 isRoot            = 1 (true)
 graphLabel        = Hoosier_Network (label in submap)
```

Figure 8.11 Contents of example GTM trap

When the NetView user opens the submap for the workstation, there will be three symbols shown, and protocol switching can be used as we saw earlier for this example.

Implementation Tip 8. 3 gives some details of how to create the *newSapTrap*.

Implementation Tip 8.3

The variable bindings in the *newSapTrap* should be as follows:

- *sapVertexProtocol*   Set this to the protocol of the higher-layer vertex (IPX or IP in our example).
- *sapVertexName*   Set this to the name of the higher-layer vertex (the vertex representing the interface in the IP or IPX protocol).
- *sapIndexId*   Set this to anything that will make the combination of protocol, name and this index unique among all SAPs you create. In most cases, 1 will do quite nicely.
- *sapServiceType*   Set this to 1 to indicate *using*. The other possibility is providing, but *using* will suffice in most cases.
- *sapProtocol*   Set this to the protocol of the lower-layer entity (Ethernet in our example).
- *sapAddress*   Set this to the name of the lower-layer entity (the name of the vertex representing the Ethernet interface).

8.3.13 Defining symbols for non-IP topology

Topology traps can specify the icons *xxMap* should use in submaps. For example, the *newGraph* trap includes the variable *graphIcon* which is set to an object ID indicating the symbol to use for the graph. These object IDs select symbols according to the file oid_to_sym.[10] For example, oid_to_sym contains the following line:

```
1.3.6.1.2.1.2.2.1.3.1.1:Cards:Generic
```

---

[10] This file is in the directory /usr/OV/conf/C.

Here the given object ID selects an icon of class *Cards* and subclass *Generic*. As we saw in Section 8.3.2, the icon will have the outline shape for *Cards* and the graphic for *Generic* inside.

8.3.14 Using the GTM programming interface

The alternative to sending topology traps is to use the GTM programming interface. Here the Topology MIB and the other concepts we have reviewed still apply, but instead of sending traps, the topology agent uses C calls to manipulate the tables in the MIB. The benefits of this approach are:

● They let you use a single call to perform a particular topology update. For example, you can create a vertex in a graph with a single call, instead of sending a trap to create the vertex and another to make it a member of the graph.
● They automatically set many of the table variables for you.
● They shield you from the long object IDs required for the variable bindings.
● They simplify the way you set certain variables. For example, instead of the four OSI status variables, you use a single variable which has easy-to-understand values.

There are quite a few of these routines, and with them you have the same capabilities you do with topology traps. The routines are documented in IBM (1995e).[11]

8.3.15 Example implementations

Appendix IV has an example shell script that generates submaps using the trap-based approach and Implementation Tip 8.4 discusses some sources of debugging information. Appendix V has a program that uses the GTM programming interface to create the same submaps.

Implementation Tip 8.4

In developing a topology agent that uses the trap-based approach, there are three files in the /usr/OV/log directory that can be useful. Two such files are gtmd.log and gtmd.trace. *gtmd* writes information about significant events to these and you can consult them when problems occur. Probably more useful will be trapd.log. Here you will find special entries for GTM traps when they are successful. For example:

```
7  Mon Mar 27 19:51:11 1995 bennett    P Graph Added
7  Mon Mar 27 19:51:18 1995 bennett    P Member Added
7  Mon Mar 27 19:51:19 1995 bennett    P Vertex Added
7  Mon Mar 27 19:51:21 1995 bennett    P Member Added
7  Mon Mar 27 19:51:23 1995 bennett    P SAP Added
```

(These have been edited slightly to fit on the page.)

---

[11] They are the series of calls beginning with *nvot*.

8.4 SUMMARY

It's impossible to manage a network effectively if you don't understand its structure and the statuses of its resources. Graphical presentation systems are the best tools anybody has yet devised for providing this information. NetView does a good job of presenting views for IP networks. For other environments, you will want to find ready-built applications and proxy agents that provide graphics. Where these are not available, you'll need to decide how important the particular environment is, and if graphics are needed, you can use NetView's GTM to build them yourself.

NINE

RUNNING IT—NETWORK OPERATIONS

In this chapter we will look at how to perform operations from NetView for the various routers, bridges, workstations and other equipment in the network. We will look at three approaches to doing this:

- The 'point and shoot' style in which commands are issued by pointing at a resource in a submap and selecting a command from a menu.
- Issuing commands directly from the UNIX shell. While the point-and-shoot style is good for the uninitiated or for the occasional command, the shell is much better for complex or repetitive commands. Here we also have shell scripts and other tools for building more sophisticated functions.
- Automatic operations, in which operations are performed in response to traps or according to a schedule.

The odd thing about this business is that while we have been very SNMP-centric up to this point, that protocol will play a less prominent part in operations. Many existing SNMP implementations allow only monitoring and trap generation, for reasons we discussed earlier.

Still, it is certainly possible to perform operations using SNMP. The basic paradigm is that for each thing you want to control you create one or more MIB variables, and issue SNMP Sets to change them. For example, if you want to control the XYZ application on a particular host, you could have a MIB variable *xyz* which when set to 1 will cause the agent to start the application, and when 0 to stop it. You could then follow up with some SNMP Gets to ensure the application started successfully.

Although the number of SNMP agents providing full control through SNMP Sets is growing, there is still much equipment that cannot be controlled in this way. Thus, we will also need to rely on other mechanisms to carry out full operations from NetView. In IP environments, where facilities such as *telnet*, *rexec* and Systems Monitor are available, or better yet when we have a ready-built application, performing operations is quite straightforward. In other cases, operations may be awkward.

9.1 REQUIREMENTS

A good operations system will:

- Support operations through SNMP Sets and Gets.
- Allow us to send any command to any device in the network, execute it there and return the response to us.
- Allow us to incorporate operations by SNMP and remote commands into the graphical network presentation system to provide point-and-shoot operations.
- Allow us to perform operations using shell scripts, C programs and other tools so that we can build custom and automatic operations tools.
- Provide the infrastructure for performing operations in response to traps or according to a schedule.
- Provide a means to control which operational functions can be used by which operators and to ensure that unauthorized people cannot use any at all.
- Provide as many ready-built operations facilities as possible for relevant networking environments and equipment.

9.2 SYSTEM DESIGN

In Chapter 6, we reviewed the NetView applications for many networking environments and their operational capabilities. Here we will focus on general operations mechanisms.

The following are the NetView and UNIX mechanisms that provide the basic infrastructure for operations:

- *rexec*   The one-shot command facility available in most TCP/IP implementations for sending commands over IP networks to remote systems.
- *telnet*   The remote login facility for use across IP networks.
- **NetView's SNMP programming interface**   For sending SNMP Sets and Gets to perform operations. These can also be used to receive traps and react automatically to them.
- **NetView's *snmpget* and *snmpset* commands**   For SNMP-based operations from the shell or from shell scripts.
- **NetView's Event Configuration and ruleset facilities**   Which allow us to have commands run in response to traps received in NetView.
- **The Systems Monitor MLM**   This can be used as an intermediate manager for operations, automatically responding to events in its portion of the network.
- **The UNIX *cron* daemon**   This provides timer-based command execution and thus can be the basis for schedule-driven operations.

In addition, NetView includes facilities for integrating these tools into its user interface, and for preventing unauthorized use of them.

9.3 IMPLEMENTATION

9.3.1 Basic infrastructure

Let's first look at the heart of the matter, the infrastructure that sends the SNMP requests and remote commands, and returns their responses.

Using *rexec* This is a straightforward tool. With *rexec*, you simply provide a command and the name or address of an IP system on which it is to be run. The command is then transported to the remote system, executed and the results returned.[1]

rexec can be easily incorporated into shell scripts and pipes since it uses standard input and output. There is also a C call in UNIX for *rexec*, so incorporating it into programs is easy as well. Figure 9.1 shows a simple example of how to use the call.

rexec has a security scheme—it requires a password and user ID for the remote system. It is important to remember, however, that as with SNMP community names, the password flows in clear text and is therefore readily available to anyone with a LAN tracing tool.

```
#include <stdio.h>
#include <sys/errno.h>

int main(int argc, char **argv) {
    int rxsocket, port, *errnum, numread;
    char **hostptr, *host, *userid, *pw, *cmd, buf[200];

    port = 512;
    errnum = 0;

    host = 'bennett'; hostptr=&host;
    userid = 'root';
    pw = 'utah';
    cmd = 'ls';

    rxsocket = rexec(hostptr, port, userid, pw, cmd, errnum);
    if(rxsocket==-1) {
        printf('Error sending command\n');
        exit(-1);
    }

    while((numread = read(rxsocket,buf,200)) != 0) {
        buf[numread] = 0;
        printf('%s', buf);
    }

    close(rxsocket);
}
```

Figure 9.1 Invoking *rexec* from a C program

Using *telnet* If the device to be remotely operated supports *telnet* natively, then you can log into it from NetView's system and do whatever you like. Most network equipment designed to run in IP networks supports *telnet* and you can normally use it to do everything required for configuration and operation. Security is available in the form of user IDs and passwords, although again these flow in clear text.

---

[1] Specifically, the standard output and standard error output of the remote command are written to the same on the local system. Also, any standard input required by the remote command is read from the local system's standard input.

NetView provides a handy interface to *telnet*, in which you point at a system and select 'Administer ... Telnet' from the main menu bar, and you are then popped into a *telnet* session with the system.

The UNIX *telnet* facility does not use standard input and output and therefore is not suitable for use in shell scripts and programs. This is not a problem as long as the device to be operated also supports *rexec* and allows you to perform all required operations using commands (and not for example panels that *rexec* cannot interact with).

Using SNMP SNMP can be used for operations in several ways:

- The manager sets a variable in an agent's MIB which controls the state of something on its system, e.g. 1 starts an application, 2 stops it.
- The manager creates an instance of an object which causes a corresponding entity to be created or started on the agent's system. Similarly the manager deletes the object to destroy or stop the entity. For example, to start an application, the manager might create an instance of the 'application' object. (To be precise, it is not possible for the manager to delete an instance. Instead the instance must be set to a special value. For example, to delete a row of a table, the manager sets one of its variables to the value *invalid*. Whether the instances are actually removed is up to the agent.)
- The manager sets a MIB variable to a command string. The agent would then execute the command and place any results in another MIB variable which the manager would subsequently Get.

In many cases, you won't have to worry about how SNMP operations are carried out since an application will do it for you, e.g. the router manufacturer provides a NetView application to perform all the Sets to its routers. In other cases, you may have to be involved, either because the vendor doesn't provide the NetView application or because you have developed the agent yourself.

There are several options for performing Sets from NetView:

- **MIB Browser** This supports Sets (as well as Gets) and can be useful for experimenting or performing occasional operations. Usually, a better choice will be . . .
- **The NetView *snmpset* and *snmpget* commands** These can be executed from the shell and are an easy way to access agents' MIBs. You can also include them in shell scripts to build your own operations functions. Implementation Tip 9.1 gives examples of using the two commands.
- **Use the SNMP programming interface** This is the best approach if you're writing relatively complicated operations functions. An example can be found in Appendix VI.

9.3.2 Adding the user interface

If you are writing programs or shell scripts to perform remote operations or indeed any other management functions, then you will most likely want to integrate these into the NetView GUI. NetView provides several facilities for doing this:

Implementation Tip 9.1

The NetView *snmpget* and *snmpset* commands can be used to read and change agents' MIB variables. For example, the following would Get a variable from the agent 'joe':

```
snmpget joe .1.3.6.1.4.1.2.6.12.7.1.0
```

The next one would Set the same variable to 1:

```
snmpset joe .1.3.6.1.4.1.2.6.12.7.1.0 integer 1
```

In both cases the results are written to standard output.

- The most basic and probably most useful are application registration files (ARFs). These allow you to add your functions and applications to NetView's main and context menus, and to the NetView Tool Palette. Once this has been done, your users can select resources in submaps and invoke your functions against them.
- Also quite handy is a little tool called *xnmappmon* that lets you wrap the output of commands into scrollable windows under the NetView GUI.
- There is also a large set of C calls available, collectively known as the *OVw* programming interface. These provide the means to:
  - Manipulate maps, submaps and symbols
  - Access the Object Database
  - Dynamically change the NetView menu structures
  - Register to be notified of various events in the GUI

  The use of these routines is really only for those who are writing full-blown applications, e.g. a configuration and control application for a particular router, and as such are beyond the scope of this book. They are documented in IBM (1995d, e).

Now let's look at the use of ARFs and *xnmappmon*, which together will let you build applications which are integrated into the NetView GUI.

xnmappmon This is a very useful tool which you can use to display the output of a command in a window. The command would be one that writes to standard output. You could use this, for example, to make a function that displays a list of the processes running on the local system. To do this, you would pass the UNIX *ps* command to *xnmappmon* as follows:[2]

```
xnmappmon cmd ps -ef
```

If the output from the command is too large to fit into the window, then scroll bars appear.

If you want to get a bit fancier, *xnmappmon* also has options to give the window a title, put a heading over the data, sort the output and so forth. To perform remote operations, you can incorporate *rexec*. Putting these features together, you could make a shell script called *do_rexec* as follows:

```
xnmappmon -commandTitle "Remote process list for $1" \
          -headingLine 1 \
```

---

[2] The *-ef* flags cause a full listing of all except kernel processes.

```
-dataLine 2\
-sort -sortColumn1 10 -sortColumn2 13 \
-cmd rexec $1 ps -ef
```

If you issued 'do_rexec joe' to the shell, a window would pop up like the one shown in Figure 9.2. The window has a heading copied from the first output line of *ps*, and the data is sorted by process ID. Note that this example assumes a '.netrc' file has been created on NetView's system to supply user IDs and passwords to *rexec*.[3] If you prefer not to use .netrc files, it will be difficult to use this example as it is, because the prompting for user ID and password will not work correctly when *rexec* runs under *xnmappmon*. In this case, you could instead build a simple command based on the C call for *rexec*, which allows you to pass user ID and password to it directly.

From this you can see that *xnmappmon* is a quick and easy way to make handy operational functions. It is especially useful in conjunction with ARFs, our next topic.

```
File  View                                        Help

    USER    PID   PPID   C    STIME    TTY   TIME  CMD

    root     1      0    0  17:44:39    -    0:03  /etc/init
    root    1813    1    0  17:47:24    -    0:00  /etc/upri
    root    2606  13101  0  17:48:17  hft/0  0:00  ksh /usr/
    root    3056    1    0  17:45:38    -    0:02  /etc/sync
    root    3116   3874  0  17:45:47    -    0:00  /etc/sysl
    root    3527   9865  0  18:32:58  pts/2  0:00  vi figtod
    root    3826    1    0  17:45:38    -    0:00  /usr/lib/
    root    3874    1    0  17:45:43    -    0:00  /etc/srcm


Messages




            Close            Stop          Restart
```

Figure 9.2 *xnmappon* window

Application registration files ARFs are an important tool for customizing NetView. They let you extend NetView's menu structure to add your own custom functions and also to integrate other applications into NetView's GUI.

Figure 9.3 is an example of a relatively simple ARF. The overall effect of the example is to add, to the 'Tools' menu of the NetView menu bar, a new item called 'Remote host processes ...'. This is shown in Figure 9.4.

When 'Remote host processes ...' is selected, a sub-menu pops up with two selections, 'Unsorted' and 'Sorted by parent PID'. Selecting either of these would drive the script *do_rexec* and display the results in an *xnmappmon* window. To support this, we would have to modify *do_rexec* slightly to make sorting optional. This is shown in Figure 9.5.

---

[3] These are files that tools such as *rexec* and FTP use, and contain user IDs, passwords and other information they require.

```
Application "Process List From Remote Host"
{
    Version "1.1";
      Copyright
      {
         "Copyright Larry Bennett, 1994"
      }

      Description
      {
         "This application lets you select an IP host from a",
         "NetView submap and list the processes running on it."
      }

      MenuBar "Tools"
      {
         <80> "Remote host processes..."    f.menu "RemoteProc";
      }

      Menu "RemoteProc"
      {
         <90> "Unsorted"                f.action "RemoteProcNoSort";
         <85> "Sorted by parent PID"    f.action "RemoteProcSort";
      }

      Action "RemoteProcNoSort"
      {
         SelectionRule isNode && isIP;
         MinSelected 1;
         MaxSelected 1;
         Command "do_rexec nosort $OVwSelection1";
      }

      Action "RemoteProcSort"
      {
         SelectionRule isNode && isIP;
         MinSelected 1;
         MaxSelected 1;
         Command "do_rexec sort $OVwSelection1";
      }
}
```

Figure 9.3 Example Application Registration File

Let's see how the ARF arranges all this. At the beginning are some clauses that add information to NetView's help system:

- The string at the top following the keyword *Application* is used to add an entry into NetView's application index.[4] If the entry is selected from this index, then the *Version*, *Copyright* and *Description* clauses are used to fill in the fields of a little window that pops up. All this provides a very basic level of help to the user.
- The *Version* clause is also placed into NetView's list of application versions.[5]

Once these little details are out of the way, the real work of the ARF begins. The *MenuBar* clause indicates the particular menu on the main NetView menu bar to which this item will be attached. This can be an existing menu or a new one, in which case the new one will be created. The number in angle brackets is a precedence value which is used to determine the position of the menu on the bar (the bigger the more left).

---

[4] The application index is accessed from NetView's menu bar with 'Help ... Indexes ... Application'.

[5] The application versions are accessed from NetView's menu bar with 'Help ... On Version'.

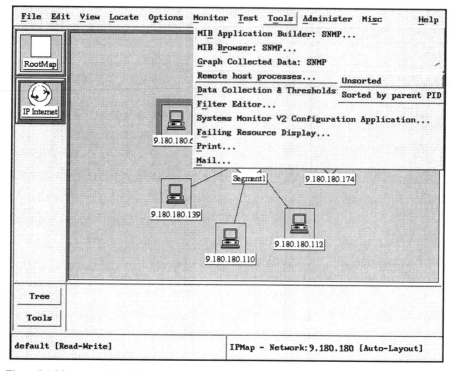

Figure 9.4 Menu created by ARF

```
if [ $1 = sort ] ; then
   xnmappmon  -commandTitle "Remote process list for $2" \
             -headingLine 1 \
             -dataLine 2\
             -sort -sortColumn1 16 -sortColumn2 20 \
             -cmd rexec $2 ps -ef

else
   xnmappmon  -commandTitle "Remote process list for $2" \
             -headingLine 1 \
             -dataLine 2\
             -cmd rexec $2 ps -ef
fi
```

Figure 9.5 Modified *do_rexec*

After this comes the text that appears in the menu, and then the action to take if the item is selected. *f.menu* means another menu will pop up, while *f.action* drives an action, e.g. a command.

In the example we also have a sub-menu, which is defined similarly. Then come the actions, both of which are invoked from the sub-menu. Each action has several clauses:

● **SelectionRule**   This determines the conditions under which this action will be available. When an action is not available, the corresponding menu item is 'greyed out'. The rule can reference object fields from the NetView Object Database to select only particular kinds of resources. In our example, they must be systems supporting IP.

- *MinSelected* and *MaxSelected*   These control how many symbols must be selected for the action to be available.
- **Command**   This is the command string that will be executed. As can be seen in the example, you can pass the names of items selected in submaps, e.g. IP hosts, using variables such as *OVwSelection1* for the first, *OVwSelection2* for the second and *OVwSelections* for all of them. The command string can also incorporate other useful variables including *OVwNumSelections* (the number of selected items) and *OVwMenuItem* (the menu item from which the action was selected).

ARFs become active once they have been placed into the /usr/OV/registration/C directory and the NetView GUI is re-started.

Other features of ARFs   Let's look at some of the other capabilities of ARFs.

Context menus   You can add items to the NetView context menu.[6] You can arrange this by putting an *ObjectMenu* clause in an ARF. For example, in our ARF, let's suppose we also want to have the 'Remote host processes ...' item in the object menu. To do this, we would add an *ObjectMenu* clause just after the *MenuBar* clause as follows:

```
ObjectMenu
{
<80> "Remote host processes..."    f.menu "RemoteProc";
}
```

Accelerators   You can also define 'accelerators' that make it possible for the user to select your menu item by typing a single character rather than using the mouse. When available, these characters are shown in the menu item and underlined to indicate they are accelerators. For example, suppose we changed the *Menu* clause in our original example to:

```
Menu "RemoteProc"
{
 <90> "Unsorted"             _U f.action "RemoteProcNoSort";
 <85> "Sorted by parent PID" _S f.action "RemoteProcSort";
}
```

Then the selection *Unsorted* could be made by typing U and *Sorted* by typing S.

Tool Palette   The NetView Tool Palette contains a set of icons, each of which invokes a corresponding tool when it is dragged into an empty area of the screen or into the Control Desk.[7] The icons may also be double-clicked to invoke their tools.

You can add your commands and applications to the Tool Palette by coding the *Toolbar* clause in your ARF. For example, the Print Tool shipped with NetView is placed into the window through this Toolbar clause:

---

[6] You will recall that this menu pops up when you move the cursor over a symbol in a submap and press the right mouse button. The action you select is executed against the symbol.

[7] You may remember that the Control Desk is the part of the NetView main window where various applications can run. Usually Events runs there, though others can run there too.

```
Tool "Print" {
    Icon Gif "/usr/OV/icons/gifs/print_tool.gif";
    DragBitmap "/usr/OV/icons/drag-bitmaps/print_tool.xbm";
    LabelColor "black";
    Action "printtool";
    SelectionMechanism double-click, drag-drop;
}
```

In addition to specifying the action for the tool, this clause also specifies its icon, the colour of the tool's label, and how it is selected.

Adding your own help NetView lets you incorporate your own information into its help system. There are several ways of doing this, and since a discussion of these would be quite long, I'll simply refer you to IBM (1995d), where they are excellently described.

9.3.3 Security

Network management systems have the power to disrupt networks severely. They can also provide a means of obtaining secret information and breaking security in other potentially harmful ways. It is therefore important that their use be restricted to those who have a legitimate need and that even authorized users can use only the particular functions required for their work.

As we've seen, it's possible to restrict which parts of the network users can see in their submaps. Also, using UNIX file permissions, you can protect NetView files that contain sensitive information like passwords, community names and the identities of agents and other network resources. Most significantly, you can control who is allowed to access the various NetView functions. Let's look at this last capability in more detail.

NetView can run in either an insecure or a secure mode. In secure mode, it requires all users to log in before they can use any of its functions. This is in addition to any login required by the system on which NetView is running. For example, on AIX the user must first log into AIX itself and then into NetView. Logging into NetView occurs in one of two ways—either the user issues the *nvauth* command to bring up the login window, or this window comes up automatically when the user tries to start the NetView GUI. The user's ID and the group to which it belongs determine which NetView functions the user may access. The login scheme, of course, also prevents unauthorized people from doing anything at all with NetView.

The security scheme works as follows:

● Each NetView function or application registers its 'resources'. These resources include its executables (i.e. commands), menu items and functions invoked from menus. They are registered in one or more Security Registration Files (SRFs).[8] An example SRF is shown in Figure 9.6.
● You then create groups to which users will belong. For each group, there are files describing access privileges for its members.[9] In particular, for each of the resources the applications register, the group will have read, write or execute access, a combination thereof or

---

[8] SRFs are placed in the directory /usr/OV/security/C/Domains/registration.

[9] These files are in several directories under /usr/OV/security/C/Domains.

```
DOMAIN_ID = xnmbrowser
DESCRIPTION = "Browser for SNMP MIB Data"
SEPARATORS = ->
VALID_PERMISSIONS = rx
ELEMENTS =
    "xnmbrowser" . FALSE executable
    "SNMP MIB Browser->Tools" . FALSE menustring
    "SNMP MIB Browser->Tools->MIB Browser" . FALSE menustring
    "SNMP MIB Browser->Tools->MIB Browser->SNMP..." . FALSE menustring
```

Figure 9.6 Security Registration File for NetView MIB browser

none at all. Execute is the most interesting privilege since it controls the ability to select a menu item, start a function from a menu or issue a command. The read privilege can be used to control whether users see particular menu items.[10]

- Finally you create user IDs. For these, you also create profiles which assign them to groups, thus determining the functions users can access. You can also define other information in the profiles, such as passwords, and the times and days of the week particular users may log into NetView. Passwords may be processed by NetView itself or may be handled by an external security product that conforms to the Generic Security Services API standard.

With this machinery, you can control the NetView functions and applications each user can access. If you extend NetView by writing your own programs, you can make use of the NetView programming interface for security. This allows your programs to check if a user has the authority to run them. The most interesting routine is *nvs_isClientAuthorized,* which a program calls to determine whether a user has a particular privilege for a resource.

An important aspect of NetView's security scheme is auditing. NetView keeps a record of logins, access to functions and changes to the security configuration. This can alert you to attempts to break security.

With NetView's security system, you can prevent the management system itself from being a security exposure. Given all the information NetView holds and the functions it can perform, this is an important first step. Still, passwords for *telnet* and FTP, community names, agent addresses and lots of other sensitive information will flow unencrypted through your network. Thus, you will still be exposed to knowledgeable people with a taste for hacking.

Today, there is not much you can do about this exposure. The solution lies in more sophisticated network management protocols. SNMPv2 has good security mechanisms and, if it is widely implemented, may be the solution. In the mean time, you can console yourself by remembering that the exposures in network management security also exist in many other areas of computer networking. So far, we have survived in spite of them.

9.3.4 Automatic operations

For simple or repetitive operational procedures, it is nice to make the computers do the work. In the world of NetView and SNMP, there are several types of actions the system can carry out automatically, including those performed:

---

[10] If a user has the read but not the execute privilege for a menu item, then it will be greyed out. If he does not have either privilege, the item will not appear in his menu at all.

- On a regular schedule
- In response to a trap received in NetView
- In response to a message written to a log somewhere in the network
- In response to data that has been collected from an SNMP agent's MIB

Let's look at how each of these types of automatic operations can be performed in a NetView-based management system.

Timer-driven actions Many operational procedures must be performed routinely, and if these are relatively simple, it is useful to have the management system carry them out according to a schedule. In UNIX systems, the *cron* daemon can execute commands, shell scripts and programs on a schedule, and can do so with considerable flexibility.

Since both NetView and the MLM run under UNIX, you can have the central and intermediate managers automatically carrying out routine operations on schedules. Implementation Tip 9.2 discusses the use of the *cron* daemon.

Trap-driven actions It's useful for the management system to run commands in response to traps it receives. Some traps indicate simple problems in the network and in many cases these can be resolved by issuing a few commands. Also, you may want the management system to notify you about certain traps in a special way, for example by sending you a voice message. Or you might want the management system to collect supplemental information automatically for certain traps, for example issuing SNMP Gets for relevant MIB variables and logging their values.

There are several options for automatically reacting to traps:

- NetView's Event Configuration facility.
- NetView rulesets. In most cases, this is a better approach than using Event Configuration.
- The NetView SNMP programming interface. This requires writing C but gives you the most flexibility in how you react to traps. The techniques for doing this are the same as those used by the sample pre-filtering daemon in Appendix II.
- The MLM. This has the advantage of being close to the source and thus improving performance and reliability. The MLM Filter Table provides the automatic reaction capability. As we saw under 'Filter Table' in Section 7.3.2, you can set up entries in this table to trigger commands when particular traps are received.

Let's consider the first two options in more detail.

Using NetView Event Configuration With NetView Event Configuration, you specify a particular trap type you want to react to by giving its enterprise ID, generic and specific code. You then indicate the name of a command that should be executed when the trap arrives, as well as the parameters for the command. These parameters may be variables provided by Event Configuration to let you access the contents of the trap, including the variable bindings. The more interesting of the variables you can pass to your command are listed in Figure 9.7.

Implementation Tip 9.2

The *cron* daemon runs commands according to schedules you specify in files. You activate these schedules using the *crontab* command.

Each line in the file defines a particular schedule for a command. The line includes five time/date fields in the following order:

- Minute
- Hour
- Day of the month
- Month
- Day of the week

The command then follows at the end of the line. For each time/date field, you can give an absolute value, a range (e.g. 15–20), a list (7,8,9) or a * to mean any valid value. The command will then be run at all times that match all fields.

The following line would cause the command *applstart* to run every morning at 7:45:

```
45 7 * * * applstart
```

The following line would cause *scanfiles* to run every hour at 10 past the hour in the remote host 'fred':

```
10 * * * * rexec fred scanfiles
```

This one would run *backups* each working day at 7:00 a.m. and 7:00 p.m.:

```
0 7,19 * * 1-5 backups
```

(Days of the week are given as numbers beginning with 0 as Sunday.)

The output from the commands is mailed to the user ID under which the *crontab* file was submitted. If you have many schedules and prefer not to be inundated with mail, you could instead redirect the output of the commands to a log file, for example:

```
45 7 * * * applstart >>usr/sys/logs/appllog
```

(The redirection operator '>>' appends the output to the file.)

For example, you might arrange to have NetView run a shell script when it receives traps with a particular enterprise ID, generic and specific code combination. The command specified in Event Configuration could be:

```
handletrap $e $1 $2
```

Here the script *handletrap* would be passed the enterprise ID and the values of the first two variables in the trap.

There are three ways you can arrange this kind of automatic trap reaction:

- Through the Event Configuration window. This approach is the easiest to learn, but can be rather cumbersome for handling a large number of traps.

```
$e    enterprise ID

$A    agent name or address

$G    generic code

$S    specific code

$T    time-stamp as 100ths of second since agent init

$#    number of variables in trap

$*    all variables bindings in trap, including the name, type and value

$n    value of the n-th variable in the trap

$-n   name and type of the n-th variable
```

Figure 9.7 Some command parameters available in Event Configuration

```
addtrap -n netView6000 \              (enterprise name)
        -l BigProblem \               (trap label)
        -i 1.3.6.1.4.1.2.6.3 \        (enterprise ID)
        -g 6 -s 12345 \               (generic, specific codes)
        -o A \                        (origin is agent)
        -c 'Error Events'\            (event category)
        -F 'Details: $A $E $G $S'  \  (trapd.log format)
        -t 2 \                        (status to assign)
        -S 3             \            (severity)
        -C /tmp/handleproblem \       (command to drive)
        -A '$A $E $G $S'              (command arguments:
                                        agent, enterprise,
                                        generic code, specific
                                        code)
```

Figure 9.8 Using *addtrap* for trap-driven command

- Using the *addtrap* command. This is the command line equivalent of the Event Configuration window and is useful if you want to configure many traps. In Figure 9.8, the command *handleproblem* will be driven when specific trap 12345 is received from enterprise 1.3.6.1.4.1.2.6.3.
- By directly editing the trapd.conf file.[11] The *addtrap* command and Event Configuration window just update this file anyway.

Using rulesets We have already seen how rulesets can be used for trap filtering and correlation. You can also use rulesets to react to traps automatically. To do this, you would take advantage of the Action node which can be placed into a ruleset to execute a command.

Suppose you want to run the command *reset_adapter* when you receive a trap with specific code 21 from an IBM 6611 router. To do this, you would use a ruleset like the one shown in Figure 9.9. Here a Trap Settings node selects those traps with the 6611's enterprise ID and the specific code 21. These traps then pass into an Action node that executes the command *reset_adapter*.

The Action node can pass parameters containing information from the trap. The variables used for doing this are shown in Figure 9.10.

---

[11] This file is in the directory /usr/OV/conf/C.

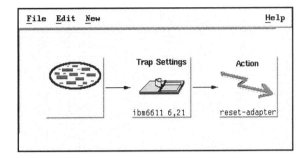

Figure 9.9 Ruleset for automatic command response

```
$NVA        agent name or address
$NVE        enterprise ID
$NVT        time-stamp
$NVC        community name
$NVG        generic code
$NVS        specific code
$NVATTR_n   n-th variable binding
```

Figure 9.10 Command parameters available in action node

It is also possible to have the ruleset cause an SNMP Set to be performed. This could be used instead of a command to carry out the automatic action. Here you use the Set MIB Variable node instead of the Action Node, and in it, specify the object ID of the MIB variable and the value to which it is to be set.

As we have seen, a given ruleset is active when one or more operators run an instance of Events which uses it. When performing automatic reaction to traps, you will usually want to have the relevant rulesets active regardless of who is using Events. Thus, it is possible to have the commands executed by the *actionsvr* daemon. You can arrange for this by listing your automatic reaction rulesets in the file ESE.automation.[12]

Message-driven actions System and application programs often write messages to log files when they encounter errors. You may want to run commands in response to certain error messages. For example, you could have a command restart an application when it logs a critical error.

If the program runs on an AIX system and uses the error logging facility there, then as we saw in Chapter 7, the *trapgend* daemon can create a trap for the error. NetView or the MLM could then react to the trap in one of the ways we have just discussed.

In other cases, you could use the Systems Monitor SIA's File Monitoring Table. This could monitor the log file and create traps when certain error messages are written there. We discussed this capability in Chapter 7.

If the system is not AIX and if it cannot run the SIA, there is another possibility. A system which *did* run the SIA could use NFS or AFS to monitor the error log remotely and generate traps when messages are logged on the remote system.

---

[12] This file is in the directory /usr/OV/conf.

Data-driven actions You may also want to drive operations in response to changes in agents' MIB variables. For example, if the MIB variable representing traffic on a link exceeds a certain level, you might want to drive a script to dial an additional ISDN line. As we will see in the next chapter, this can be done using NetView or the MLM.

In the case of NetView, the SNMP collection function can be used to monitor particular MIB variables and generate traps when thresholds are exceeded. These traps can then drive commands using the techniques we have just seen. In the case of the MLM, its Threshold Table can monitor MIB variables and either directly drive commands itself or send traps to NetView.

9.4 SUMMARY

Effective tools for network operations allow you to respond quickly to network problems and to keep the network running efficiently. In a NetView-based management system, there are many tools available to handle the operational requirements. There are tools such as *telnet*, *rexec* and SNMP to provide the basic infrastructure for operating remote systems. There are facilities such as *xnmappmon* and ARFs to integrate operations into the NetView GUI. There are also capabilities for restricting who can use NetView's functions. In addition, NetView and the MLM can perform automatic operations on a schedule and in response to events in the network.

KEEPING AN EYE ON IT—MONITORING AND REPORTING

Problem reporting systems provide a certain amount of information about the state of a network, but it's a limited view. Systems send traps and users complain when network conditions are intolerable, but it's also important to know about more subtle degradations and impending problems. There is also much other information managers need about the network in order to understand its performance, availability and many other characteristics.

A key aspect of the network management system is therefore its ability to collect a wide range of information from the network, to store it in a useful form, and to provide or enable tools that can generate reports from the information.

SNMP is at its best when it comes to collecting this sort of information. The basic MIB-II contains a lot of good data—especially for IP networks—and the MIB extension mechanism makes it possible for virtually any kind of data to be provided by an agent. NetView and Systems Monitor are very strong in this area, both having good SNMP-based tools for gathering information about the network and thus providing the basis for reporting functions.

10.1 REQUIREMENTS

First let's look at the kinds of data we need to collect from the network.

10.1.1 Topology information

It's clearly important to have graphics showing the network topology and status in real time, but it's also useful to have network documentation that can be printed or pulled up on systems other than NetView. If all you need are printed versions of NetView's submaps, these can easily be produced using NetView's Print Tool.

If you want to generate your own reports from NetView's topology data, the difficulty of doing so will depend on the networks' protocols. It can be done relatively easily for IP networks since NetView can store IP topology information in a relational database. For non-IP networks, it is more difficult since GTM uses a private database and this can be accessed only using programming interfaces.

10.1.2 Inventory information

This is information providing details of the hardware and software in the network. It's needed for a variety of purposes including financial asset management and supporting problem management. This can be thought of as topology information in higher focus.

For each hardware device, this information ideally includes the model, manufacturer, serial number and any other identifying information, as well as similar information for each of its features. For the software installed on a particular device, we need to know its identifying name or number, its version and fix level, license information and a list of any installed software features.

We would also like to know about each communications facility in the network, including LAN and WAN links. Here we need to know the type of each facility (e.g. Ethernet, E1 link, Frame Relay interface), details of its provider, its speed and physical characteristics (e.g. 10BaseT versus 10Base2 Ethernet), as well as information about any virtual resources provided by the facility (e.g. X.25 or Frame Relay virtual circuits).

Agents generally will include this kind of information in their MIBs, though they may not provide everything you require. Still, with SNMP data collection it will usually be possible to obtain at least basic inventory information. The collection itself can be driven from topology information, so that for example you could periodically collect from all resources listed in the Topology Database. It must be admitted, however, that in many cases collection would have to be performed uniquely for each type of agent. Much of the required information will be available only in MIB extensions which differ among agents. If agents use standard MIB extensions, however, e.g. a Frame Relay MIB extension, some common collection will be possible.

10.1.3 Fault information

It is important to understand not just the urgent or disastrous faults that agents report in traps, but also more subtle problems and degradations. Agents generally provide a great deal of information about these in their MIBs, often as counters of various exceptional events. These include errors sending or receiving individual messages, brief outages and conditions that may foreshadow serious problems. The basic MIB-II includes much of this kind of information, as do MIB extensions, and the NetView and MLM collection functions can be used to obtain it.

10.1.4 Performance information

This information is important for diagnosing problems in the network and for knowing when you need to change the capacities of the network's components. The information required here includes:

- LAN and WAN link data:
  - Utilization

- Speed
- Packet or frame size
- Number of messages sent and received
- Number of octets sent
- Queue length

In addition to aggregate information for each link, it is also useful to have information broken down by each protocol running on the link.
- Communications devices data:
  - Processor utilization
  - Memory utilization
  - Queues within various processes in the device
- Response time measurements:
  - Time required for various kinds of end user transactions
  - Time required for messages to cross links or pass through communications devices
  - In protocols such as SNA and ATM, the time required for messages to cross logical connections such as virtual routes and virtual path connections

For links, the basic MIB-II provides most of the required information, and MIB extensions usually contain a lot of performance information. In LANs, the RMON MIB is especially useful. For communications devices, MIB-II does not contain any performance information. However, MIB extensions for routers, bridges, concentrators and other equipment usually have at least processor and memory utilization. Response time measurements are relatively rare in agents' MIBs.

NetView and the MLM can collect performance information using SNMP.

10.1.5 Accounting information

This consists of the amount of time users are connected to the network and the amount of traffic they send. It also includes identifying information such as user IDs, group IDs and account numbers. It may also include information such as the type of service used, e.g. batch, interactive, high priority, isochronous. In protocols such as ATM and FDDI, where users can request particular amounts of bandwidth, it may also include measurements of the amounts they use.

Here, as with performance information, the data must be available in the relevant agents' MIBs and, if it is, NetView and the MLM can collect it.

10.1.6 Availability information

There are two major kinds of availability measurements:

- Measurements for individual components of the network. For example, routers, bridges and links
- Measurements of overall services. For example, whether the network path from London to Los Angeles is available

For measuring the availability of individual components, one option is to analyse trap logs. For example, the Node Down and Node Up traps that NetView generates can be used. There is some danger here that a trap will get lost, though this is probably not a big problem if it happens only occasionally. Another possibility is to use Trouble Ticket's information to calculate the lengths of outages for individual resources.

A better way to understand components' availability is to have the manager poll them periodically. NetView of course does this for IP resources—this is the basis for the Node Up and Node Down traps. This approach could be extended to non-IP networks by periodically polling their proxy agents in a way that forces them to query the actual components.

It is more difficult to measure the availability of overall services. For example, in an IP network there may be several possible paths between London and Los Angeles. It is quite complicated to determine from individual component data whether at least one path is available at a given time. A much more effective approach is to have monitors that periodically attempt to use services and report their findings. If you're trying to monitor network connectivity, then a system in London could periodically try PINGing a router in Los Angeles. It could make its findings available to NetView through its MIB extensions or by writing them to a log.

In IP networks, the MLM's status monitoring process could be subverted to check network availability. Placing an entry in its Status Monitoring Table for a remote system will cause it to PING the system periodically and generate traps when connectivity is lost.

10.1.7 Collecting and processing the data

For each of these kinds of data, we want more than just a single snapshot. The management system must collect it periodically and maintain it in a form that is easy for report-generation programs to use. This may be a flat file, but in most cases a relational database is much better.

Finally, once we have the data in a useful form, we need the actual programs to do the report generation.

10.2 SYSTEM DESIGN

NetView and the Systems Monitor MLM are good at collecting the several kinds of required data and can store it in useful forms. Either can store the data in flat files and NetView can also place it into relational databases. Neither, however, addresses report generation. Here you will need to provide your own solutions and in this section we will look at how to do this.

The overall monitoring and reporting system based on NetView and Systems Monitor will be as shown in Figure 10.1. The sources of the data will be the following:

1. Traps from agents, NetView itself or its applications.
2. Topology data generated by the NetView IP discovery process. For IP networks, this meets many of the requirements for inventory and topology data.
3. Agents' MIBs. This will account for the majority of our data and will be gathered by SNMP Gets from NetView and the MLM.

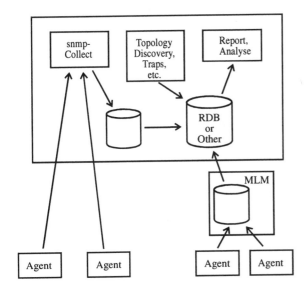

Figure 10.1 Monitoring and reporting system

4. Other data sources such as NetView applications. These would include non-IP topology data or any other kind of data that applications produce but do not make available via traps or SNMP MIBs.

In all but the third case, the information will usually be delivered to the NetView system automatically. In the third case, you will need to determine what is collected and how this is done.

There are two primary methods for collecting data using SNMP:

- **NetView** The MIB Data Collector will be configured to collect the desired MIB variables from agents, and store the values in flat files or relational databases. It will also be possible to have NetView compare the data to thresholds during collection and to generate traps when the thresholds are crossed.

  Using NetView for collection is the simplest approach, requiring the least amount of configuration and other arranging. However, there is a drawback. Frequently sending SNMP Gets and their responses across the network can consume substantial amounts of bandwidth. Furthermore, a more flexible collection mechanism is available in the MLM.

- **The MLM** If you place MLMs strategically, then the collection traffic occurs across only a limited portion of the network, most often on high-bandwidth LANs. The collected data is compared to thresholds at the MLM. Thresholding can cause traps to be sent to NetView and can also cause commands and scripts to be driven. The MLM stores the collected data locally and you can later move it up to NetView if you like, possibly after having done some filtering or pre-processing to reduce its size.

  As we'll see, the MLM's collection mechanism is more flexible than NetView's. In particular, you can specify more sophisticated threshold conditions. If you need to use these conditions at the central site as well, you can also run the MLM on NetView's system. As long as you disable the MLM's trap reception, there will be no problems with conflicting ports.

Once the data has been collected, it must be assembled into a useful form for reporting. The first task will usually be to move it all to a single location, which means moving the MLM-collected data up to NetView and translating it into a standard format. The MLM includes a tool to do this, translating the data into the NetView collection format. When used in conjunction with remotely mounted file systems, i.e. NFS or AFS, it can move the data to NetView's system while translating it. Alternatively, tools such as FTP can be used to move the data.

Once all the data has been moved to NetView's system, you may also want to copy it into a relational database. NetView provides tools for doing this.

Finally, the actual report generation will be carried out at the central site or wherever you have assembled the data.

10.3 IMPLEMENTATION

The SNMP collection mechanisms in NetView and the MLM are by far the most powerful tools available to us since they provide access to many different kinds of information. Thus, most of this chapter will be devoted to their use and to related topics. Still, the other kinds of relevant data—specifically topology, traps and data from NetView applications—are also important. Topology and trap data are sufficiently general to warrant further discussion. Thus, we will review these two topics first and then spend the rest of the chapter on SNMP collection.

10.3.1 Trap data

In Chapter 7 we saw that Trouble Ticket can generate reports from problem data. It is also possible to perform this kind of reporting without Trouble Ticket, using the information NetView maintains about traps.

As we've seen, trapd.log contains entries for the traps received by NetView. This log, while useful for people to read, is not in a particularly good form for programs since it is a relatively unstructured ASCII file. If you have a relational database, however, you can transfer this information into a database table, which will be much easier for programs to use.

The process of transferring information from trapd.log into a relational database is described in IBM (1995b). The result is that it is placed into a database table called the *trapdlog* table. This has several columns containing information about each trap:

- The time the trap was generated.
- The category of the trap, e.g. threshold events, error events, status events.
- The name of the system sending the trap.
- The type of the trap sender, e.g. application, agent, *netmon, tralertd*.
- A description of the trap. This is the text written in trapd.log and will be either the default NetView dump of the complete trap information or whatever is defined through the Event Configuration process.

A program can use an SQL query to select the traps of interest, using time, source, category and so forth as criteria. It would then parse the details of the traps' contents from the text description fields.

Depending on how you have done Event Configuration, the descriptions may not include details such as the traps' enterprise IDs, generic and specific codes, and variable bindings. This may not be a problem if all you are doing is searching for particular traps, perhaps counting them or calculating the lengths of outages. In that case, your program can simply search for the text descriptions you have defined in Event Configuration.

If you do require trap details not available in the descriptions, the best approach is to create a custom logging function which writes to a flat file or relational database. The pre-filtering daemon in Appendix II could be easily modified to do this.

10.3.2 Topology data

Reporting an IP network's topology is relatively easy since NetView can maintain IP topology in a relational database instead of the usual flat files. With this information in a relational database, you can write SQL and programs that list the inventory of the network, list equipment of certain types and so forth.

With topology information, you do not have to copy from flat files into the relational database, as you do with trap data. Instead, you configure NetView to maintain it directly in the relational database as described in IBM (1995b). The IP topology information is maintained in a set of several tables there (as described in the box 'IP topology tables').

While obtaining IP topology information is therefore relatively easy, it is more difficult for non-IP topology. GTM cannot store its information in a relational database. Instead, it maintains it in flat files whose format is not documented, and there are no tools for copying this into a relational database.

It is possible to obtain GTM's topology information using the *nvotGet* series of routines, which can be called from C programs. Thus, the best approach is to write a program which obtains the topology information you require and writes it to a flat file or a relational database. Your reporting programs can then access the information there.

10.3.3 Extending the MIB with Systems Monitor SIA

Let's now turn to the main subject of this chapter, collecting data using SNMP.

In most cases, you must rely on agents MIBs to supply the performance, fault and inventory information you require. If they don't, you will need to add it yourself. If the agents support SMUX or DPI multiplexing, then you could write some code to implement the objects you require, though this is a fairly significant programming task. For systems that support the Systems Monitor SIA, a better alternative is to use its Command Table to implement new MIB objects.

The new MIB objects can be ones which the manager Gets or Sets. The basic mechanism is that you provide a command that the SIA executes when the manager accesses the object. In the case of a Get, the command would obtain the required information; for a Set, it would carry out an action.

To implement a new MIB object, you add a new entry to the SIA's Command Table. As with other Systems Monitor tables, you would do this using one of the techniques discussed in Section 3.5.4.

IP topology tables

- *topoinfo* This table contains summary information about the IP topology, including counters of various sorts.
- Tables describing the networks, segments, systems and interfaces in the overall IP internetwork:
  - *networkclass* table—describes the IP networks
  - *segmentclass* table—describes the segments
  - *nodeclass* table—describes the systems
  - *interfaceclass* table—describes the interfaces

  In these tables, each 'object', i.e. network, segment, system or interface, is uniquely identified with an 'object ID'.
- *objectclass* This table describes the class to which each object belongs. This table can be used when you know the ID of an object but not its class and hence cannot determine which of the tables above contains its information. For example, if an interface has object ID 123, then there would be an entry indicating that object 123 belongs to the interface class. The class is identified here not by name but by a 'class ID' used in conjunction with the next table.
- *classtable* This table gives the class name for each of the class IDs.
- *memberof* This table describes the system to which each interface belongs, and the network to which each segment belongs. Each row describes one 'member of' relationship with the columns *containedobjid* and *containerobjid*.
- *coupledwith* This table describes the segment and network to which each interface belongs. Each row contains two object IDs which describe a 'coupled with' relationship. Thus, for one interface there would be one row describing the segment it is coupled with and another describing the network. Between the *memberof* and *coupledwidth* tables, the complete topology of the internetwork can be deduced. Note that the table structure allows for multiple interfaces on hosts and routers and thus for their membership in multiple segments and networks.

Let's first consider the case of a MIB object the manager will Get. In the Command Table entry, you place a command string into a variable. Then when the manager performs the Get, this command string will be executed and its output placed into another variable in the entry, the 'result variable'. This result is then returned to the manager in the GetResponse.

Let's now consider these result variables in more detail. In each command table entry, there are actually four of these—one for text results, one for INTEGERs, one for *Gauge* results and one for *Counters*. The standard output from the command is placed into as many of these as make sense. For example, if the output is a message it will go into only the text result variable. If the output is a positive number it will go into all of them.

The manager performs the Get against one of these result variables.

Let's look at an example of a MIB object the manager would Get (see Figure 10.2). Suppose you want to implement a variable that returns a list of the processes running on the SIA's system. You would add a new entry to the Command Table, with the usual *State*, *Name* and *Description* variables. You would then set up additional variables in the entry to define the details (the objects in the Command Table all have the common prefix *smSiaCommand*):

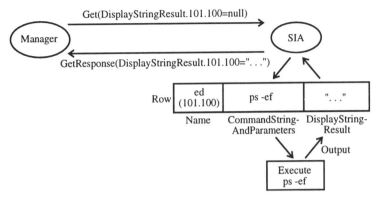

Figure 10.2 SIA Command Table Get example

- *GetStringAndParameters*—'**ps -ef**'   This is the command string itself, in this case, the UNIX *ps* command which returns a list of processes running in the system.
- *TimeOutValue*—**5**   This is the number of seconds the SIA will allow the command to run.
- *TimeToLive*—**10**   This is the length of time the SIA will keep and re-use the result. Thus, if the manager performed a Get for the variable twice in rapid succession, the command would be executed only once.
- *OutputResultIndex*—*DisplayString*   This indicates that the result is to be converted to type *DisplayString*. Thus, only the *DisplayString* result variable will get the command's output. It is also possible to specify that the output should be converted to INTEGER, *Gauge* or *Counter*, in which case it will be placed into as many of the result variables as possible.
- *OutputRowIndex*—**0**   This object lets you select a particular row of the output to be placed into the result variable. Here we're indicating we want all of it.
- *OutputColumnIndex*—**0**   This lets you select a field of the output. Fields are delimited by white space. Here we're indicating we want all the output.

When the manager performs a Get against the *DisplayStringResult* variable in this entry, the entire output of the 'ps -ef' command will be returned in the GetResponse.

Sets work similarly to Gets, but now the command will carry out an action based on the value sent in the Set (see Figure 10.3). You can pass this value to the command as a parameter, using the $SM6K_COMMAND_SET_VALUE environment variable.

Suppose you want to implement an object that controls an application, so that setting the object to 1 starts the application and 0 stops it. To do this, you would create an entry in the Command Table similar to the one for the Get example, but this time using *SetStringAndParameters* instead of *GetStringAndParameters*. You would place in *SetStringAndParameters* a command to start and stop the application. For example, if you had a command named *applctl* which started the application when passed a 1 and stopped it when passed a 0, you would use the following command string:

```
applctl $SM6K_COMMAND_SET_VALUE
```

To start the application, the manager would Set the INTEGER result variable to 1. The command string would then be executed, with 1 being substituted for $SM6K_COMMAND_SET_

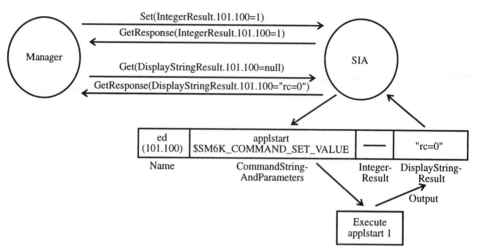

Figure 10.3 SIA Command Table Set example

VALUE. *applctl* would start the application and *applctl*'s output would then be placed into the result variables—just as with Gets. A response would then be returned to the manager with the same value it passed in the Set.[1]

If we are picky, this means the object that the manager Set (the result variable) may have a different value from the one carried in the Set request. For example, if *applctl* wrote a message saying it started the application, then this message—and not the value 1 sent by the manager— would be in the result variable. This could be considered violating the spirit of SNMP, but it is a useful feature since the manager can perform a subsequent Get to the result variable and see the command's output.

The command table can also be used to create MIB variables based on shared or kernel memory segments. The idea here is that a Get request would obtain a value from the segment and a Set would update it. This facility is documented in IBM (1995f).

10.3.4 NetView MIB collection and thresholding

Let's now consider the manager's side of the collection process.

NetView MIB collection is carried out by the *snmpCollect* daemon, which you configure to collect particular objects from particular agents. *snmpCollect* does this at regular intervals you specify and places the collected data into a group of flat files. This collection may involve thresholding so that traps are generated when variables exceed values you define. NetView MIB collection is possible only for variables of type INTEGER, *Gauge, Counter, TimeTicks* and *IpAddress*. Thus, you can collect numeric data but not text strings. The assumption is that you will not want to collect non-numeric data repeatedly, since it normally does not change.

---

[1] SNMP requires that the response to the Set have identical variables bindings to those in the Set itself.

The collection is performed according to the configuration file snmpCol.conf.[2] The entries in this file indicate to *snmpCollect* which MIB variables it should collect, which agents to collect them from, how frequently to do so, and all other parameters it requires for collection.

The most usual way to define this configuration is using NetView's MIB Data Collection window. This is shown in Figure 10.4. Alternatively, you can use the *setthresh* command, which would be more appropriate when you have a large number of collections you wish to arrange. In either case, the result is that the configuration file is updated. If you feel adventurous or impatient, you might also decide to edit the configuration file directly.[3]

Regardless of which method you use, you will supply some or all of the following information:

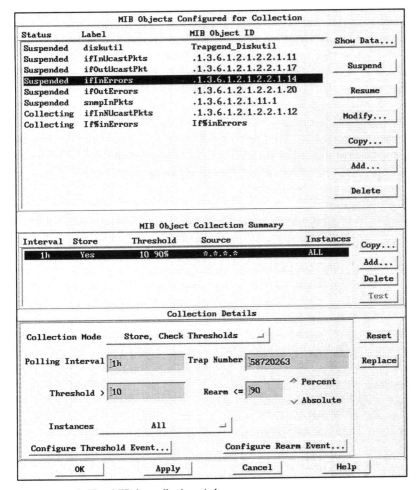

Figure 10.4 NetView MIB data collection window

[2] snmpCol.conf is in the directory /usr/OV/conf.

[3] If you do this you will need to recycle the *snmpCollect* daemon to ensure it picks up the changes.

- The ID of the MIB object you wish to collect
- The instances to collect for this object
- The agent or agents from which you wish to collect it[4]
- Whether to save the data, compare it to thresholds, or both
- A polling interval to indicate frequency of collection
- A threshold and rearm value. We saw how these work under 'MIB Data Collection' in Section 3.2.6
- Codes to use in threshold and rearm traps

Figure 10.5 shows an example of using the *setthresh* command to arrange collection.

```
setthresh    -o ip.ipInReceives \      (MIB object)
             -i 0 \                     (Instance ID)
             -s R \                     (Start or resume collection)
             -n 9.180.180.208 \         (Agent address)
             -c C \                     (Agent addr is not a pattern)
             -m s \                     (Collect and save data)
             -p 2s \                    (Polling interval)
             -v 50 \                    (Threshold value)
             -r 50 \                    (Rearm value as a percentage)
             -t % \                     (Rearm is percentage of threshold)
             -T 58720263                (Specific code for traps)
```

Figure 10.5 Command to configure NetView MIB collection

snmpCollect stores the collected data in the /usr/OV/databases/snmpCollect directory. Here, for each collected instance of each MIB object, there will be two files:

- The first, a 'bang file' that contains general information about the instance, including its data type, the units it's expressed in, its object ID and instance ID. Figure 10.6 shows an example bang file. This file will have a name of the form:

  mnemonic.instanceID!

  The mnemonic is the name of the collected object as defined in its MIB module. For example, if you were collecting instance 1 of *ifInOctets*, then the bang file would have the name 'ifInOctets.1!'.
- The second, a binary data file, which contains the actual collected values. It has the same name as the bang file, but without the '!'.

If you are collecting the same instance from different agents, all data for all agents will be in the same binary data file. Different instances though will have different collection files.

```
units/sec
COUNTER
.1.3.6.1.2.1.2.2.1.12
1
```

Figure 10.6 Example 'bang file'

---

[4] In the case of multiple agents, you can use wildcard characters and address ranges, e.g. 9.180.180.* or 9.180.180.10–20. You can also specify particular agents to exclude from collection.

The traps *snmpCollect* generates for crossed thresholds are enterprise specific, with the NetView for AIX enterprise ID (1.3.6.1.4.1.2.6.3) and the specific code you select. The specific code 58720263 is used by default and traps with this code will be nicely displayed in the Events window and trapd.log.[5] You can, however, use any specific code in the range from 1001 to 1999, as long as it is odd. The reason for this 'oddity' is that the corresponding rearm trap will have a specific code equal to this value plus one, and thus the threshold and rearm traps form nice little pairs.

The threshold traps from *snmpCollect* contain several variable bindings:

- The name or address of the agent from which the data was collected
- A line of text describing the event, e.g.

```
ipInReceives 0 threshold exceeded (>100.00): 241.00
```

- The ID of the MIB object being collected
- The instance ID

The rearm traps contain similar information.[6]

The way *snmpCollect* stores and thresholds a particular variable depends on its data type. If the variable is an INTEGER, *Gauge* or *TimeTicks*, then the actual collected value is stored and compared to the threshold. If it is a *Counter*, the change in the value per second is used. Thus, suppose that you collect an object which is counting the number of times a particular event occurs. If it is 1000 at 12:00 and 1120 at 12:01, then the value stored and compared to the threshold would be 2. This is how we would want it to work since absolute values of counters are generally not very meaningful.

As we saw earlier, it is also possible for *snmpCollect* to perform collection based on MIB expressions. Here you define expressions made of MIB objects and arithmetic operators in the file *mibExpr.conf*.[7] You could, for example, define an expression which added the incoming and outgoing octets on a line, multiplied by 8 to convert to bits, and then divided by the line speed to get the line's utilization. Then you could treat this expression as if it were a MIB object.

10.3.5 Systems Monitor collection and thresholding

The Systems Monitor MLM can also perform collection from SNMP agents' MIBs, and its collection function has all the major features NetView's does. It can periodically poll agents for their MIB variables, store the collected values locally and generate traps when threshold values are exceeded or rearmed. As we've seen, one of the major advantages of using the MLM is it allows you to perform collection in a distributed manner, close to the agents.

Another advantage is that its thresholding mechanism is quite flexible. The MLM can generate traps when any one of several conditions occurs:

[5] There is Event Configuration for these in /usr/OV/conf/C/trapd.conf.

[6] In addition to the information found in threshold traps, rearm traps also contain a binding that indicates the highest value collected between the time the threshold was exceeded and subsequently rearmed.

[7] In the directory /usr/OV/conf.

- When the collected value is greater than, less than, equal to or not equal to a threshold.
- When a particular variable exists or does not exist.
- When a particular variable changes or does not change.

These conditions can be combined to form expressions using AND, OR and NOT logical operators. The same conditions are available for rearming a threshold.

When a threshold or rearm condition is met, the MLM can either send a trap to NetView or execute a command locally. Thus, the MLM could automatically react to simple problems and notify NetView of more serious ones.

Like NetView, the MLM handles *Counter* variables specially. For these, it applies thresholds based on the change since the last collection. This behaviour can be modified if you prefer to test the absolute value. On the other hand, you can test types other than *Counter* for changed values if you prefer.[8]

The MLM places collected data into a file using a straightforward, readable format.[9] The file has one line for each collected value, and includes:

- Collection time and date
- MIB variable data type
- Name or address of the agent from which the value has been collected
- Object ID of the MIB variable
- The collected (and not delta) value

To configure the MLM for collection, you add entries to the Threshold Table. Each entry will cause collection of an object instance from a particular agent. An entry can also cause collection of all instances of an object, or collection from a group of agents.

To configure an entry in the Threshold Table, you first set the *Name* and *Description* objects as usual. Then you set additional objects controlling the details of collection and thresholding. For example, you could create an entry as follows (the Threshold Table objects all have a common prefix of *smMlmThreshold*):

- *State = enabledThresholdStore*   Perform both thresholding and storing.
- *LocalRemoteMIBVariable = 'serverx:.1.3.6.1.2.1.4.3.0'*   The name of the agent and the object ID for the variable. You can use the Alias Table to point to pre-defined lists of agents.
- *Condition = '>'*   Perform a greater-than comparison for thresholding.
- *Value = 800*   The threshold is 800.
- *PollTime = '30s'*   Collect the variable every 30 seconds.
- *SpecificTrap = 1234*   Use specific code 1234 in the threshold traps. By default, the enterprise ID will be that of Systems Monitors, though you can also specify your own with the object *ArmEnterprise*.
- *ReArmCondition = '<'*   Perform a less-than comparison for rearming.
- *ReArmValue = '500'*

---

[8] You override the default by specifying, for example, 'value >' instead of '>' to force comparison to the absolute value, and 'delta >' to force comparison to the change in the value.

[9] By default the collected data is placed in /var/adm/smv2/collect/midmand.col.

In this example, there will be no rearm trap.

The MLM can be a very flexible way of collecting data from agents. If MLMs are placed strategically throughout the network, they can also significantly reduce the burden collection places on the network.

10.3.6 Data staging and preparation

Once the data has been collected, either by NetView or the MLM, you will want to prepare it for use by reporting programs.

Collating MLM data You will probably want to move data collected by remote MLMs to a central location, most likely the NetView system since there are tools in NetView to further massage it. A good way to do this is to use the MLM *smconvert* utility in conjunction with a remote file system such as NFS or AFS. *smconvert* will convert the data in an MLM collection file into the NetView format and append it to the files in a NetView collection directory.

The overall scheme for conversion and transfer would be:

- At each MLM, you would first remotely mount the NetView directory into which the data will be assembled. This directory could be /usr/OV/databases/snmpCollect. However, in most cases you will want to do it elsewhere so that you can separate the data you are assembling from any data being collected by NetView.
- You would then copy any data from NetView itself into this directory. It would be a good idea to stop the *snmpCollect* daemon while you do this to avoid any overlapping data in the static and dynamic collection directories.
- You would then run the *smconvert* utility at each MLM, instructing it to add the converted data to the remotely mounted NetView directory.

In this process, there is a certain amount of synchronization that must be performed to prevent MLMs from simultaneously appending data to the NetView files. It would be possible to have a timer in each MLM which popped periodically and caused the data to be sent to NetView. However, it would be difficult to guarantee correct synchronization. Therefore, a much more attractive approach is to drive the process centrally from NetView. A script there could drive the collation process on the MLMs, one after another. This would be quite easy to do using *rexec* to run *smconvert* on the MLMs.

Converting NetView data As we have seen, NetView data—or MLM data converted into NetView format—is stored in pairs of files in the NetView collection directory. You may want to convert this to some other form so your programs can easily access it. One possibility is to convert it to an ASCII format using the NetView *snmpColDump* utility. Another possibility is to copy it into a relational database. Alternatively, you may want to have programs access it directly, in which case the discussion in Implementation Tip 10.1 will be of interest to you.

snmpColDump The *snmpColDump* utility will convert the data in binary collection files into a readable ASCII format. It writes to standard output. (One thing to beware of is that *snmpColDump* places tabs and not blanks in its output.)

Implementation Tip 10.1

NetView's SNMP collection function places the collected data into binary data files. These are unreadable except with a program. Each file contains a series of data quadruplets, one quadruplet for each value that has been collected, in the following format:

- A four-byte unsigned integer giving the start of the period for which collection was performed. This is given as the number of seconds since the beginning of 1970, in Co-ordinated Universal Time (a.k.a. GMT).
- A four-byte unsigned integer giving the end of the period for which collection was performed.
- A four-byte unsigned integer containing the agent's address.
- An eight-byte floating-point collected value.

A program to read a binary data file and write a formatted version to standard output is in Appendix VII.

---

snmpColDump has flags you can use to control which fields are displayed and how they are formatted. You can control, for example, whether the collected variables' object IDs are displayed and how the collection times are formatted.

You can use UNIX tools such as *grep* and *awk* to manipulate the output from *snmpColDump* and quickly produce little reports. For example, suppose you want to sift some data to get the values collected from agent 'serverx'. You also want to sort them by the collected value, and display only the collection time and the value. The following command will do that:

```
snmpColDump tcpInSegs.0 | grep serverx | sort +3 -n | \
awk '{printf('%s %s\n', $2, $4)}'
```

and produce this output (for example):

```
21:47:45 10
21:47:49 12
21:47:43 18.5
21:47:47 26
```

In addition to formatting collected data, *snmpColDump* can be used to maintain binary collection files. It allows you to update them in place, for example by periodically removing all entries written before a certain time. This is described in Appendix VIII.

Copying to a relational database You can transfer *snmpCollect* data into any of the relational databases supported by NetView. There are two basic methods for performing the transfer — 'snapshot' and 'archive'.

As its name suggests, the snapshot method is for when you want to put a complete copy of the data into the relational database, while leaving the original data unchanged. The archive method is for when you want to move current *snmpCollect* data into the relational database and remove it from the *snmpCollect* directory.

The details of the transfer process are described in IBM (1995b). The major steps involved are:

- Set up the configuration options for the transfer, e.g. which transfer method to use. There is a SMIT screen provided to do this.
- Clear the relational database tables if you want to replace the data already in them. The NetView command *nvColTable* will do this.
- Perform the transfer using the NetView *nvColToSQL* command.

10.3.7 Report generation

Once data has been collected and assembled, you will probably want to generate reports and graphs from it. Let's look at some techniques that can be used for doing this.

Graphs Once you understand the format of the data collected by *snmpCollect*, it is relatively easy to use it as input to your favourite graphics package. You can also take advantage of a handy NetView tool called *xnmgraph* which is designed specifically to graph *snmpCollect* data. *xnmgraph* can take its input from:

- The collection files in /usr/OV/databases/snmpCollect
- Data being collected in real time by *snmpCollect*
- Data from some other source—a file or standard input

Its output can be sent to a window for on-line viewing, to a printer, or to a file. Earlier in Figure 3.19 we saw an example of *xnmgraph*'s output, in that case as generated by the MIB Application Builder.

On-line graphing To see graphs on your NetView screen, there are several approaches you can use, all of which amount to calling *xnmgraph*. The simplest is to take advantage of one of the pre-defined graphs from the NetView menu pull-downs or Tool Palette, for example:

- Selecting 'Tools ... Graph Collected Data: SNMP' from the menu bar will create a graph of all data in the *snmpCollect* directory or just the data for a system selected in a submap.
- 'Monitor ... System Activity ... CPU Performance' will create a real time graph showing CPU utilization for a host running the *trapgend* daemon (using the MIB extension this daemon provides).
- 'Monitor ... Network Activity ... Interface: Traffic' produces a real time graph of the number of incoming, outgoing and error packets for a selected system.
- The MIB Application Builder. This tool can generate forms, tables and graphs, and in the last case gives you an easy way to hook a graphing application into the NetView menu structure. This can graph either real-time data or that already in the *snmpCollect* directory.

Regardless of how you get into an *xnmgraph* graph, you have many options in the graph window itself. Under the window's View menu, you will find controls for line colours and widths, polling interval, scaling and all sorts of other options. You can also page back and forth in the graph by clicking on its left or right edges or centre the graph around a particular time by clicking it.

All the above ways of invoking *xnmgraph* are useful for quickly generating graphs. If you need more control over their generation, you will need to invoke the *xnmgraph* command directly.

When doing this, you specify one or more MIB objects to graph, and some options controlling the graph details.

The more interesting options are:

- *-browse* **or** *+browse*   Determines whether only previously collected data is graphed (*-browse*) or real-time data as well (*+browse*).
- *-poll*   Polling interval used for real-time collection.
- *-title*   Title for the graph.
- *-displayWidth*   Amount of time one page of the graph represents.
- *-resolution*   Amount of time each segment of a line represents. For example, if you are collecting a particular variable once per minute, but set resolution to be five minutes, then the average value over each five minute period will be graphed.
- *-printonly* **and** *-printCommand*   Used to produce hard-copy graphs.
- *-mib*   The specifications for the lines in the graph.

With the *-mib* flag, you give one specification for each line to be included in the graph. Each specification is a text string with fields that are separated by colons. The fields you specify for each line are (respectively):

- *mibOID*   The ID of the MIB object for this line (without the instance ID).
- *mibLabel*   A label to be used in the graph legend for the line. The host name for the collected data is placed at the beginning of this.
- *instanceRE*   The instance ID for this line. It can be an actual instance ID, e.g. 0 or 1.2.3.4, or it can be a regular expression, e.g. [34] to indicate instances 3 or 4. If nothing is specified, then all instances are graphed. Thus, a single line specification can create multiple graph lines.
- *instMatchOID*   This and the next field are an alternative to *instanceRE* for specifying which instances are to be graphed.
- *instMatchRE*   There are cases where you may want to graph only some instances of an MIB object. For example, if the object is one of the Interface Group's counters, e.g. *ifInOctets*, then you may want to filter out certain kinds of interfaces, for example the loopback interface, or those of type Other. To do this, you would specify *instMatchOID* as the object ID for *ifType* and then specify *instMatchRE* as a regular expression that matches only relevant interface types. (There is an example of this in Figure 10.7.)
- *instLabelOID*   This is the ID of an object whose value will be put into the label for this line. For example, if you were graphing *ifInOctets* you could specify this as *ifType*'s object ID. Then the value of the appropriate *ifType* instance would be appended to the label for the line.
- *instLabelTrunc*   This is used in conjunction with *instLabelOID*, and allows you to truncate the label. Here you specify a regular expression to match the character in the label where truncation will occur. For example, if you gave the regular expression ([,;]) then the label would be truncated at the first comma or semicolon.
- *mult*   A factor by which each value in the line is multiplied. This allows scaling.

- **node** A list of one or more systems (separated by spaces) for which data will be graphed.

Here's a simple example of using *xnmgraph* to graph *ipInReceives* from host massimo:

```
xnmgraph \
    -poll 2s \
    +browse \
    -title "Collected ipInReceives" \
    -mib \
    ".1.3.6.1.2.1.4.3:ipInReceives:0::::::massimo"
```

This would graph already collected values and also initiate collection for real-time values using a polling interval of two seconds. The legend for the single line in the graph would be 'massimo ipInReceives'.

As another example, suppose you wanted to graph two lines, one for *ipInReceives* and one for *tcpInSegs*, on hosts massimo and joe. The following command will do that:

```
xnmgraph \
    +browse \
    -title "ipInReceives and tcpInSegs" \
    -mib \
    ".1.3.6.1.2.1.4.3:ipInReceives:0::::::massimo joe,
    .1.3.6.1.2.1.6.10:tcpInSegs:0::::::massimo joe"
```

For another example, suppose you wanted to graph the previously collected values of *ifOut-Octets* for each interface of an AIX host named helen. You want to exclude the software loop-back interface (type 24) and those of type Other (type 1). The command shown in Figure 10.7 would do this. A sample of its output is shown in Figure 10.8. The system used for the sample has only one interface (other than software loopback).

In the example command, the *instMatchOID* and *instMatchRE* are arranged so that the *ifType* instances will be collected and matched to anything other than 1 and 24. The *instLabel-OID* is *ifDescr* and the *instLabelTrunc* is ';'. Thus, the interface description in *ifDescr*, up to the first semicolon, will be used in the legend for each line.

xnmgraph streams *xnmgraph* can also serve as a more general graphing tool, reading from standard input any data you like. This can be useful for cases where you want to graph something other than *snmpCollect* data, but give the graphs the same look and feel. You might, for example, wish to graph the data generated by a program you write to reduce a large amount of raw collected data.

To do this, you organize the data into 'streams', each of which contains the data for a particular line in the graph. You tag each item of data with a number identifying its stream. You can then treat the stream number as if it were a MIB object ID.

The input data for *xnmgraph* must be in text lines of the following form:

```
streamnum starttime stoptime min avg max
```

in which:

- **streamnum** indicates the stream to which this data point belongs.

```
xnmgraph \
  -browse \
  -title "Collected and Real-Time ifOutOctets" \
  -mib \
".1.3.6.1.2.1.2.2.1.16:\                    (mibOID)
ifOutOctets:\                               (mibLabel)
:\                                          (instanceRE)
.1.3.6.1.2.1.2.2.1.3:\                      (instMatchOID)
^[2-9]$|^1.$|^2[0-3]$|^2[5-9]$|^3.$:\       (instMatchRE)
.1.3.6.1.2.1.2.2.1.2:\                      (instLabelOID)
;:\                                         (instLabelTrunc)
:\                                          (mult)
helen"                                      (node)
```

Figure 10.7 Example *xnmgraph* command

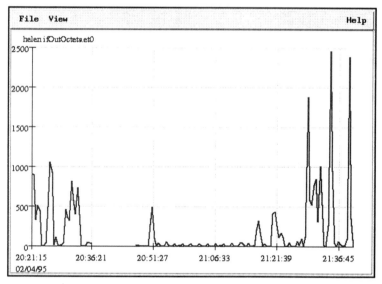

Figure 10.8 Example *xnmgraph* output

- *starttime* is the beginning of the 'collection period' for the data point. This can be given either as seconds since the beginning of 1970 or in the form mm.dd.yy-hh:mm:ss. If you specify it as 0, then the start time is the same as the stop time for the last data point in this stream.[10]
- *stoptime* is the end of the collection period.
- *min* is the data point itself if *avg* and *max* are not given. If they *are* given, then this is the minimum value for the collection period.[11]
- *avg* and *max*, if given, are the average and maximum values for the collection period.

For example, suppose the data shown in Figure 10.9 is in the file /tmp/data. Then this command would display a graph with two lines:

---

[10] Unless this is the first data point, in which case the start time is taken to be one second before the stop time.

[11] If you specify all of *min*, *avg* and *max*, then in the *xnmgraph* window you can request which of the three you wish to see.

```
1  12.01.94-23:25:27   12.01.94-23:25:28   1.0 1.5 1.9
1  12.01.94-23:25:28   12.01.94-23:25:29   2.0 2.5 2.9
1  12.01.94-23:25:29   12.01.94-23:25:30   3.0 3.5 3.9
1  12.01.94-23:25:30   12.01.94-23:25:31   4.0 4.5 4.9
2  12.01.94-23:25:27   12.01.94-23:25:28   5.0 5.5 5.9
2  12.01.94-23:25:28   12.01.94-23:25:29   6.0 6.5 6.9
2  12.01.94-23:25:29   12.01.94-23:25:30   7.0 7.5 7.9
2  12.01.94-23:25:30   12.01.94-23:25:31   8.0 8.5 8.9
```

Figure 10.9 Stream-oriented input data for *xnmgraph*

```
cat /tmp/data | xnmgraph \
-displayWidth 5s \
-mib \
"+1:Line 1:::::::,
+2:Line 2:::::::"
```

The line labelled 'Line 1' will be made from the data points flagged as stream 1 in the file, and 'Line 2' will be made from the stream 2 points.

This technique of producing your own data and then feeding it into *xnmgraph* is quite powerful and flexible and, when combined with the techniques we'll explore below for digesting raw MIB data into more interesting statistics, can produce very useful graphs.

Hard-copy graphs You may also decide to print the graphs. Here there are several options:

- Use the NetView Print Tool which can take a snapshot of an *xnmgraph* or other NetView window. It can send the snapshot to a printer or save it in a file in printer-ready format, e.g. PostScript. The tool supports black and white, greyscale and colour.
- Use another X window capture program, for example XV which is available as shareware.[12]
- Use the printing capabilities of *xnmgraph*. Depending on how you configure *xnmgraph*, this approach can support black and white, greyscale and colour.

Let's look more closely at this last approach. To generate print output with *xnmgraph*, you invoke it with the *printOnly* option. This causes *xnmgraph* to create the graph in a window, carry out the printing tasks, and then close the window. The process is depicted in Figure 10.10.

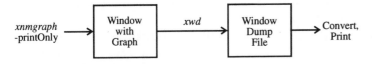

Figure 10.10 Printing with *xnmgraph*

Doing this actually drives two commands, both of which are defined by settings in the file XNm.[13] The first such setting is *xnmgraph.xwdCommand*. By default, it is the command:

```
/usr/bin/X11/xwd -nobdrs -id 0x%x -display %s | %s
```

---

[12] You can get this from the Internet for example from ftp.cis.upenn.edu in directory /pub/xv.

[13] XNm is in the directory /usr/OV/app-defaults.

This first invokes the *xwd* command to capture the screen and produce an encoded version of it.[14] This is then piped into whatever command has been defined for the second setting in the XNm file, which is *xnmgraph.printCommand*. By default, it is the command:

```
cat > /tmp/xnmgraph.xwd
```

This simply writes the output into the file /tmp/xnmgraph.xwd. Thus, the overall default behaviour of *xnmgraph* for printing is to produce a file containing an *xwd*-encoded version of the graph.

You can change this default behaviour, although it isn't too bad since it gives you a file which you can then transform into something you can print. One technique is to use the *xpr* command, which will create a black-and-white printer file. For example, to create a black-and-white PostScript file you could use:

```
cat /tmp/xnmgraph.xwd | xpr -rv -device ps > \
   /tmp/xnmgraph.ps
```

If you want to do something fancier, you would need to get a more powerful program than *xpr*, one that is capable of converting *xwd* format into greyscale or colour files for your printer. Note that *xwd* captures all the colour information from the window. It's just a question of finding a conversion program than can use it.

One possibility is to take advantage of the (free) *pbmplus* package.[15] This includes several utilities that translate among various graphics formats.

Three of the more interesting translators in this package are:

- **xwdtopnm** Translates the window dumps created by *xwd* into an intermediate graphic format called PNM (Portable Any Map).
- **pnmtops** Translates PNM format into colour PostScript suitable for printing.
- **ppmtopgm** This can convert PNM format to a greyscale format suitable for input to *pnmtops*. Thus, to create greyscale PostScript, you insert this into the conversion process.

To get a colour PostScript file, you could build a pipe to convert the *xwd* file as follows:[16]

```
cat /tmp/xnmgraph.tmp | xwdtopnm | pnmtops | \
   /tmp/xnmgraph.ps
```

Tables and reports You will probably want to see tables and other sorts of reports about the measurements collected from agents' MIBs. As with graphing, you may want to pre-process the MIB data to obtain more refined information.

NetView provides some basic tools to display MIB data and provides some samples to show you how to do fancier things. Beyond these, you will need to develop your own techniques. Let's look at how we can display collected data on-line, and also produce reports for off-line viewing.

---

[14] *xwd* and *xpr* (discussed below) are provided with the X Windows support normally available in AIX systems.

[15] This is available on the Internet, for example from ftp.x.org in directory /R5contrib, and is also included in the softcopy materials for this book available on the Internet at www.mcgraw-hill.co.uk (check on editorial information for professional computing).

[16] If you're printing to A4 instead of American 8.5 × 11 paper you should use the *pnmtops* options '-width 8.26 -height 11.69'.

On-line display The main NetView tool for displaying MIB data on-line is in the Data Collection window. Here you can press the Show button for a particular collection entry and you will see a table with both the data that has already been collected as well as the data being collected in real time.

The other option is to use the *snmpColDump* command to see data that has already been collected. For example, if you wanted to make it easy to see the last 10 collected values of *ipIn-Receives* for a particular system, you could combine *snmpColDump* with *xnmappmon* and make a little window that popped up from a menu selection.

To do this, suppose we made the following script (named *last10_iprs*):

```
snmpColDump \
/usr/OV/databases/snmpCollect/ipInReceives.0 | \
grep $1 | \
tail -10 | \
awk '{printf("%s %s: %s\n", $1, $2, $4)}'
```

This invokes *snmpColDump* to dump the *ipInReceives* binary data file. It then pipes that into *grep* to select the lines for the desired system. This is then piped into *tail* to get the last 10 values, and then into *awk* for formatting.

Then we would create another script to invoke *last10_iprs* within *xnmappmon*:[17]

```
xnmappmon \
    -commandTitle 'Last 10 Values of ipInReceives for $1' \
    -cmd last10_iprs $1
```

We could then make the application registration file (ARF) shown in Figure 10.11. A NetView user could now invoke our tool from the NetView menu, and see the incoming IP traffic for a system selected in a submap.

Thus, using NetView tools such as *snmpColDump*, *xnmgraph* and ARFs in conjunction with UNIX utilities, it is fairly easy to create custom displays of data collected from agents' MIBs.

```
Application "Show Last 10 ipInReceives for Selected Host"
{ Version "1.1";
    Copyright { "Copyright Larry Bennett, 1995" }

    Description
    { "Pop up and xnmappmon window showing the last 10 ipInReceives",
    "for the host selected on a submap." }

    MenuBar "Monitor"
    { <80> "Last 10 ipInReceives..." f.action "ShowLast10"; }

    Action "ShowLast10" {
        SelectionRule isSNMPSupported || isSNMPProxied;
        MinSelected 1;
        MaxSelected 1;
        Command "xnmappmon_last10_iprs $OVwSelection1"; } }
```

Figure 10.11 ARF to invoke *xnmgraph*

---

[17] This second script avoids the headaches caused by invoking *xnmappmon* directly from the application registration file we are about to see. Otherwise, untangling the syntax gets tricky.

Off-line display without an RDB If you don't have a relational database, there is still a fair amount you can do to create reports. In general, the technique is to use *snmpColDump* and pipe its output into other UNIX tools such as *awk, sed, sort, join, grep* and so forth. Appendix IX gives an example report-generating program using these techniques.

The main trick to report generation is being familiar with the techniques of script writing. UNIX has many commands that can make this job quite easy—some of which are used in the example scripts. If you're familiar with these, you'll have an easy time. If not, you would do well to get a book on the subject, for example Rosenblatt (1994), which explains script writing, or Schwartz (1993), which explains the more modern Perl language.

Off-line display with an RDB With a relational database, you can rely on SQL to generate reports much more easily. Once the collected data has been copied from the normal flat files into the database, it is stored in three tables:

- The *colData* table, in which each row contains the data for one collection of a particular variable.
- The *varInfo* table, in which each row describes a variable that has been collected. This serves the same purpose as the bang files we reviewed earlier. Each row here contains the variable's object ID, mnemonic, units and data type.
- The *expInfo* table, in which each row describes a MIB expression. Each row here contains the information defined for the expression in mibExpr.conf.

The most interesting of these is the *colData* Table. Its columns are explained in the box. Let's consider an example of generating a report from it.

Columns of the *colData* Table

varID Object ID of variable collected

expName MIB expression name (if this is an expression collection)

collectTime Time at which this collection occurred, in readable format, e.g. 1995-01-29 17:48:37

startTicks Time at which this collection interval began, expressed as seconds since the beginning of 1970

stopTicks Time at which this collection interval ended, expressed as seconds since the beginning of 1970

hostName Name of the agent from which the value was collected

ipAddr IP address of the agent

instance Instance ID collected, e.g. 0 or 1

stringValue The collected value represented as a string (used for IP addresses)

floatValue The collected value as a floating point (used for types INTEGER, *Counter, Gauge* and *TimeTicks*)

Suppose there are several RMON probes scattered over a network, and that each probe monitors one or more Token-Rings. NetView is collecting statistics from them periodically. One very interesting statistic is how frequently a ring is in the 'beaconing' state, as this indicates that something is very wrong in the ring, for example someone has installed an adapter in his PC with the speed set incorrectly. Let's assume we want to create a report showing which rings have been beaconing.

The RMON MIB has the Token-Ring Mac-Layer Statistics Table. As we saw earlier, each entry of this table contains information for a monitored ring and includes, among other things, the object *tokenRingMLStatsBeaconEvents*. This counts the number of times the ring has been in the beaconing state. This object can be the basis for a report that will show which segments are beaconing during each collection interval, and which are doing so the most.

An SQL query can generate the report. The query will get all the collected instances of the beacon counter which are greater than zero, and return a results table with these sorted by the beacon counter in descending order. It will also use the agent's address and the collection time as secondary sort criteria. Each row in the final results table will include the agent's IP address, the instance ID of the counter, the collection time and the collected value.

The query is:[18]

```
select ipAddr, instance, collectTime, floatValue \
    from colData \
    where \
        varID = '.1.3.6.1.2.1.16.1.2.1.8' and \
        floatValue > 0 \
    order by \
        floatValue desc, ipAddr asc, collectTime asc
```

10.4 SUMMARY

SNMP is very good at collecting all sorts of data from the network. Nearly all networking equipment sold today includes an SNMP agent with at least the basic MIB-II, and often a MIB extension as well. Generally these MIBs will provide good fault, performance and inventory information. For other kinds of information, e.g. accounting and availability, agents may not always provide what you need and the only hope is to write or acquire software to generate it.

NetView and Systems Monitor are quite good at collecting whatever data is available from SNMP agents. They also provide good tools for screening it in real time to determine whether it indicates problems. They do not address reporting of this data, but there are many packages on the market for taking data and easily generating snappy reports and graphs. It is also fairly easy to do this yourself, especially with the help of a relational database.

---

[18] This was tested with DB2/6000.

ELEVEN
CONCLUSION

In multiprotocol networks, NetView, Systems Monitor, Trouble Ticket and the several NetView applications can be used to carry out four of the most important management activities—problem reporting, graphical network display, operations and network monitoring. Still, there is more to network management. Today, you can buy many other management functions from IBM and other vendors, but in many cases they are not particularly well integrated with each other. Yet if anything is clear in this field, integrated management systems are extremely important.

IBM is working to build this sort of integrated system in a project called 'Karat', which for the UNIX-based management market has led to the product 'SystemView for AIX'. The idea is to take the many AIX-based systems and network management products and essentially meld them together into an integrated whole, while adding more functions. NetView will be the key management platform in SystemView for AIX.

In its first incarnation, SystemView for AIX has taken an initial step towards integration with a nice GUI called the Visual Launch Panel from which NetView and other products can be invoked. The GUI is arranged by management disciplines to provide a sensible structure for the many management products involved. Also, all the components of SystemView for AIX are packaged together on two CDs. IBM plans, in future releases of SystemView for AIX, to make this integration more substantial so that the different products can share data and work together more effectively. By the time you read this, some of the integration may already be available.

As SystemView for AIX develops, NetView will continue to be the key underlying platform for the other functions and will continue to be enhanced. Its identity may be less clear as integration becomes more substantial, but it will still be there, carrying out the functions we have looked at in this book and, with its connections to other products, doing so more effectively.

TRAP VARIABLE BINDINGS FOR *TRAPGEND*

The NetView daemon *trapgend* generates traps for certain entries made to the AIX error log, as discussed in Section 7.3.1. The traps include many variable bindings which describe the error log entry. The object IDs used in the bindings are from the IBM sub-tree under *enterprises*. The traps are constructed in a way that makes them easy to translate into SNA alerts, and much of the terminology involved is from the SNA Management Services Architecture. For example, the term 'alert' is used instead of 'error'.

The variables bindings in *trapgend*'s traps are:

- Several variables describing the hardware and software (the RS/6000 and AIX) on which the trap was created. These are in the style of information that would be included in the Product Set ID Subvectors of an SNA Management Services alert. There are usually 15 to 20 of these variables.
- A variable containing the error type from the error template.
- A variable containing the error description code from the template.
- Several variables, each of which contains a probable cause, failure cause, user cause, install cause or recommended action codepoint, copied exactly from the error template.
- Several more variables, each group of which conveys a detailed data field from the error log entry. For each detailed data field, there are four variable bindings: a product ID code (which all but the extreme architectural purists may ignore), a data ID code (which is the codepoint for the detail data field in the error template), an encoding ID (which again may be ignored), and finally the value of the detail data field.
- In some cases there are variables containing throttling information for the error log entry. *trapgend* has a throttling value that can be employed to limit the frequency with which it converts error log entries into traps. By default, it is configured so that it will convert the same error message no more than once per minute. (You can change this value through SMIT.)

There is much documentation of these trap variables in the file:

/usr/OV/snmp_mibs/ibm-alert.mib.

EXAMPLE PRE-FILTERING DAEMON

This appendix contains the C code for the pre-filtering daemon discussed in Section 7.3.5.

II.1 REGISTERING THE DAEMON

Let's review a few details of how daemons are integrated into NetView's infrastructure. As you can see from the code below, such a program can register itself to NetView by calling the routines *OVsInit*, *OVsInitComplete* and *OVsDone*.

We must also create a definition file for the daemon, a Local Registration File (LRF). This defines the daemon's name, the path for its executable file, its initialization parameters and other information.

The one I used for the pre-filtering daemon is:

```
filterd:/usr/local/bin/filterd:
OVs_YES_START:pmd,ems_sieve_agent::OVs_WELL_BEHAVED:15:
```

The file would normally be placed in the directory /usr/OV/lrf along with the other LRFs for NetView and its applications. It must be activated by issuing the *ovaddobj* command (e.g. 'ovaddobj /usr/OV/lrf/filterd.lrf').

Once this all has been done, the daemon can be controlled with *ovstart* and *ovstop*, and its status displayed with *ovstatus*. It will also terminate gracefully when NetView is stopped.

II.2 RECEIVING TRAPS

When using *nvSnmpTrapOpenFilter* to connect to the SNMP interface, there are two ways to receive traps. One is using *select* to wait for a trap to arrive. Here the daemon simply waits for a trap, doing nothing else. This is the simplest method and suitable in most cases. The code below uses this method.

The other method is to use 'callback routines'. In this case, your program does not wait but instead is free to perform other processing until a trap arrives. When one does arrive, the callback routine is driven to receive it.

II.3 CODE

```
/*****************************************************************/
/* Sample program to receive traps from the NetView            */
/* SNMP API using a filter string that passes only             */
/* enterprise-specific traps from enterprise                   */
/* 1.3.6.1.4.1.2.6.3.1 with specific code 123456.  For         */
/* each such trap received the program checks if               */
/* the variable bindings contain an object with ID             */
/* 1.3.6.1.2.1.99.  If so and this object is bound to an       */
/* integer with value 2 then it creates an incident report     */
/* and sends it to Trouble Ticket using cmd_in.                */
/*****************************************************************/

#include <stdio.h>
#include <stdlib.h>
#include <string.h>
#include <OV/OVsnmp.h>
#include <OV/OVsPMD.h>
#include <sys/select.h>
#include <sys/errno.h>

#define filt_string "SNMP_TRAP=6 && SNMP_SPECIFIC=123456 &&
CLASS=1.3.6.1.4.1.2.6.3.1"

extern int errno;

/*****************************************************************/
/********************** main ************************************/
/*****************************************************************/

int main(int argc, char **argv) {
    OVsnmpSession      *trapSession;
    OVsnmpPdu          *trapResponse;
    OVsnmpVarBind      *varBindPtr;
    OVsPMDCommand      pmdcmd;
    struct fd_set      readFDs;
    struct timeval     timeVal;
    int                responseID,
                       count,
                       numFDs,
                       i, j,
                       rc,
                       error,
```

```
                        pmd_socket,
                        dotted[4],
                        workint,
                        mo_len = 7; /* Length of object in match_oid */
ObjectID                match_oid[] = {1,3,6,1,2,1,99};
char                    cmdstring[1000],
                        msg[500];


/****************************************************************/
/* First indicate we are starting initialization and get       */
/* the socket for pmd communication.  If the call fails         */
/* things are really screwed up with the pmd and so we          */
/* just ditch.                                                  */
/****************************************************************/
if(OVsInit(&pmd_socket) != 0) exit(-1);


/****************************************************************/
/* Open session for receiving traps and process any            */
/* errors.  Specify the filter string to accept only traps     */
/* with the desired enterprise and trap codes.  With this      */
/* and the rest of the initialization any errors will mean     */
/* that not only do we exit but also we must call              */
/* OVsInitComplete to indicate to pmd that initialization      */
/* failed.                                                     */
/****************************************************************/
trapSession = nvSnmpTrapOpenFilter(NULL, NULL, filt_string);
if (trapSession == NULL) {
  sprintf(msg,
    "nvSnmpTrapOpenFilter: Trap Filter Session failed to open.\n"
    "    %d: %s \n"
    "    %d: %s \n"
    "    %d: %s \n",
    OVsnmpErrno,   OVsnmpErrString(OVsnmpErrno),
    nvSnmpErrno,   OVsnmpErrString(nvSnmpErrno),
    nvSnmpSubsys,  OVsnmpErrString(nvSnmpSubsys));
  OVsInitComplete(OVS_RSP_FAILURE, msg);
  exit(1);
}

if (trapSession->session_flags && RECV_TRAPS == 0) {
  sprintf(msg,"RECV_TRAPS flag is not set in trapSession.\n");
  OVsInitComplete(OVS_RSP_FAILURE, msg);
  exit(1);
}


/****************************************************************/
/* Now that we have finished initialization we must            */
/* indicate this to the pmd.                                   */
/****************************************************************/
OVsInitComplete(OVS_RSP_SUCCESS, "Initialization complete.");
```

```
/***************************************************************/
/* Main loop of program.  Wait for either a trap to come    */
/* in or for a signal from pmd.  The only signal pmd will   */
/* send us is that it is time to terminate.  If a trap has */
/* arrived check if we are interested in it and if so        */
/* build an incident report and send to Trouble             */
/* Ticket                                                    */
/***************************************************************/
numFDs = trapSession->sock_fd + pmd_socket + 2;
FD_ZERO(&readFDs);

while(1) {
  FD_SET(trapSession->sock_fd, &readFDs);
  FD_SET(pmd_socket, &readFDs);
  if ((count = select(numFDs, &readFDs, NULL, NULL, NULL)) < 0) {
    sprintf(msg,"Select failed.\n");
    OVsDone(msg);
    exit(1);
  }
  /***************************************************************/
  /* If we received something from pmd it must be the exit    */
  /* signal so we issue the OVsReceive for form sake but      */
  /* without bothering to check result.  Then just exit.      */
  /***************************************************************/
  if(FD_ISSET(pmd_socket, &readFDs)) {
    OVsReceive(&pmdcmd);
    OVsDone("Normal completion.");
    exit(0);
  }

  /***************************************************************/
  /* Otherwise if SNMP receive occurred then attempt to       */
  /* receive the trap.                                         */
  /***************************************************************/
  else if(FD_ISSET(trapSession->sock_fd, &readFDs)) {
    trapResponse = OVsnmpRecv(trapSession);

    /***************************************************************/
    /* If we had a problem getting the trap then handle error   */
    /* case.                                                     */
    /***************************************************************/
    if (trapResponse == NULL)
    {
      error = errno;
      sprintf(msg,"%d OVsnmpRecv: %s\n"
              "    %d: %s \n"
              "    %d: %s \n"
              "errno = %d\n",
              OVsnmpErrno, OVsnmpErrString(OVsnmpErrno),
```

```
                    nvSnmpErrno, OVsnmpErrString(nvSnmpErrno),
                    nvSnmpSubsys, OVsnmpErrString(nvSnmpSubsys),
                    error);
      OVsDone(msg);
      exit(1);
   }
   /******************************************************************/
   /* Otherwise we have a trap -- scan through the variable   */
   /* bindings looking for object with desired ID.            */
   /******************************************************************/
   else {
      varBindPtr = trapResponse->variables;
      while(varBindPtr != NULL) {
         if(varBindPtr->oid_length == mo_len) {
         for(i=0;i<mo_len && match_oid[i] == varBindPtr->oid[i];i++);
         if (i==mo_len) break;
         }
         varBindPtr = varBindPtr->next_variable;
      }
      /******************************************************************/
      /* If we found the object then check if its type is       */
      /* integer and its value is 2.  If so then create the      */
      /* incident report by creating the string of file format  */
      /* required by cmd_in and then invoking cmd_in by piping  */
      /* the string into it.  The agent address must be        */
      /* in dotted decimal.  We must invoke cmd_inv using env   */
      /* command to have NX_ROOT properly set in environment.   */
      /******************************************************************/
      if (varBindPtr!=NULL && varBindPtr->type==ASN_INTEGER &&
          *varBindPtr->val.integer==2) {
         workint = trapResponse->agent_addr;
         for (j=0;j<=3;j++) {
            dotted[j] = workint % 256;
            workint = workint / 256;
         }
         sprintf(cmdstring,"echo 'Incident_Report_Submission {\n"
                           "Summary = \"The magic trap occurred\"\n"
                           "Impact =  3\n"
                           "Organization = TechSpt\n"
                           "Resource = \"%d.%d.%d.%d\"}'"
                           "| env -i NX_ROOT=/usr/lpp/tt6000"
                           "/usr/lpp/tt6000/bin/cmd_in",
                           dotted[3],dotted[2],dotted[1],dotted[0]);
         system(cmdstring);
      }
      OVsnmpFreePdu(trapResponse);
   } /* end else we have a trap */
   } /* end if trap receive fd set */
   } /* end while (1) */
} /* end main */
```

DEFINITION OF GRAPH TABLE

This appendix contains the section of the Topology MIB which defines the Graph Table. This is discussed in Section 8.3.9.

```
graphTable        OBJECT-TYPE
                          SYNTAX     SEQUENCE OF GraphTableEntry
                          ACCESS     not-accessible
                          STATUS     mandatory
                          DESCRIPTION
                            "There is entry in the graph table for each
                             graph defined by an agent."

                  REFERENCE    "AWP-7603, Graph"
                  ::= {graph 1}

graphTableEntry           OBJECT-TYPE
                          SYNTAX     GraphTableEntry
                  ACCESS    not-accessible
                          STATUS     mandatory
                          DESCRIPTION
                            "Each entry defines the basic information
                             about a graph."
                  REFERENCE    "AWP-7603, Graph"
                  INDEX {graphProtocol, graphName}
                  ::= {graphTable 1}

GraphTableEntry ::=
    SEQUENCE {
              graphType          GraphType,
              graphProtocol      OBJECT IDENTIFIER,
              graphName          OCTET STRING,
              layoutAlgorithm    LayoutAlgorithm,
```

```
            userDefinedLayout      DisplayString,
            graphLocation    OCTET STRING,
            backgroundMap    DisplayString,
            graphManagementExtension      OBJECT IDENTIFIER,
            graphManagementAddr  OCTET STRING,
            graphIcon        OBJECT IDENTIFIER,
            isRoot           INTEGER{ true(1), false(2)},
            graphLabel       OCTET STRING
            }

graphType       OBJECT-TYPE
            SYNTAX     GraphType
            ACCESS     read-only
            STATUS     mandatory
            DESCRIPTION
               "This variable indicates if the row is valid or
               invalid. If this variable has a value of invalid
               then the table row is invalid and must be
               ignored."
            DEFVAL { graph }
             ::= {graphTableEntry 1}

graphProtocol  OBJECT-TYPE
                  SYNTAX     OBJECT IDENTIFIER
                  ACCESS     read-only
                  STATUS     mandatory
                  DESCRIPTION
                  "The context in which the graph name is
                    defined."
                  REFERENCE   "AWP-7603, Naming"
            ::= {graphTableEntry 2}

graphName      OBJECT-TYPE
                  SYNTAX     OCTET STRING
            ACCESS     read-only
                  STATUS     mandatory
                  DESCRIPTION
                   "This is the unique name for the graph.  It
                     must be unique among all graphs with the
                     same graphProtocol values."
            REFERENCE    "AWP-7603, Naming"
            ::= {graphTableEntry 3}

layoutAlgorithm         OBJECT-TYPE
                  SYNTAX     LayoutAlgorithm
                  ACCESS     read-only
                  STATUS     mandatory
                  DESCRIPTION
                  "The layout algorithm to use when displaying
                    this graph on a topology display."
```

```
                    REFERENCE  "AWP-7603, Graph"
                    DEFVAL     {none}
          ::= {graphTableEntry 4}


userDefinedLayout        OBJECT-TYPE
                         SYNTAX    DisplayString
                         ACCESS    read-only
                         STATUS    mandatory
                         DESCRIPTION
                          "The name of the user-defined layout
                           algorithm when layout Algorithm is equal to
                           userdefined. Support of this algorithm must
                           be arranged with the management platform."
                         REFERENCE  "AWP-7603, Graph"
                         DEFVAL { "" }
          ::= {graphTableEntry 5}


graphLocation   OBJECT-TYPE
                         SYNTAX    OCTET STRING
                         ACCESS    read-only
                         STATUS    mandatory
                         DESCRIPTION
                          "This variable contains the location of the
                            graph."
                REFERENCE  "AWP-7603, Correlation"
                DEFVAL { '00'h }
                ::= {graphTableEntry 6}


backgroundMap   OBJECT-TYPE
                SYNTAX    DisplayString
                ACCESS    read-only
                STATUS    mandatory
                DESCRIPTION
                "This is the background map to use as a backdrop on
                  the topology display.  The valid values for this
                  variable are management platform specific."
                DEFVAL          { "" }
                ::= {graphTableEntry 7}


graphManagementExtension      OBJECT-TYPE
                         SYNTAX    OBJECT IDENTIFIER
                         ACCESS    read-only
                         STATUS    mandatory
                         DESCRIPTION
                          "This object identifies a table containing
                            additional information about the graph."
                         DEFVAL          { {0} }
          ::= {graphTableEntry 8}
```

```
graphManagementAddr          OBJECT-TYPE
                             SYNTAX     OCTET STRING
                             ACCESS     read-only
                             STATUS     mandatory
                             DESCRIPTION
                              "This variable contains the address of the
                              agent that is the source of the table
                              identified by graphManagementExtension.
                              It can be used as the destination address
                              for management operations."
                   DEFVAL           {'00'h}
                   ::= {graphTableEntry 9}


graphIcon          OBJECT-TYPE
                   SYNTAX     OBJECT IDENTIFIER
                   ACCESS     read-only
                   STATUS     mandatory
                   DESCRIPTION
                     "This variable identifies the icon to use for the
                     graph on a topology display."
                   DEFVAL { {0} }
                   ::= {graphTableEntry 10}


isRoot             OBJECT-TYPE
                   SYNTAX     INTEGER{ true(1), false(2) }
                   ACCESS     read-only
                   STATUS     mandatory
                   DESCRIPTION
                     "This variable identifies if this is a root graph."
                   DEFVAL     {false}
                   ::= {graphTableEntry 11}


graphLabel         OBJECT-TYPE
                   SYNTAX     DisplayString
                   ACCESS     read-only
                   STATUS     mandatory
                   DESCRIPTION
                     "This is the label to be used on the topology
                     display. It is either administratively or user
                     defined. If it has the value of the null string,
                     graphName should be used on the display."
                   DEFVAL     {""}
                   ::= {graphTableEntry 12}
```

TOPOLOGY TRAPS EXAMPLE

This script in this appendix generates non-IP topology submaps by sending traps to NetView's GTM. It relies on the *snmptrap* command to create and send the traps. The script creates the set of submaps depicted in Figure IV.1, in which there are two protocols, Frame Relay and DS1. The idea is that the Frame Relay 'logical interface' runs over the DS1 'physical interface'. To keep the example to a reasonable length, I have just one workstation with one interface.

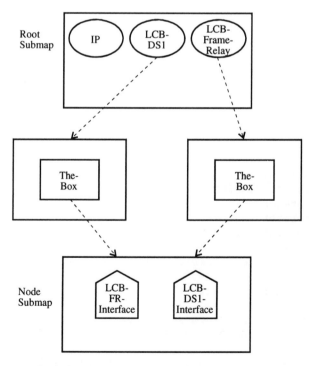

Figure IV.1 Submaps created by shell script

```
# Create the root graph for DS1 (newGraph trap).
# .1 = graphType (3=graph graph), .2 = graphProtocol, .3=graphName
# .4 = layoutAlgorithm (7=row/column), .5 = userdefinedLayout,
# .6 = graphLocation, .7 = backgroundMap,
# .10 = graphIcon, .11 = isRoot, .12 = graphLabel
#
snmptrap helen .1.3.6.1.4.1.2 helen 6 1879048213 0 \
.1.3.6.1.4.1.2.5.3.4.1.1.1 integer 3 \
.1.3.6.1.4.1.2.5.3.4.1.1.2 objectidentifier .1.3.6.1.2.1.2.2.1.3.18 \
.1.3.6.1.4.1.2.5.3.4.1.1.3 octetstringascii LCB_DS1 \
.1.3.6.1.4.1.2.5.3.4.1.1.4 integer 7 \
.1.3.6.1.4.1.2.5.3.4.1.1.5 octetstringascii not_used \
.1.3.6.1.4.1.2.5.3.4.1.1.6 octetstringascii Closet \
.1.3.6.1.4.1.2.5.3.4.1.1.7 octetstringascii "" \
.1.3.6.1.4.1.2.5.3.4.1.1.10 objectidentifier .1.3.6.1.2.1.2.2.1.3.1.11 \
.1.3.6.1.4.1.2.5.3.4.1.1.11 integer 1 \
.1.3.6.1.4.1.2.5.3.4.1.1.12 octetstringascii LCB_DS1

# Create the root graph for Frame Relay (newGraph trap)
snmptrap helen .1.3.6.1.4.1.2 helen 6 1879048213 0 \
.1.3.6.1.4.1.2.5.3.4.1.1.1 integer 3 \
.1.3.6.1.4.1.2.5.3.4.1.1.2 objectidentifier .1.3.6.1.2.1.2.2.1.3.32 \
.1.3.6.1.4.1.2.5.3.4.1.1.3 octetstringascii LCB_Frame_Relay \
.1.3.6.1.4.1.2.5.3.4.1.1.4 integer 7 \
.1.3.6.1.4.1.2.5.3.4.1.1.5 octetstringascii not_used \
.1.3.6.1.4.1.2.5.3.4.1.1.6 octetstringascii Outside \
.1.3.6.1.4.1.2.5.3.4.1.1.7 octetstringascii "" \
.1.3.6.1.4.1.2.5.3.4.1.1.10 objectidentifier .1.3.6.1.2.1.2.2.1.3.57.11 \
.1.3.6.1.4.1.2.5.3.4.1.1.11 integer 1 \
.1.3.6.1.4.1.2.5.3.4.1.1.12 octetstringascii LCB_Frame_Relay

# Create the box graph for DS1 (newGraph trap).
# Fields same as for graphs above except that graphType (.1) is
# 4 for box graph.
snmptrap helen .1.3.6.1.4.1.2 helen 6 1879048213 0 \
.1.3.6.1.4.1.2.5.3.4.1.1.1 integer 4 \
.1.3.6.1.4.1.2.5.3.4.1.1.2 objectidentifier .1.3.6.1.2.1.2.2.1.3.18 \
.1.3.6.1.4.1.2.5.3.4.1.1.3 octetstringascii The_Box \
.1.3.6.1.4.1.2.5.3.4.1.1.4 integer 7 \
.1.3.6.1.4.1.2.5.3.4.1.1.5 octetstringascii not_used \
.1.3.6.1.4.1.2.5.3.4.1.1.6 octetstringascii Desk \
.1.3.6.1.4.1.2.5.3.4.1.1.7 octetstringascii "" \
.1.3.6.1.4.1.2.5.3.4.1.1.10 objectidentifier .1.3.6.1.2.1.2.2.1.3.6.10 \
.1.3.6.1.4.1.2.5.3.4.1.1.11 integer 2 \
.1.3.6.1.4.1.2.5.3.4.1.1.12 octetstringascii The_Box

# Create the box graph for Frame Relay (newGraph trap).
snmptrap helen .1.3.6.1.4.1.2 helen 6 1879048213 0 \
.1.3.6.1.4.1.2.5.3.4.1.1.1 integer 4 \
.1.3.6.1.4.1.2.5.3.4.1.1.2 objectidentifier .1.3.6.1.2.1.2.2.1.3.32 \
```

```
.1.3.6.1.4.1.2.5.3.4.1.1.3 octetstringascii The_Box \
.1.3.6.1.4.1.2.5.3.4.1.1.4 integer 7 \
.1.3.6.1.4.1.2.5.3.4.1.1.5 octetstringascii not_used \
.1.3.6.1.4.1.2.5.3.4.1.1.6 octetstringascii Desk \
.1.3.6.1.4.1.2.5.3.4.1.1.7 octetstringascii "" \
.1.3.6.1.4.1.2.5.3.4.1.1.10 objectidentifier .1.3.6.1.2.1.2.2.1.3.6.10 \
.1.3.6.1.4.1.2.5.3.4.1.1.11 integer 2 \
.1.3.6.1.4.1.2.5.3.4.1.1.12 octetstringascii The_Box

# Make the box graph a member of the graph for DS1 # (newMemberTrap).
# .1 = memberProtocol (protocol of containing graph)
# .2 = memberName (name of containing graph),
# .3 = memberIndexId (to make triplet protocol, name, index unique)
# .4 = memberComponentProtocol, .5 = memberComponentName
#
snmptrap helen .1.3.6.1.4.1.2 helen 6 1879048222 0 \
.1.3.6.1.4.1.2.5.3.4.4.1.2 objectidentifier .1.3.6.1.2.1.2.2.1.3.18 \
.1.3.6.1.4.1.2.5.3.4.4.1.3 octetstringascii LCB_DS1 \
.1.3.6.1.4.1.2.5.3.4.4.1.4 integer 1 \
.1.3.6.1.4.1.2.5.3.4.4.1.6 objectidentifier .1.3.6.1.2.1.2.2.1.3.18 \
.1.3.6.1.4.1.2.5.3.4.4.1.7 octetstringascii The_Box

# Make the box graph a member of the graph for Frame Relay
# (newMemberTrap).
snmptrap helen .1.3.6.1.4.1.2 helen 6 1879048222 0 \
.1.3.6.1.4.1.2.5.3.4.4.1.2 objectidentifier .1.3.6.1.2.1.2.2.1.3.32 \
.1.3.6.1.4.1.2.5.3.4.4.1.3 octetstringascii LCB_Frame_Relay \
.1.3.6.1.4.1.2.5.3.4.4.1.4 integer 1 \
.1.3.6.1.4.1.2.5.3.4.4.1.6 objectidentifier .1.3.6.1.2.1.2.2.1.3.32 \
.1.3.6.1.4.1.2.5.3.4.4.1.7 octetstringascii The_Box

# Create a vertex in the box graph for DS1 (newVertex trap).
# .2 = vertexProtocol, .3 = vertexName, .4 = vertexLabel,
# .6 = vertexLocation, .9 = vertexIcon,
# .10 = vertexOperationalState (2=enabled),
# .11 = vertexUnknownStatus (2=false),
# .12 = vertexAvailabilityStatus (0 = empty, i.e.  no problems)
# .13 = vertexAlarmStatus (0 = empty, i.e.  no alarms)
#
snmptrap helen .1.3.6.1.4.1.2 helen 6 1879048192 0 \
.1.3.6.1.4.1.2.5.3.1.1.1.2 integer 18 \
.1.3.6.1.4.1.2.5.3.1.1.1.3 octetstringascii LCB_DS1_Interface \
.1.3.6.1.4.1.2.5.3.1.1.1.4 octetstringascii LCB_DS1_Interface \
.1.3.6.1.4.1.2.5.3.1.1.1.6 octetstringascii The_Box \
.1.3.6.1.4.1.2.5.3.1.1.1.9 objectidentifier .1.3.6.1.2.1.2.2.1.3.1.1 \
.1.3.6.1.4.1.2.5.3.1.1.1.10 integer 2 \
.1.3.6.1.4.1.2.5.3.1.1.1.11 integer 2 \
.1.3.6.1.4.1.2.5.3.1.1.1.12 integer 0 \
.1.3.6.1.4.1.2.5.3.1.1.1.13 integer 0
```

```
# Create a vertex in the box graph for Frame Relay (newVertex trap).
snmptrap helen .1.3.6.1.4.1.2 helen 6 1879048192 0 \
.1.3.6.1.4.1.2.5.3.1.1.1.2 integer 32 \
.1.3.6.1.4.1.2.5.3.1.1.1.3 octetstringascii LCB_FR_Interface \
.1.3.6.1.4.1.2.5.3.1.1.1.4 octetstringascii LCB_FR_Interface \
.1.3.6.1.4.1.2.5.3.1.1.1.6 octetstringascii The_Box \
.1.3.6.1.4.1.2.5.3.1.1.1.9 objectidentifier .1.3.6.1.2.1.2.2.1.3.1.1 \
.1.3.6.1.4.1.2.5.3.1.1.1.10 integer 2 \
.1.3.6.1.4.1.2.5.3.1.1.1.11 integer 2 \
.1.3.6.1.4.1.2.5.3.1.1.1.12 integer 0 \
.1.3.6.1.4.1.2.5.3.1.1.1.13 integer 0

# Make the vertex a member of the box graph for DS1 (newMemberTrap).
# Same trap as used above to make box graphs members of graphs.
# Use of integer rather than object identifier for protocol of
# contained entity (.6) indicates that this entity is a vertex rather
# rather than a graph.
#
snmptrap helen .1.3.6.1.4.1.2 helen 6 1879048222 0 \
.1.3.6.1.4.1.2.5.3.4.4.1.2 objectidentifier .1.3.6.1.2.1.2.2.1.3.18 \
.1.3.6.1.4.1.2.5.3.4.4.1.3 octetstringascii The_Box \
.1.3.6.1.4.1.2.5.3.4.4.1.4 integer 1 \
.1.3.6.1.4.1.2.5.3.4.4.1.6 integer 18 \
.1.3.6.1.4.1.2.5.3.4.4.1.7 octetstringascii LCB_DS1_Interface

# Make the vertex a member of the box graph for Frame Relay
# (newMemberTrap).
snmptrap helen .1.3.6.1.4.1.2 helen 6 1879048222 0 \
.1.3.6.1.4.1.2.5.3.4.4.1.2 objectidentifier .1.3.6.1.2.1.2.2.1.3.32 \
.1.3.6.1.4.1.2.5.3.4.4.1.3 octetstringascii The_Box \
.1.3.6.1.4.1.2.5.3.4.4.1.4 integer 1 \
.1.3.6.1.4.1.2.5.3.4.4.1.6 integer 32 \
.1.3.6.1.4.1.2.5.3.4.4.1.7 octetstringascii LCB_FR_Interface

# Correlate the two vertices with a SAP trap (newSAPTrap).
# .2 = sapVertexProtocol (of using vertex in this case),
# .3 = sapVertexName (of using vertext in this case),
# .4 = sapIndexId (integer to make unique)
# .5 = sapServiceType (1 = using), .6 = sapProtocol (of providing
# vertex in this case), .7 = sapAddress (name of used vertex in this
# case)
#
snmptrap helen .1.3.6.1.4.1.2 helen 6 1879048196 0 \
.1.3.6.1.4.1.2.5.3.1.2.1.2 integer 32 \
.1.3.6.1.4.1.2.5.3.1.2.1.3 octetstringascii LCB_FR_Interface \
.1.3.6.1.4.1.2.5.3.1.2.1.4 integer 1 \
.1.3.6.1.4.1.2.5.3.1.2.1.5 integer 1 \
.1.3.6.1.4.1.2.5.3.1.2.1.6 integer 18 \
.1.3.6.1.4.1.2.5.3.1.2.1.7 octetstringascii LCB_DS1_Interface
```

GTM C CALLS EXAMPLE

This program creates the same non-IP topology submaps as the script in Appendix IV. Here however it is done using C calls instead of traps.

```c
#include <stdio.h>
#include <errno.h>
#include <string.h>
#include <nvot.h>
#include <OV/ovw_obj.h>

int main(int argc, char **argv) {
  nvotReturnCode rc;

  /* Initialize, specifying parms 1) connect to local host, 2) arc
     naming is independent of vertex order, 3) check for existing
     objects before re-creating. */
  if (rc = nvotInit(NULL, TRUE, TRUE) != NVOT_SUCCESS) {
    fprintf(stderr, "NVOT initialization failed:\n");
    printf("  %s\n", nvotGetErrorMsg(rc));
    exit(-1) ;
  }

  /* Create the root graph graph for DS1 */
  rc = nvotCreateRootGraph("1.3.6.1.2.1.2.2.1.3.23",       /* protocol */
                  "LCB_DS1",                        /* name */
                  POINT_TO_POINT_LAYOUT,            /* layout */
                  "",                               /* background */
                  "1.3.6.1.2.1.2.2.1.3.1.11",       /* icon obj id */
                  "LCB_DS1",                        /* label */
                  "");                              /* details */
  if (rc != NVOT_SUCCESS)
    fprintf(stderr, "Error: %s\n", nvotGetErrorMsg(nvotGetError()));
```

```
/* Create the root graph graph for Frame Relay */
rc = nvotCreateRootGraph("1.3.6.1.2.1.2.2.1.3.32",/* protocol */
                "LCB_Frame_Relay",                 /* name */
                POINT_TO_POINT_LAYOUT,             /* layout */
                "",                                /* background */
                "1.3.6.1.2.1.2.2.1.3.57.11",       /* icon obj id */
                        "LCB_Frame_Relay",         /* label */
                        "");                       /* details */
if (rc != NVOT_SUCCESS)
   fprintf(stderr, "Error: %s\n", nvotGetErrorMsg(nvotGetError()));


/* Create the box graph for DS1 inside root graph graph */
rc = nvotCreateBoxInGraph("1.3.6.1.2.1.2.2.1.3.23",   /* parent
                                                         proto */
                "LCB_DS1",                         /* parent name */
                "1.3.6.1.2.1.2.2.1.3.23",          /* box proto */
                "The_Box",                         /* box name */
                ROWCOL_LAYOUT,                     /* box layout */
                "",                                /* background */
                "1.3.6.1.2.1.2.2.1.3.6.10",        /* icon */
                "The_Box",                         /* label */
                "");                               /* details */
if (rc != NVOT_SUCCESS)
   fprintf(stderr, "Error: %s\n", nvotGetErrorMsg(nvotGetError()));


/* Create the box graph for Frame Relay inside root graph graph */
rc = nvotCreateBoxInGraph("1.3.6.1.2.1.2.2.1.3.32",/* parent proto */
                "LCB_Frame_Relay",                 /* parent name */
                "1.3.6.1.2.1.2.2.1.3.32",          /* box proto */
                "The_Box",                         /* box name */
                ROWCOL_LAYOUT,                     /* box layout */
                "",                                /* background */
                "1.3.6.1.2.1.2.2.1.3.6.10",        /* icon */
                "The_Box",                         /* label */
                "");                               /* details */
if (rc != NVOT_SUCCESS)
   fprintf(stderr, "Error: %s\n", nvotGetErrorMsg(nvotGetError()));


/* Create a vertex in the box graph for DS1 */
rc = nvotCreateVertexInBox("1.3.6.1.2.1.2.2.1.3.23",/* parent proto */
                "The_Box",                         /* parent name */
                DSL,                               /* vertex proto */
                "LCB_DS1_Adapter",                 /* vertex name */
                "1.3.6.1.2.1.2.2.1.3.1.1",         /* icon */
                "LCB_DS1_Adapter",                 /* label */
                "",                                /* details */
                STATUS_NORMAL);                    /* status */
if (rc != NVOT_SUCCESS)
   fprintf(stderr, "Error: %s\n", nvotGetErrorMsg(nvotGetError()));
```

```
/* Create a vertex in the box graph for Frame Relay */
rc = nvotCreateVertexInBox("1.3.6.1.2.1.2.2.1.3.32",  /* parent proto */
                  "The_Box",                      /* parent name */
                  FRAME_RELAY,                    /* vertex proto */
                  "LCB_FR_Interface",             /* vertex name */
                  "1.3.6.1.2.1.2.2.1.3.1.1",     /* icon */
                  "LCB_FR_Interface",             /* label */
                  "",                             /* details */
                  STATUS_NORMAL);                 /* status */
if (rc != NVOT_SUCCESS)
  fprintf(stderr, "Error: %s\n", nvotGetErrorMsg(nvotGetError()));

/* Correlate the two vertices with a SAP */
rc = nvotCreateUsingSap  (FRAME_RELAY,
                          "LCB_FR_Interface",
                          DSL,
                          "LCB_DS1_Adapter");
if (rc != NVOT_SUCCESS)
  fprintf(stderr, "Error: %s\n", nvotGetErrorMsg(nvotGetError()));

/* Disconnect from GTM and exit. */
nvotDone() ;
}
```

EXAMPLE SNMP PROGRAM

This program is an example of how to use the NetView SNMP programming interface to perform SNMP Gets and Sets. The program first gets the value of the variable *smMlmFilterDefaultAction.0* from the Systems Monitor MLM MIB extension, and then inverts it logically. Thus, if it is 1 (*sendTraps*), it is changed to 2 (*blockTraps*), and vice versa.

```
#include <stdio.h>
#include <malloc.h>
#include "/usr/OV/include/OV/OVsnmp.h"

int main(int argc, char **argv) {
  OVsnmpSession *session;
  OVsnmpPdu *getRequest, *getResponse, *setRequest, *setResponse;
  OVsnmpVarBind *varBind;
  char *destination;
  ObjectID target_oid[MAX_SUBID_LEN] = {1,3,6,1,4,1,2,6,12,7,1,0};
  int target_oid_len = 12;
  OVsnmpVal obj_val;
  long setval, getval;

  obj_val.integer = &setval;

  /* Check args */
  if (argc != 2) {
    fprintf(stderr, "Gotta give me just one argument -- destination "
                    "name or address\n");
    exit(-1);
  }

  /* Open session with destination, with NULL as community name to
     use community name defined to NetView.  Also pass NULL callback
     info (last two parms) since we are using blocking calls. */
```

```
session = OVsnmpOpen(NULL,
                     *(argv+1),
                     SNMP_USE_DEFAULT_RETRIES,
                     SNMP_USE_DEFAULT_INTERVAL,
                     SNMP_USE_DEFAULT_LOCAL_PORT,
                     SNMP_USE_DEFAULT_REMOTE_PORT,
                     NULL,
                     NULL);
if (session == NULL) {
  fprintf(stderr, "Error initializing SNMP session:\n  %s\n",
          OVsnmpErrString(OVsnmpErrno));
  exit(-1);
}


/* Create the GET PDU */
if ((getRequest = OVsnmpCreatePdu(GET_REQ_MSG)) == NULL) {
  fprintf(stderr, "Error creating GET PDU:\n  %s\n",
          OVsnmpErrString(OVsnmpErrno));
  exit(-1);
}


/* Add our target variable to the bindings in the GET PDU */
if (OVsnmpAddNullVarBind(getRequest, target_oid, target_oid_len)
    == NULL) {
  fprintf(stderr, "Error adding varbinds to GET PDU:\n  %s\n",
          OVsnmpErrString(OVsnmpErrno));
  OVsnmpFreePdu(getRequest);
  OVsnmpClose(session);
  exit(-1);
}


/* Issue the send, blocking until a response is received or error
   occurs */
getResponse = OVsnmpBlockingSend (session, getRequest) ;
if (getResponse == NULL) {
  fprintf(stderr, "Error sending GET PDU:\n  %s\n",
          OVsnmpErrString(OVsnmpErrno));
  if (OVsnmpErrno != SNMP_ERR_NO_RESPONSE) OVsnmpFreePdu(getRequest);
  OVsnmpClose (session) ;
  exit(-1);
}


/* Check the PDU error_status field */
if (getResponse->error_status != SNMP_ERR_NOERROR) {
  fprintf(stderr, "Error from agent in GET PDU response:\n  %s\n",
          OVsnmpErrString(getResponse->error_status));
  OVsnmpFreePdu(getResponse);
  OVsnmpClose (session) ;
  exit(-1);
}
```

```
/* The response will contain only one variable binding, the one we're
   interested in.  Get the value from it, increment, and throw away
   the PDU */
getval = *(getResponse -> variables) -> val.integer;
if (getval == 1) setval = 2;
  else setval = 1;
OVsnmpFreePdu(getResponse);


/* Now create a SET PDU, add a variable binding to set the target
   variable to the incremented value, and send to destination. */

if ((setRequest = OVsnmpCreatePdu(SET_REQ_MSG)) == NULL) {
  fprintf(stderr, "Error creating SET PDU:\n  %s\n",
          OVsnmpErrString(OVsnmpErrno));
  exit(-1);
}

if (OVsnmpAddTypedVarBind(setRequest,
                          target_oid,
                          target_oid_len,
                          (u_char) ASN_INTEGER,
                          &obj_val,
                          1) == NULL) {
  fprintf(stderr, "Error adding varbinds to SET PDU:\n  %s\n",
          OVsnmpErrString(OVsnmpErrno));
  OVsnmpFreePdu(setRequest);
  OVsnmpClose(session);
  exit(-1);
}

setResponse = OVsnmpBlockingSend (session, setRequest) ;
if (setResponse == NULL) {
  fprintf(stderr, "Error sending SET PDU:\n  %s\n",
          OVsnmpErrString(OVsnmpErrno));
  if (OVsnmpErrno != SNMP_ERR_NO_RESPONSE) OVsnmpFreePdu(setRequest);
  OVsnmpClose (session) ;
  exit(-1);
}

/* Check the PDU error_status field */
if (setResponse->error_status != SNMP_ERR_NOERROR) {
  fprintf(stderr, "Error from agent in SET PDU response:\n  %s\n",
          OVsnmpErrString(setResponse->error_status));
  OVsnmpFreePdu(setResponse);
  OVsnmpClose (session) ;
  exit(-1);
}
```

```
/* Echo the incremented value as obtained from response to SET, ditch
    the PDU and exit normally. */
varBind = setResponse->variables;
getval = *varBind -> val.integer;
printf("Variable updated to %d\n", getval);

OVsnmpFreePdu(setResponse);
OVsnmpClose(session);
exit(0);
}
```

PROGRAM TO READ *SNMPCOLLECT* DATA

This appendix contains the C program referred to in Implementation Tip 10.1. It reads an *snmp-Collect* binary data file and writes its contents in ASCII to standard output. Its single parameter is the name of the input binary data file.

```c
#include <stdio.h>
#include <stdlib.h>
#include <string.h>

void main(int, char**, char**);
void main(argc, argv, envp)
int argc;
char **argv;
char **envp;

{
  struct collect_rec {
      unsigned int start_time;
      unsigned int end_time;
      unsigned int agent_addr;
      double value;
  } crec;
  FILE *fp;

  if (argc != 2) {
    fprintf(stderr, "Wrong number of parameters\n");
    exit(4);
  }

  if ( (fp = fopen( *(argv+1), "r" )) == NULL) {
    fprintf(stderr, "Error opening input file\n");
    exit(4);
  }
```

```
while( fread( &crec, sizeof(crec), 1, fp ) != NULL ) {
  printf("%u %u %s %.5f\n",
    crec.start_time,
    crec.end_time,
    inet_ntoa(crec.agent_addr),
    crec.value);
}

exit(0);
}
```

MAINTAINING DATA WITH *SNMPCOLDUMP*

In addition to formatting data collected by NetView's *snmpCollect* daemon, the *snmpColDump* command can be used to maintain binary collection files. It allows you to update them in place, for example by periodically removing all entries written before a certain time.

You do this by using the -r flag of *snmpColDump*, which works in a somewhat strange way, but is nonetheless effective. When you run *snmpColDump* with the -r flag, it reads an *asciifile*. This contains the same information fields as a binary data file, but in an ASCII format. *snmpColDump* then writes a new binary data file whose values are taken from the *asciifile*.

Here's an example of an *asciifile*:

```
785368061    785368063    9.180.180.60     18.5
785368061    785368063    9.180.180.208    1.5
785368063    785368065    9.180.180.60     10
785368063    785368065    9.180.180.208    0
```

The fields in each line are (respectively):

1. The beginning time of the collection period
2. The time the collection occurred
3. The agent's IP address
4. The collected value

The following command would replace the file 'tcpInSegs.0' with the data from an *asciifile* named 'af':

```
snmpColDump -r af tcpInSegs.0
```

To maintain a binary data file, the idea would be to:

● Use *snmpColDump* to write the file in readable format.

- Pipe the output into a process that eliminates the undesired lines and writes the remainder in *asciifile* format.
- Pipe this into *snmpColDump* (this time using its -r flag) to create the replacement binary data file.

You could do this for example with the following pipe:

```
snmpColDump -tTI tcpInSegs.0 | filtold |
   snmpColDump -r - tcpInSegs.0
```

This assumes a program called *filtold* which carries out the second step.

VIII.1 PROGRAM *FILTOLD*

This program reads data from standard input as formatted by *snmpColDump*, filters out all entries older than one week, and then writes the remaining entries to standard output in *asciifile* format.

```c
/* Read snmpColDump-output-format lines from standard input, and write
   to standard output only those which are less than one week old */

#include <stdio.h>
#include <stdlib.h>
#include <string.h>

#define delims " \x09"

void main(int, char**, char**);
void main(argc, argv, envp)
int argc;
char **argv;
char **envp;

{
   char inline[500], *value, *start, *stop, *agentaddr;
   unsigned long earliest;

   /* Get earliest time (in seconds since beginning 1970) a
      record may have and pass this filter -- ie a week ago */

   earliest = time( NULL ) - 7 * 24 * 60 * 60;

   /* Read and parse each line, compare to earliest, and write out if
      not too old. */
   while( gets(inline) != NULL ) {

      /* Skip three fields (date, time and name/addr) */
      strtok( inline, delims );
```

```
    strtok( NULL, delims ); strtok( NULL, delims );

    /* Get value, start time, stop time and agent addr */
    value =   strtok( NULL, delims );
    start =   strtok( NULL, delims );
    stop = strtok( NULL, delims );
    agentaddr = strtok( NULL, delims );

    /* If this line not too old then write to stdout in asciifile
       format */
    if ( atoi(stop) >= earliest )
      printf( "%s %s %s %s\n", start, stop, agentaddr, value );
  }

  exit(0);
}
```

EXAMPLE REPORT-GENERATING SCRIPT

This appendix contains the report-generating script referred to under 'Off-line display without an RDB' in Section 10.3.7.

The script will produce a report showing how busy the interfaces are on a set of systems—routers for example. It assumes you have collected *ifInOctets* and *ifOutOctets* from each system and placed the data in /usr/OV/databases/snmpCollect. The data will have been collected at some interval, e.g. once every hour, over some period, e.g. a week. The script also assumes that collections from all systems occur at roughly the same times, i.e. the collection intervals are roughly synchronized.

The report will give:

- Octets and utilization, both incoming and outgoing, for each router interface, for each collection period
- The 10 busiest hours for each router interface
- The 10 busiest hours across all the router interfaces

The main script relies on two other scripts, *get_instances* and *scdjoin*. I've broken these out into separate scripts not just for modularity but also because some people may find them useful either as they are or with minor modifications.

Script *get_instances* is used to look in /usr/OV/databases/snmpCollect and return the instances of *ifInOctets* and *ifInOctets* that have been collected. It allows a filtering expression to be specified as well. Here, this is applied to the MIB object *ifType* to eliminate all instances of type Software Loopback and Other. This feature works similarly to *instMatchOID* and *inst-MatchRE* in *xnmgraph* (which are discussed in Section 10.3.7).

Script *scdjoin* performs a function very similar to the standard *join* command in UNIX, except that it performs 'fuzzy joining' to allow for collection intervals that end at slightly different times.

A language such as Perl could make this sort of report-generation program easier to write. Here I've used the Korn shell script language since it is supplied with AIX.

IX.1 MAIN SCRIPT

```
# This script generates a report of the input and output traffic for
# the IP hosts passed as parameters.  The report is based on
# ipInOctets and ipOutOctets for each interface (other than loopback
# and type other) for each host.  It assumes that SNMP collection has
# already been performed for the hosts and the resulting data stored
# in directory /usr/OV/databases/snmpCollect.

# The report is in three sections.  First for each host/interface
# combination, there is a table sorted by time giving -- for each
# collection interval -- ifInOctets, IfOutOctets and in and out
# utilization (based on in/out octets and interface speed).  Next
# there is a section showing the ten busiest collection intervals for
# each host/interface comination.  Finally is a section showing the
# ten busiest collection intervals for all host/interface
# combinations.

# Define some tempfiles and clean up any existing copy of tempfile3
tempfile1="/tmp/genrep.tmp1"
tempfile2="/tmp/genrep.tmp2"
tempfile3="/tmp/genrep.tmp3"
rm $tempfile3 2>/dev/null

# Check syntax
if [ -z "$*" ]
then
  echo 'Syntax is' $0 'node_names' >&2
  exit 1
fi

# For each host n passed as argument ...
for n in $*
do

  # Call script get_instances to determine which MIB-2 ifTable
  # instances exist on this host and are also in the collection
  # database.  Request only interfaces that are not of type
  # Software Loopback or Other.  (Note the use of back-quote.)
  instances=`get_instances /usr/OV/databases/snmpCollect/ifInOctets \
                    $n \
                    .1.3.6.1.2.1.2.2.1.3 \
                    -v "softwareLoopback|other"`

  # For each ifTable instance i returned by get_instances ...
  for i in $instances;
  do

    # Do SNMP gets to obtain the speed and ifType of the interface
    snmpget $n .1.3.6.1.2.1.2.2.1.5.$i | read junk1 junk2 junk3 speed
    snmpget $n .1.3.6.1.2.1.2.2.1.3.$i | read junk1 junk2 junk3 iftype
```

```
  # Write heading for table we are about to create
  echo "Host: $n  Interface: $i ($iftype)"
  echo \
  " Date      Time           InOct/Sec   InUtil    OutOct/Sec  OutUtil"
  echo " ----------------------------------------------------------------"

  # Call snmpColDump to format ifInOctets and ifOutOctets for the
  # interface, grep out the lines for this host, then sort the result
  # based on the host address and timestamp as preparation for calling
  snmpColDump -tpI /usr/OV/databases/snmpCollect/ifInOctets.$i | \
    egrep $n | sort -b -k6 -k5 >$tempfile1
  snmpColDump -tpI /usr/OV/databases/snmpCollect/ifOutOctets.$i | \
    egrep $n | sort -b -k6 -k5 >$tempfile2

  # Call scdjoin to join together the ifInOctets and ifOutOctets
  # data.  The join is based on host address and collection timestamp
  # so that we will have in each joined line the ifInOctets and
  # ifOutOctets for a given collection time.  The output of scdjoin
  # is piped into awk to compute and format each line of the first
  # section of the report (stats per collection interval).  Tee is
  # then invoked to save a copy of this output in a tempfile and to
  # pipe the output into another invocation of awk to generate the
  # final format output for this first section of the report.  (The
  # reason for two format steps is that in the first step some
  # additional info is added to the beginning of each output line to
  # be used in later stages of the script when they access the copy
  # saved in the tempfile.)
  scdjoin $tempfile1 $tempfile2 | \
    awk -v speed=$speed -v n=$n -v i=$i -v iftype=$iftype \
      '{printf("%s!%s!%s %9.2f $ %s %s %12.2f %8.2f %12.2f %8.2f\n",
                n, i, iftype, ($4+$11)*8/speed*100, $1, $2,
                $4, $4*8/speed*100, $11, $11*8/speed*100)}' | \
      tee -a $tempfile3 | \
        awk '{ gsub(/.*\$/, ""); printf("%s\n",$0) }'
    echo " ----------------------------------------------------------------"
    echo
  done
done


# Now go on to generate second stage of the report (ten busiest
# collection intervals for each host/interface.  First use sed and
# uniq on the tempfile to get all unique instances of each
# host/interface.  (Each line of the tempfile will have the host,
# interface_number and ifDesc concatenated together into a single
# token with the "!" character separating them.
interfaces=`cat $tempfile3 | sed "s/ .*//" | uniq`
echo
echo "TEN BUSIEST PERIODS FOR EACH HOST/INTERFACE:"
```

```
# For each host/interface i generate the ten busiest collection
# intervals.  First break up the token to get the host, interface and
# ifDesc.  Then generate heading, and use grep to select all entries
# in the tempfile corresponding to this host/interface.  Sort the
# result in descending order by sum of ifInOctets and ifOutOctets
# (which was put into tempfile above).  Then use head command to pick
# first ten entries of sorted output, and format each line with awk.
for i in $interfaces
do
  echo $i | sed "s/!/ /g" | read host interface iftype
  echo
  echo "Host: $host  Interface: $interface ($iftype)"
  echo " Date      Time          InOct/Sec   InUtil   OutOct/Sec  OutUtil"
  echo " ---------------------------------------------------------------"
  grepexp="^$i"
  cat $tempfile3 | egrep "$grepexp" | sort -brn -k2 | head -10 | \
    awk '{ gsub(/.*\$/, ""); printf("%s\n",$0) }'
  echo " ---------------------------------------------------------------"
done


# Now produce final stage of report (ten busiest collection intervals
# for all host/interfaces).  Sort the tempfile in descending order
# (based on utilization) to get 10 busiest, then format the output
# with awk.  In this awk invocation the line is split on the "$"
# character which separates the first half of the line (containing
# host, interface number and ifDesc) and the second half (containing
# the statistics).
echo
echo "TEN BUSIEST PERIODS FOR ALL HOST/INTERFACES:"
echo
echo " Date      Time          InOct/Sec   InUtil   OutOct/Sec  OutUtil" \
     " Host:ifnum"
echo " ---------------------------------------------------------------"\
"------------"
cat $tempfile3 | sort -brn -k2 | head -10 | \
awk '{ \
  split($0,half,"$"); \
  sub(/!/, ":", half[1]); \
  sub(/!.*/, "", half[1]); \
  gsub(/.*\$/, "", half[2]); \
  printf("%s  %s\n",half[2], half[1]) \
}'
echo " ---------------------------------------------------------------"\
"------------"


# Clean up and exit
rm $tempfile1 $tempfile2 $tempfile3 2>/dev/null
exit 0
```

IX.2 SCRIPT *GET_INSTANCES*

```
# This script returns a list of all the instances of a given MIB
# object for which data exists in OV/databases/snmpCollect.  The MIB
# object must be specified by the filename stem into which it is
# collected.  Thus for example if instances of ifInOctets are being
# collected then the MIB object must be specified as
# "/usr/OV/databases/snmpCollect/ifInOctets".  The script will write
# to standard output a list of numbers -- separated by blanks --
# giving the instances of ifInOctets being collected.
#
# The MIB object is passed as the first argument.  In addition this
# script can filter the list of instances by a criterion applied to a
# related MIB object.  For example, in the case of ifInOctets there is
# a corresponding MIB object ifType whose instances describe the
# type of each interface.  In this example, it is possible to filter
# instances by specifying three or four more parameters as follows:
#
#  2) a host name or address to query
#  3) the object ID (in dotted decimal without an instance) of the
#     object to query
#  4) the first argument to pass to egrep
#  5) the second (optional) argument to pass to egrep
#
# When these additional parameters are passed, then for each instance
# found in the collection directory an snmpget command is issued to
# the given host for the given object with the instance ID in
# question.  The output of this snmpget is passed to egrep using the
# given parameters, and if egrep returns other than 0 return code
# (failure to find pattern) then the instance is filtered and not
# included in the final result.

# Check syntax
if [ $# != 1 ] && [ $# != 4 ] && [ $# != 5 ]
then
  echo "Syntax is:" >&2
  echo " " $0 "MIB_data_file_stem [node_name test_variable egrep_args]" \
    >&2
  exit 1
fi

# Get instances that exist in collection database
instances=`ls -1 $1.*! 2>/dev/null | \
  awk '{ gsub(/.*\.|!/, ""); printf("%s ",$0) }'`

if [ -z "$instances" ]
then
  echo "No instances of" $1 "found by" $0
  exit 2
fi
```

```
# If additional parameters supplied, then perform filtering
if [ $# != 1 ]
then
  selected=
  for i in $instances
  do
    result=`snmpget $2 $3.$i 2>&1`
    if [ $? = 1 ]
    then
      if echo $result|egrep -v "This variable does not exist">/dev/null
      then
        echo $result >&2
      fi
    else
      if echo $result|awk '{printf("%s", $4)}'|egrep $4 $5 >/dev/null
      then
        selected="$selected $i"
      fi
    fi
  done
  echo $selected
else
  echo $instances
fi
```

IX.3 SCRIPT *SCDJOIN*

```
# This script joins two input files, both of which must be 1) produced
# by the snmpColDump command using the -t, -p and -I flags, and 2)
# sorted (ascending) with field 6 (IP address) as the major key and
# field 5 (timestamp as seconds since beginning 1970) as the minor
# key.  The join is performed in a fuzzy way so that collection
# intervals that vary only slightly will still match.  To do this two
# temporary files are created from the two inputs, each of which has
# as its first field a "join key" made by concatenating the IP address
# with a "fuzzy timestamp".  The fuzzy timestamp is created by taking
# the timestamp in field 5 and changing it to the nearest integer that
# is a multiple of the variable round (which is set in this script).
# If round is 10, and a timestamp is 87654321, then the fuzzy
# timestamp will be 87654320.

# Set up constants
round=3
tempfilestem="/tmp/scdjoin.tmp"

# Check syntax
if [ $# != 2 ]
then
  echo 'Syntax is' $0 'infile1 infile2' >&2
```

```
  exit 1
fi

# For each input file, create the temporary file with the join key
for i in 1 2
do
  tempfile=$tempfilestem$i
  cat $1 | \
    awk -v round=$round '{
      newstamp = int(($5 + round/2)/round) * round;
      printf("%s%s$ %s\n", $6, newstamp, $0) }' >$tempfile
  shift
done

# Perform the join and sed out the fuzzy timestamp
join $tempfilestem"1" $tempfilestem"2" | sed 's/.*\$ //'

# Clean up and exit
rm $tempfilestem"1" $tempfilestem"2" 2>/dev/null
exit 0
```

Automated Network Management
27134 Paseo Espada #222, San Juan Capistrano, CA 92675, USA
Phone: +714 493 2925
Fax: + 714 493 2655

Bridgeway Corporation
800 Turnpike Street, Suite 300, North Andover, MA 01845, USA
Phone: +508 683 3626
Fax: +508 685 1048

Diederich & Associates, Inc.
625 Fair Oaks Avenue, Suite 290, South Pasadena, CA 91030, USA
Phone: +818 799 9670
Fax: +818 799 9521

ki Networks
6760 Alexander Bell Drive, Columbia, MD 21046, USA
Phone: 800 945 4454 (North America)
Phone: +410 290 0355 (Worldwide)
Fax: +410 290 0397

PEER Networks
3375 Scott Blvd., Suite 100, Santa Clara, CA 95054, USA
Phone: +408 727 4111
Fax: +408 727 4410
E-mail: phil@peer.com

WilTel Incorporated
One Williams Center, P.O. Box 21348, Tulsa, OK 74121, USA
Phone: +918 588 4912
Fax: +918 588 5054
E-mail: dante_artadi@wiltel.com

Many of the references here are IBM publications, nearly all of which are available in CD format as part of the *IBM Networking Softcopy Collection Kit* (IBM order number SK2T-6012). Unless you want only one or two of these publication, this is the easiest and least expensive way to get them. I've marked with an asterisk the publications that are available in the kit.

The NetView publications listed below are for version 4, the current level at the time of writing.

Comer, D. E. (1991). *Internetworking with TCP/IP,* Vol. 1. Prentice-Hall, Englewood Cliffs, NJ.

IBM (1993a). *AIX NetView Service Point: Installation, Operation, and Programming Guide.* IBM order number SC31-6120.

*IBM (1993b). *Systems Network Architecture Formats*. IBM order number GA27-3136.

*IBM (1994). *IBM AIX SNA Manager/6000 User's Guide, Version 1 Release 1*. IBM order number SC31-7157.

IBM (1995a). *NetView Association Catalog*. IBM order number G325-6553.

*IBM (1995b). *NetView for AIX: Database Guide, Version 4*. IBM order number SC31-8167.

*IBM (1995c). *NetView for AIX: Host Connection, Version 4*. IBM order number SC31-8161.

*IBM (1995d). *NetView for AIX: Programmer's Guide, Version 4*. IBM order number SC31-8164.

*IBM (1995e). *NetView for AIX: Programmer's Reference, Version 4*. IBM order number SC31-8165.

*IBM (1995f). *Systems Monitor User's Guide for AIX, Version 2.2*. IBM order number SC31-8173.

Rose, M. T. (1991). *The Simple Book: an introduction to management of TCP/IP-based internets*. Prentice-Hall, Englewood Cliffs, NJ.

Rose, M. T. (1994). *The Simple Book: an introduction to internet management*, 2nd edition. Prentice-Hall, Englewood Cliffs, NJ.

Rosenblatt, B. (1994). *Learning the Korn Shell*. O'Reilly and Associates, Sebastopol, CA.

Schwartz, R. L. (1993). *Learning Perl*. O'Reilly and Associates, Sebastopol, CA.

Stallings, W. (1993). *SNMP, SNMPv2, and CMIP: the practical guide to network management standards*. Addison-Wesley, Reading, MA.

The ATM Forum (1994). *ATM User-Network Interface Specification, Version 3.1*. Contact info@atmforum.com.

SOFTCOPY MATERIALS

There is a set of softcopy materials available from the World Wide Web that will be of interest to those who wish to use any of the sample programs in this book, or who wish to study the RFCs and MIB extensions I've referred to.

Specifically, the materials are:

● All RFCs mentioned in the book
● The NetView General Topology Manger MIB extension
● The Systems Monitor SIA and MLM MIB extensions
● The LMU for AIX MIB extension
● All the sample programs

The materials can be obtained from the Internet at www.mcgraw-hill.co.uk (check on editorial information for professional computing).